THE
QUEEN
MOTHER

By the same author

Documents in British Economic and Social History

British History 1760–1914

The Industrial Revolution

A History of Post-War Britain

Our Future Monarch, Prince Charles

THE
QUEEN
MOTHER

Peter Lane

LONDON
ROBERT HALE

Robert Hale Limited
Clerkenwell House
Clerkenwell Green
London, EC1R oHT

Photoset by Jarrold & Sons Ltd,
and printed in Great Britain by
Redwood Burn Ltd, Trowbridge & Esher

Contents

Illustrations

The Duchess of York visits the children's ward at the Harrow and Wealdstone Hospital (*Radio Times Hulton Picture Library*)

Opening new buildings at the Middlesex Hospital (*Topical Press Agency Ltd*)

The Duke and Duchess of York leaving St Paul's Cathedral (*Popperfoto*)

The only known photograph of the Duchess of York in uniform (*Radio Times Hulton Picture Library*)

The Duchess of York with the two Princesses in the garden at Royal Lodge, Windsor (*Radio Times Hulton Picture Library*)

King George V's coffin on its last sad journey (*Keystone Press Agency Ltd*)

The interment of King George V's body in St George's Chapel, Windsor (*Fox Photos Ltd*)

King George VI and Queen Elizabeth on their way to the Coronation Service (*Keystone Press Agency Ltd*)

The new King and his family on the balcony of Buckingham Palace (*Popperfoto*)

The King and Queen in Paris (*Radio Times Hulton Picture Library*)

The King and Queen with Franklin D. Roosevelt (*Keystone Press Agency Ltd*)

Between pages 128 and 129

The Queen and the two Princesses in the garden of Royal Lodge, Windsor (*Radio Times Hulton Picture Library*)

The King and Queen visiting one of the districts destroyed by bombing (*Radio Times Hulton Picture Library*)

The Queen supervising the Princesses at their lessons, Windsor Castle (*Radio Times Hulton Picture Library*)

The Queen visits the East End after it had suffered from heavy bombing (*Fox Photos Ltd*)

Inspecting the harvest at Sandringham (*Radio Times Hulton Picture Library*)

A family photograph taken after a party to celebrate Princess Elizabeth's eighteenth birthday (*The Press Association Ltd*)

On the balcony of Buckingham Palace on VE Day (*Popperfoto*)

The King and Queen with Prime Minister Smuts (*Keystone Press Agency Ltd*)

The King and Queen enjoying a village concert (*Radio Times Hulton Picture Library*)

The King and Queen on their way to St Paul's Cathedral (*The Press Association Ltd*)

The christening day of Prince Charles (*Radio Times Hulton Picture Library*)

The christening day of Princess Anne (*Popperfoto*)

Three sorrowing Queens at the lying-in-state of King George VI (*Popperfoto*)

The royal cortège *en route* for St George's Chapel for the burial of King George VI (*Syndication International Ltd*)

The Queen Mother and Prince Charles at his mother's Coronation (*Odhams*)

Queen Elizabeth II and her family on the balcony of Buckingham Palace after the Coronation (*Popperfoto*)

Between pages 144 and 145

The Queen Mother with Prince Charles and Princess Anne (*Radio Times Hulton Picture Library*)

Waterloo Station: the Queen Mother returns from her tour of Canada and the
United States (*The Press Association Ltd*)

The Queen Mother with her horse, Devon Loch (*Radio Times Hulton Picture Library*)

Talking to children at John Brown's shipyard, Clydebank (*Glasgow Herald/Evening
Times*)

The Queen Mother fishing in New Zealand (*High Commission for New Zealand*)

"One of the most amazing Queens since Cleopatra . . ." Harold Nicolson
(*Photographs supplied by: Radio Times Hulton Picture Library, Syndication
International Ltd, Fox Photos Ltd, Keystone Press Agency Ltd*)

Trooping the Colour, 1970 (*Popperfoto*)

The Queen Mother, August 1975 (*Syndication International Ltd*)

4th August 1976, the Queen Mother's seventy-sixth birthday (*Syndication International
Ltd*)

The Queen Mother walks with Prince Charles in the procession of Knights of the
Garter (*Syndication International Ltd*)

Trooping the Colour, 1978 (*Popperfoto*)

Acknowledgements

I am very grateful for the considerable help which I received during the writing of this biography from the staff at Clarence House. In particular, I wish to thank the Queen Mother's Press Secretary, Major John Griffen, CVO, for his unfailing help and courtesy.

I am pleased to ackowledge the gracious permission of Her Majesty the Queen to use material held in the Royal Archives. I wish to thank the following for permission to quote from copyright material: The Rt Hon. David Ogilvie, thirteenth Earl of Airlie, for the extracts from *Thatched with Gold* by Mabell the Countess of Airlie; Lady Diana Cooper for the extracts from her book, *The Light of Common Day*; Lady Alexandra Metcalfe for the extracts from her husband's letters; George Allen & Unwin Ltd, for the extracts from *Queen Mary* by Sir James Pope-Hennessy; Jonathan Cape Ltd, for the extracts from *Certain People of Importance* by A. G. Gardiner; Cassell Ltd, for the extracts from *A King's Story* by the Duke of Windsor, and *The Little Princess* by Marion Crawford; Chatto & Windus Ltd, for the extracts from *Dawson of Penn* by Francis Watson; Collins Ltd, for the extracts from *Times to Remember* by Rose Kennedy, and *Harold Nicolson, Diaries and Letters, 1930–39* and *1945–62*, edited by Nigel Nicolson; Constable & Co. Ltd, and Nigel Nicolson for the extracts from *King George V* by Sir Harold Nicolson; Curtis Brown Ltd, for the extracts from *Recollections of Three Reigns* by Sir Frederick Ponsonby, *Cosmo Gordon Lang* by J. G. Lockhart, and *Monarchy in the Twentieth Century* by Sir Charles Petrie; André Deutsch for the extracts from *Eleanor and Franklin* by Joseph P. Lash; Evans Bros. Ltd, for the extracts from *A Crowded Life* by Lady Cynthia Colville; John Farquharson Ltd, for the extracts from *Loyal to Three Kings* by Lady Helen Hardinge; Hamish Hamilton Ltd, for the extract from *The Crossman Diaries*, vol. 1; The Hamlyn Group for the extracts from *Princess Elizabeth* by Dermot Morrah; Heinemann Ltd, for the extracts from *As It Happened* by (Lord) Clement Attlee; David Higham Associates Ltd, for the extracts from *Haply I may Remember* by Lady Cynthia Asquith, and *King Edward VIII* by Hector Bolitho; Hodder & Stoughton Ltd, for the extracts from *Queen Elizabeth, the Queen Mother* by Dorothy Laird, and *Fisher of Lambeth* by W. Purcell; Hutchinson Publishing Group Ltd, for the extracts from *Diaries, 1915–18* by Lady Cynthia Asquith, *Queen Elizabeth* by Lady Cynthia

Acknowledgements

Asquith, *Majesty* by Robert Lacey, *Lloyd George: A Diary* by Frances Stevenson, and *This I Remember* by Mrs Eleanor Roosevelt; Michael Joseph Ltd, for the extracts from *More Equal than Others* by Lord Montagu of Beaulieu, *The Sport of Queens* by Dick Francis, *Out on a Wing* by Sir Miles Thomas, and *The Heart has its Reasons* by the Duchess of Windsor; Longman Group Ltd, for the extract from *Philip* by J. Basil Boothroyd; Macmillan Ltd, for the extracts from *King George VI* by Sir John Wheeler-Bennett, *An Edwardian Youth* by L. E. Jones, and *Notes on the Way* by Lady Rhondda; Methuen & Co. Ltd, for the extract from *Britain between the Wars* by C. L. Mowat; John Murray for the extracts from *A Good Innings* by Viscount Lee of Fareham, and *King George V* by John Gore; Oxford University Press for the extracts from *A Diary with Letters, 1931–50* by Thomas Jones, and *Lloyd George: Family Letters, 1885–1936* ed. K. O. Morgan; A. D. Peters & Co. Ltd, for the extracts from *Memoirs* by Lord Woolton, *The Memoirs of Lord Chandos*, and *The Twenties* by John Montgomery; Weidenfeld and Nicolson Ltd, for the extracts from *Edward VIII* by Frances Donaldson, and *Chips: The Diaries of Sir Henry Channon*, ed. R. R. James.

I also wish to thank the editors and proprietors of the following for permission to quote extracts from their publications: The *Glasgow Herald;* The *Times; New Statesman;* The *Yorkshire Herald;* The *Scotsman;* The *Daily Express; Evening News; Glasgow Herald;* The *People;* and *Country Life.*

And finally, I would like to thank my wife and children for their great patience throughout the long period of writing this book.

Author's Note

This book was in the hands of the publishers when *Edward and Mrs Simpson* appeared on television. The then Duchess of York was given only a small part in that series. I hope that the material in Part III of this book helps to explain the role she played during the Abdication crisis. Like the writers of the television scripts, I have relied heavily on Lady Frances Donaldson's definitive work on *Edward VIII*, but have been able to draw on other sources to bring out the part played in 1936 by the present Queen Mother.

In memory of my father, who was
born in 1900

Introduction

IN A REVIEW OF *A King's Story*, the historian Noel Annan wrote of Court memoirs in which "reflections of inconceivable banality succeed descriptions of Court life so bizarre that the characters seem permanently to be playing charades...."[1] In this tribute to Queen Elizabeth, the Queen Mother, I have of necessity used some of these 'memoirs' as source material and have again, of necessity, had to write about 'Court life'. But I trust that this book will escape the wrath of critics such as Noel Annan. For the life of the Queen Mother has been far from banal; nor has it been bizarre. And no one would presume to say that she had spent her eighty years 'playing charades'.

In 1900, Queen Victoria still reigned over an empire 'on which the sun never sets'. There were twenty reigning monarchs in continental Europe. The Wright brothers had not yet flown nor had Marconi received the first faint radio signals across the Atlantic. The 'horseless carriage' was still largely a plaything for the very rich, and millions of horses still worked their way through agricultural, industrial and urban Britain. The world had not yet heard of vitamins, penicillin or nylon. The Labour Party was only a few months old.

During her lifetime the Queen Mother has seen the dissolution of the German, Russian, Austro-Hungarian and Turkish Empires. These have disappeared from the map while the British Empire has become a Commonwealth of self-governing nations, with the Indian Empire split into three parts. She has seen the break up of the United Kingdom, with the Republic of Ireland taking advantage of the constitutional crisis of 1936 to loosen its ties with the Mother Country before finally contracting out of the Kingdom and the Commonwealth in 1948.

The Queen Mother has played a role in each of the two wars, both of which helped the progress of that social revolution which may be said to have been started by the Liberals in the reign of her father-in-law, to have been developed in the inter-war years under her father-in-law and her husband, and to have reached a temporary climax during the period of Labour government after 1945.

When Queen Elizabeth was born, the British people thought of ageing Victoria with a reverential awe. Her son, Edward VII, won public popularity with his extrovert manner and sporting successes. Queen Elizabeth's father-in-law and Queen Mary gained the affection of the British people with their close attention to public duty and their apparently unruffled family life. The institution of the monarchy came under great strain during the crisis of 1936, and public affection for the institution was weakened by the behaviour of Edward VIII during that crisis. At that time the then Duke of York (later King George VI) wrote of having "to clear up the inevitable mess".[2] On 31st December 1936, shortly after he had become King, he wrote of making "amends for what has happened".[3] His Queen played a major role in helping clear up "the inevitable mess" and in helping George VI to "make amends". Their joint success was such that they won a new respect from the British people for the institution of the monarchy. That this respect is widespread and earnest has been publicly demonstrated during the Jubilee of Queen Elizabeth II. The Queen Mother can claim a major part of the success of her daughter as Queen for it was she who played the major role in the lives of the two Princesses.

So this volume will not be a series of banalities or bizarre descriptions of charade-playing characters. All the people who know her well and all who work with her insist that she be described as "charming" and "great fun". It would be a travesty of the truth if, to please Annan-like critics, we were to try to avoid explaining and examining these facets of her character. But there has been much more than "charm" and "fun" to her life, as supporter of a shy, over-modest and uncertain husband, the wife of the monarch during the dark days of 1936 and the darker days of 1939-45 and the mother of the present Queen. I hope that the following pages will be taken as a tribute to both the "charm" and "fun" and what I can only call the steely resolve of a very popular Queen Mother.

PART 1: 1900–1920

1

The Bowes-Lyon family

LADY ELIZABETH BOWES-LYON was born on 4th August 1900. She was the ninth child and the fourth daughter of Lord and Lady Glamis, who became Earl and Countess of Strathmore in 1904 on the death of Lord Glamis's father. The news of her birth attracted none of the attention that will be given to her eightieth birthday, for the British people have learned to respect and to give a special affection to Lady Elizabeth, later Queen Elizabeth and now the Queen Mother.

If she had not become Queen, would people have wanted to read her life story? Perhaps, because people still read the autobiographies of ladies from upper-class families, such as the Countess of Airlie, the Duchess of Argyll and Lady Cynthia Colville, on whose memoirs I have drawn for some parts of this story. And there is little doubt that Lady Elizabeth would have lived a life as interesting to the general reader and to the social historian as any of these.

And her life story, even if she had not become a member of 'the royal firm', might have attracted the attention of students of Scottish history, for the history of the Glamis family was closely interwoven with the nation's history from 1370 until the collapse of the Jacobite Rebellion in 1745. The downfall of the Stewart kings of Scotland and England was due, in part, to the advent to power of William III and Mary II, the daughter of James II, in 1688: it is ironic that the history of the family of Lady Elizabeth's mother was closely interwoven with the fortunes of the new monarchs, and it is at least possible that historians would have been interested in the fortunes of the Bentinck family.

The first documentary mention of the Lyon family is dated 1372. King Robert II, grandson of Robert Bruce, had come to the Scottish throne in 1371. Shakespeare might have had this Robert in mind when he wrote: "Uneasy lies the head that wears a crown." Since the death of Bruce in 1329, the feudal nobles of Scotland had tried to extend their own power, while various descendants of Bruce's old rival, John Balliol, tried to regain the throne. The situation was much as it had been in England during the civil war between King Stephen and Queen Matilda when: "Men said openly that Christ slept and His saints; such things, and more than we can say, did we endure nineteen winters for our sins." Edward III of England added to Scotland's problems. He took advantage of the internecine wars to invade Scotland to try to gain revenge for the defeat which the English had suffered at Bannockburn and to regain that control of Scotland which had been won by Edward I of England.

So it was "an uneasy head" that wore the Scottish crown in 1371 when the first of the Stewarts came to the throne. Robert II, fully aware of the weakness of his position, tried to win the support of some of the leading nobles by marrying his children into the great and powerful families of Scotland. He chose his Chamberlain, Sir John Lyon, as the husband for his daughter Lady Jean Stewart, a sign that the Lyon family, even then, was of some distinction and fit for a king's daughter.

Sir John was known as "the White Lyon" because of his fair complexion. As part of the marriage settlement he was raised to the peerage as Lord Lyon and given a royal estate, Glamis, along with the title Thane of Glamis, once held by Macbeth. Sir John Wheeler-Bennett, the official biographer of George VI, writing of the engagement of Lady Elizabeth Bowes-Lyon to Prince Albert the Duke of York, noted: "The fact that she was a Scotswoman also delighted the nation, and the genealogists derived much pleasure from showing that both she and the Duke were descended from King Robert I of Scotland."[1]

King Robert II's plans did not ensure a peaceful future for Scotland. Throughout the fifteenth century the feudal nobles continued to wage war on each other and on their kings. Scotland experienced its own equivalent of the Wars of the Roses which were weakening England at roughly the same period. The Lyon family played a leading role during this period of turbulent history. During the minority of James II (1437–60), the Earl of Douglas acted as Regent and was continually involved in war against other nobles anxious to capture the young King and so enhance their own fortunes. In 1445 the grandson of the White Lyon was created Lord Glamis as a reward for his loyalty to the Douglas and the Stewart child-King. During the reign of the lazy and inefficient King James III (1460–88), the Glamis family fought alongside most of the other nobles of Scotland at the Battle of Sauchieburn, when the King's eldest son took the field at the head of the nobles determined to rid their country of the worthless King. James IV (1488–1513) married Henry VII's daughter, Margaret Tudor, an attempt by the first Tudor monarch to strengthen his uncertain hold on the English throne. While Henry VII lived, relations between England and Scotland were peaceful, but the accession of the youthful, energetic and ambitious Henry VIII led to bickering between the two countries. When Henry VIII went to war against

France, James IV went to the aid of the French. He invaded England at the head of a very large army which included a contingent led by the then Lord Glamis. On 9th September 1513 the Scots met a large and powerful English army at Flodden, just over the Border. The battle that followed was an utter disaster for the Scots. The King himself, thirteen earls, innumerable other nobles – including Lord Glamis – and some ten thousand ordinary soldiers were killed. It was perhaps the memory of Flodden, where "fell the flower of Scottish nobility", that inspired Queen Elizabeth to make a remark which received wide publicity, during the Royal Tour of South Africa in 1947. She was introduced to some Boer veterans who had fought against the British Army between 1899 and 1902. One Boer told her: "Pleased to meet you, Ma'am, but we still feel sometimes that we can't forgive the English for having conquered us." "I understand that perfectly," said the Queen. "We feel very much the same in Scotland, too."

The eighth Lord Glamis entertained Mary Queen of Scots, daughter of James V (1513–42), during her uneasy progress through her kingdom. While she was there, the English Ambassador wrote to Queen Elizabeth I that, "In spite of extreme Fowle and Colde weather, I never saw her merrier, never dismayed." Much the same might well be written of the Queen Mother, who lived much of her life in Glamis, surrounded, as it were, by the memories of many kings and at least one other queen.

Mary's son, James VI of Scotland (1567–1625) became King James I of England (and Ireland) in 1603, on the death of Elizabeth I. When he moved down into England, James took with him the ninth Lord Glamis as an adviser. In 1606 he was created the first Earl of Kinghorne. The family fortunes had taken an upward step in terms of rank; there was also opportunity for this first Earl to use his political influence to rebuild the family estates, so that his son, on his inheritance, was the wealthiest peer in Scotland.

This second Earl was a personal friend of the great Marquess of Montrose, whom he followed in signing the Covenant (1638), the Scottish national protest against the high-handed policies of Charles I. He spent large sums of money to raise an army to fight for the Covenanters under Montrose and, when the latter turned to support the King, Kinghorne spent even more money to help raise a Covenanting army against Montrose. It is not surprising that the man who had been the wealthiest peer on his inheritance should have died the poorest. His son, the third Earl, "by prudence and frugality", paid off the debts of £400,000 which encumbered the estate. He also managed to win his way into the confidence of Charles II, who was restored to the throne in 1660. As one sign of that new-found friendship with the Stewarts, in 1677 he was created the first Earl of Strathmore.

It is hardly surprising that the Strathmores were fervent Jacobites in 1715 and 1745. The Old Pretender stayed at Glamis in 1715, the castle servants having to make up beds for the eighty-eight gentlemen who travelled with the Stewart claimant to the throne. In 1745 the Young Pretender, "Bonnie Prince Charlie", stayed at Glamis during his flight from his foray into northern England while on his way to the butcher's field at Culloden. With the failure of the 1745 rebellion, the Strathmores, like many other Scottish noble families, accepted the inevitable. The Hanoverians were firmly established on the throne. There seemed little point in looking only to a proud past.

In 1767 the history of the family took a decisive step into the new world then being created by the Industrial Revolution. The nineteenth Lord Glamis (the ninth Earl of Strathmore), in an attempt to solve the family's monetary problems, married the heiress of George Bowes, a wealthy land-owning Member of Parliament. This marriage was, as we shall see, of some interest to social historians. It was also a sign that the Strathmores no longer looked only to Scotland. Like many other Scottish noble families, they had become increasingly anglicized as they served the Stewarts on the throne of Great Britain and Ireland after 1603. The marriage to Mary Eleanor Bowes confirmed this anglicization. In fact, George Bowes agreed to transfer all his wealth to the Lyon family only on condition that the family agree to the promotion of a private Act of Parliament which changed the family name from Lyon to Bowes. It cannot have been an easy matter to have decided to give up an honoured name with long historic connections with Scotland and to take up the essentially English name. But change they did, in order that their Scottish past might be more securely buttressed by the English wealth of the Bowes family.

The Bowes had first come into prominence during the reign of Elizabeth I (1558–1603). There are many other great families who can trace their claim to fame to a wise Tudor ancestor. One outstanding example is the Cecil family which today includes the noble families of Salisbury, Exeter, and Burghley. In 1601 a William Hansley of Market Rasen complained that "there was none of the noble blood left in the Privy Council. What are the Cecils? Are they better than pen-gents?" But in serving the Tudors and, later, the first Stewarts, these "pen-gents" and other courtier-lawyer-politicians became wealthy. They used some of their wealth to buy their way into the nobility. Other gentlemen served the new monarchy in lesser ways and earned lesser, if still substantial, rewards. One such was John Bowes, who became Elizabeth I's first Ambassador to Russia. By 1770 his descendant George Bowes owned vast areas of County Durham, with its coal fields and iron deposits then being developed during the first days of the Industrial Revolution.

In his time, this George Bowes had married wisely. His wife inherited the family estate at St Paul's Walden Bury in Hertfordshire. Bowes's daughter, Mary Eleanor, heiress to estates in Durham and Hertfordshire, was an attractive match for the ninth Earl of Strathmore in 1767. From this time the

Strathmores devoted most of their efforts to running their English estates in Durham and Hertfordshire, using Glamis mainly as a summer retreat.

The marriage, between the representative of the old nobility and the daughter-representative of the new wealth, serves as a reminder that one of the striking features of the British peerage has been its willingness to recognize that its members are, as it were, passengers on a train moving along the lines of history. At one stop, some passengers get out, as a once noble family dies out for one reason or another. At another halt, new passengers board the train and, after some initial problems, are accepted by the others as fully fledged members of the peerage. So it was that the Cecils and other courtier-politicians joined the ranks of the peerage. In the eighteenth century merchants, bankers, lawyers and industrialists could buy a country estate and, if they wished, turn themselves into gentry. As Defoe wrote:

> Fate has but little Distinction set
> Betwixt the Counter and the Coronet.

When a family had only a female heiress, it could still buy its way into the ranks of the nobility by a wise marriage. So it was that the Bowes fortune was used to purchase a noble hand for Mary Eleanor and a change of name for the noble family. The tenth Earl, son of that marriage, altered the family name by taking Lyon before Bowes. The thirteenth Earl made a further change when he altered the family name to its present form of Bowes-Lyon. The family history-tapestry had another strand firmly sewn into the pattern.

In 1880 the heir to the thirteenth Earl was Claud George Bowes-Lyon, Lord Glamis. He was then aged twenty-five and an officer in the Life Guards. He spent part of his time on duty at Windsor Castle, where he was horrified at the drunkenness which was commonplace among his fellow-officers, disgusted by the heavy gambling which took place at the Barracks and shocked at the easy morals of the Court gathering around Edward, Prince of Wales. It is another irony that one of Lord Glamis's earliest resolutions was that no child of his should ever be exposed to the false tinsel of courtly life. For Lady Elizabeth was the ninth child of this very Court-hating Lord Glamis.

In 1881 Lord Glamis's grandmother died. She had been born Charlotte Grimstead, daughter and heiress of a substantial Hertfordshire land-owning family. In her will she left to her favourite grandson, Lord Glamis, "my public house known as the Strathmore Arms at St Paul's Walden, the beer house known as the Woodman at Whitewell with the paddock adjoining and all my other real estate in the parish of St Paul's Walden or any adjoining parish referred to as my Walden property". This "other real estate" consisted of the Georgian mansion of St Paul's Walden Bury and hundreds of acres of some of the best farming land in Hertfordshire. This estate was valued at £40,000 in 1882. It is almost impossible to say what this represents in today's inflation-ridden currency. As standards of comparison we might take the price of beef on the London market, in 1880 – 5½ pence a pound, or the average wage paid to skilled workmen in Birmingham in 1886 – thirty shillings (£1·50) per week, or indeed, the wage paid to maids at the Glamis house at St Paul's – £10–£12 a year.

Lord Glamis was now a wealthy man. He felt able to propose marriage to Cecilia Cavendish-Bentinck, the eighteen-year-old daughter of a younger son of the fourth Duke of Portland. The marriage took place at Petersham parish church on 16th July 1881, the fifth Duke of Portland giving his cousin away. So was woven yet another thread into the family history-tapestry. For the Cavendish-Bentincks were another rich, politically powerful and noble family.

The Bentincks first came to prominence when their Dutch ancestor, Hans Bentinck, became adviser to William III, Prince of Orange. It was Bentinck who arranged the marriage of that monarch to Mary, the daughter of James II. It was Bentinck who negotiated on behalf of William with those English politicians who wanted to get rid of James II in 1688. Bentinck took part in the short war that followed the landing of William III in 1688; he fought at the Battle of the Boyne in 1690 and had earned the thanks of a grateful monarch. In 1690 Bentinck was created the first Earl of Portland.

The downfall of the last of the Stewart kings – the centre of the hopes of the Lyon family – was the cause of the rise of the Portland family. The second Earl married a very rich heiress, Mary Cavendish Harley. In *Landlords to London*, Simon Jenkins has shown how these families – the Harleys, Cavendishes and Portlands – played a major role in the development of eighteenth-century London: they not only gave their names to streets, squares and estates; they also consolidated and extended their families' fortunes, which enabled them to have time to devote to political activity whenever they wished. The third Duke was Prime Minister in 1783 and 1807. He used his political influence to get a royal licence which allowed the family to use the name Cavendish-Bentinck. One of his sons became famous as a Governor-General of India, while his heir, the fourth Duke, came to the forefront as the leader of the anti-Peelite Tories after the repeal of the Corn Laws in 1846.

Lady Elizabeth was born at St Paul's Walden Bury. When her mother had first come to St Paul's in 1881, she found the old red-brick house with its well-laid-out gardens and spacious and elegant seclusion very different from gloomy Glamis. Here she had to supervise the work of a large number of domestic servants with the aid of her housekeeper and the butler. In *Remember and Be Glad*, Lady Cynthia Asquith gives an account of the "vast amount of organization" that running such a house involved: "Morning after morning I would find my mother what we called 'coping' – her breakfast tray pushed to one side, her bed littered with sheets and sheets of paper scribbled all over with tangled plans for the day. . . ."[2] The problems of running St Paul's were increased as the years went by and the Glamis family grew seemingly continuously. The first child, Violet, was born in April 1882. She died of diphtheria in 1893. Mary Frances was born in August 1883. She married Lord Elphinstone in 1919 and died in 1961. Just eleven days before her own twenty-second birthday, Lady Glamis gave birth to Patrick (September 1884). He married Lady Dorothy Osborne and died in 1949. John Herbert was born in April 1886. He married Miss Fenella Hepburn-Stuart-Forbes-Trefusis and died in 1930. Alexander Francis was born in April 1887 and died in 1911. Fergus was born in April 1889. He was killed in action with the Black Watch at Loos in 1915. Rose Constance was born in May 1890. She married the Hon. William Spencer Leveson-Gower, who became the fourth Earl Granville and died in 1953. Michael Claude was born in October 1893. He married Miss Elizabeth Cator and died in 1954.

This recital of births, marriages and some deaths helps to explain why friends considered that "the Glamises are not so much a family as a clan". Personal friends as well as relations by marriage came to regard the Glamises' home as one where they would always be welcomed. There were, by 1893, three groups of children requiring Lady Glamis's attention. There were three older ones – Violet, Mary and Patrick. Then there were the three boys, John, Alexander and Fergus. Finally, or so it seemed, there were the two smaller ones, Rose and Michael. The house at St Paul's had to be enlarged to accommodate the children, their nurses, tutors and other servants. A new wing in neo-Elizabethan red brick was 'home' for the children and their staff.

The death of Violet, just seventeen days after Michael's birth in October 1893, was taken by the Glamis parents as a sign that their child-bearing days were over. And for seven years there were no more babies. By 1900 the house was, in term time at least, somewhat quieter and less crowded. The four older boys were away at boarding-school, and only Rose (aged nine) and Michael (aged six) were still in the schoolroom.

On 1st January 1900 Queen Victoria wrote in her diary: "I begin a New Year and a New Century," so ending, for herself at least, the argument as to whether the twentieth century began on 1st January 1900 or 1st January 1901. For the Bowes-Lyons the start of the new century brought the news that Lady Glamis was expecting another baby. And on 4th August Lady Elizabeth was born at the family home at St Paul's. Fortunately for her, another child, David, was born in 1902. These two were nicknamed "the two Benjamins" by their mother (who became Countess of Strathmore in 1904) who joked that, aged forty when David was born, she was often mistaken for the babies' grandmother.

Lady Glamis employed Clare Cooper Knight as nursemaid to the baby Elizabeth. The daughter of a farmer on the family estate in Whitwell,

Hertfordshire, she later became nannie to David and remained with the Bowes-Lyon family throughout the rest of her life. She worked for Mary, Lady Elphinstone, before becoming nannie to Lady Elizabeth's own children – our present Queen and Princess Margaret. The children were unable to get their tongues around her name 'Clara'; it was their efforts to do so which gave her the family nickname 'Alah'. She died at Sandringham House on 2nd January 1946 and was buried at St Paul's Walden Bury, her 'family', including the then Queen Elizabeth, attending the burial service. On the coffin lay a simple wreath of violets with the Queen's message, "In loving and thankful memory – Elizabeth R."

It was Alah who supervised the Bowes-Lyon nursery with its high fender, oil lamps and baby's clothing airing on a fireguard. It was she who told of the little Elizabeth, "an exceptionally happy, easy baby, crawling early, running at thirteen months and speaking very young". Neither the fond nannie, nor Lord Glamis with his jaundiced view of royalty, dreamed then that this baby was to become the much-loved Duchess of York, then Queen Consort and finally Queen Mother.

In *More Equal than Others*, Lord Montagu of Beaulieu discusses the merits and demerits of the hereditary peerage. Lord Montagu's family, like the Cecils, first came into prominence during the Tudor period. His ancestor Thomas Wriothesley sided with Henry VIII during the quarrel with the Pope over 'the King's Matter' of divorce from Catherine of Aragon. Among his rewards was a title – the earldom of Southampton – and an estate – the former Cistercian Abbey of Beaulieu. Lord Montagu has some right to claim that he has some inside knowledge of the importance of heredity, breeding and training. As he says,[3] "When people bet on horses or dogs, raise pedigree cattle or choose gun dogs, they pay a great deal of attention to breeding and training. It is strange that it is now fashionable to dismiss, as irrelevant, breeding and background in human beings." In an attempt to be fair, Lord Montagu quotes Lady (Barbara) Wootton, a left-wing life peeress: "It's an absolute toss up whether you get wisdom out of certain people's sons." And a hereditary peer, the Earl of Lichfield, is also quoted: "... My great-great-great-grandfather was bright, or clever, or a pirate (which he was) [while] ... I could be his moronic great-great-great grandson. ..."

But Lord Montagu quotes Lord Mancroft: "I think there is a good deal to be said for the hereditary principle. When Herbert Morrison on one occasion was caught out by Lord Salisbury [a Cecil], I remember one peer saying to another, 'You know, Salisbury has all the political nous and cunning of Morrison, but he's been at the game four hundred and fifty years longer!' There's a lot in that, you know."

And if we have to have kings and queens, there's a lot to be said for having people who have "been at the game" for a long time. There is no guarantee, as

Lichfield pointed out, that it will always work. We may, indeed, get a stupid, lazy or otherwise unsuitable king. Indeed the history of the Queen Mother would have taken a different line if we had not had one such king in 1936. But if a king has to choose someone to be his queen, there is a good deal to be said for his choosing someone from a family that has been at the business of being used to royalty for a long time. As we have seen, the Lyon family had that history of attachment to and service to the Stewart family. There was nothing strange in living in historic surroundings for Elizabeth Bowes-Lyon. Her home, Glamis, had a longer history and link with royalty than any royal home in which she has since lived, except for Windsor and Holyroodhouse in Scotland. The family history-tapestry had been woven over many years and contained many strands of varying strengths and importance. If her ancestor the White Lyon was fit for a king's daughter, then she herself was, by background and breeding, fit for the son of a king and one who was to be, albeit unwillingly, king himself.

2

Growing up, 1900–12

"GIVE ME THE CHILD for the first seven years and you may do what you like with him afterwards" is allegedly a Jesuit saying. Wordsworth made the same point, if more poetically, when he wrote: "The child is father of the man." Modern theories of child-development are based on the belief that a person's character is largely determined by the experiences of early childhood. What was the nature of the experiences of the Queen Mother during her formative years? What were the forces which helped mould the childhood of this youngest daughter of a wealthy and noble family?

The Queen Mother herself acknowledges that one important feature of her childhood was the nature of the homes in which she lived. In 1904 her father succeeded to the earldom of Strathmore, inheriting not only Glamis Castle but a fortune of £250,000. This was a considerable addition to the sizeable fortune he had inherited along with St Paul's Walden Bury. Even if he had only put this fortune into government stock paying about three per cent interest, he would have had an annual income of about £7,500 – about a hundred times the income of an Edwardian schoolteacher.

A number of people have looked back through the dark and destructive days of the First World War to a 'golden age' of falling prices, stable money-values and low taxation – for the Celtic wizardry of Lloyd George did not cast any spells until 1909 when he raised income tax to the then unbelievably high rate of 1s 2d (about 6p) in the pound on incomes over £3,000 a year with a super-tax of 5d (about 2p) in the pound on incomes above £5,000 a year. As Donald Read writes: "By later-twentieth-century standards these rates seem Elysian. . . ."

The Queen Mother's childhood was spent as one of the privileged inhabitants of Read's Elysium. She spent most of that childhood at St Paul's, a fortnight each year at the Bowes's home, Streatlam Castle, three months at Glamis and two months at the family's London house in St James's Square.

In 1937 the Queen Mother provided her friend Lady Cynthia Asquith with a very long account of her memories of life at St Paul's, which seems to have formed the basis for a piece which appeared in *The Times* Coronation Supplement of 1937:

> Home was not Glamis (for holidays) or Streatlam Castle (for visits) but St Paul's Waldenbury [sic], a comely red-brick Queen Anne house, much grown upon by magnolia and honeysuckle, in pleasant Hertfordshire. Here were all the things that children could desire – dogs and tortoises, Persian kittens and Bobs, the Shetland pony, hay to make, chickens to feed, a garden, a friendly stillroom, the attic of a tumbledown brewhouse to play truant in, bullfinches to tame, fields to roam, flowers to love, ripe apples to drop, providentially, about the head, and on wet days, the books that are best read on the floor in front of the fire, and a wonderful chest full of periodic costumes and the wigs that went with their gorgeousness.[1]

It is not surprising that Lady Cynthia Asquith concluded: "It must have been lovely to be a child in the surroundings of St Paul's Waldenbury [sic]."[2]

Equally pleasant, at least for the children, must have been the three-month summer holiday at Glamis. The whole household had to be moved – nursemaids, footmen, ladies' maids, valet, butler, governess, books, toys and children's pets all travelled in the 'Flying Scotsman' the five-hundred-mile-long journey to Scotland. At Glamis the Queen Mother learned to love fishing, partly as an antidote to her dislike for one of the family's favourite pastimes – shooting. Here too she enjoyed the pleasures and the influence of a wider family life. Her father was happier at Glamis than in any other of their homes. He enjoyed entertaining his neighbours and friends, his relations and their friends, so that there were usually at least twenty people to dinner, when his pipers marched three times around the table.

One uncle had been lawn tennis champion of Scotland, another had helped win the Doubles Championship at Wimbledon – and the castle tennis courts were in constant use. There was also a seemingly endless series of cricket games between teams from the castle and teams from various parts of Scotland. This is hardly surprising when we remember that the Strathmores were close friends of the Leveson-Gowers, one of whom, affectionately nicknamed "Shrimp", was chairman of the English selectors in 1930. One of the Queen's brothers, Michael, wrote: "I always loved the cricket up there. Do you remember one special umpire, Mr Arthur Fossett, short, round, red-faced and fat, who was perfectly trained never to no-ball father and always gave his appeals out?"[3]

For the youngest of the Glamis girls there was the sociability that went along with entertaining the almost innumerable 'clan' which packed the large and always hospitable home. She was encouraged to play the part of hostess, to show guests to their rooms and to lead newcomers over the ancestral home. One such guest was Lady Scott, wife of the famous explorer, who wrote to tell her husband, then in the Antarctic, about her visit and about the "little Lady Elizabeth Lyon" who had shown her over the castle.[4]

In the evening after dinner, family and friends gathered in the Great Hall of the castle, a room dominated by the thirteen-foot-wide fireplace in which a huge log fire took the chill off the Scottish evenings. Sometimes Lady Strathmore or one of the girls played the piano while everyone sang – Scottish ballads as well as popular tunes of the day. Sometimes the family and guests played at charades – which gave them a chance to dress up and indulge in acting, a pastime which the Queen Mother taught her children. Mrs Roosevelt played this game with the royal family when she stayed at Windsor Castle (Chapter 21); she also described Winston Churchill's dislike of such light-hearted frivolity.

The Strathmores, like most other upper-class families, had a town-house in London. It is difficult for us to imagine how London must have looked when Mayfair and Belgravia were 'home' for members of this class. Some of their houses have been pulled down and replaced by office blocks or showrooms; others have been converted into clubs, offices or flatlets. Mabell, Countess of Airlie, gives us a glimpse of life as seen from the windows of a town-house in late Victorian England. In *Thatched with Gold*, this friend of Queen Mary's wrote:

> From the barred windows of the nursery on the third floor, my sisters and I could watch the familiar sights of the London of our day [1880s–1890s] – the jingling hansoms, the lamplighter speeding through the dusk with his long pole, the white-coated muffin-man heralded by his bell. . . . Every great family had its own turn-out, ranging from the enormous four-horse barouches with postillions to the lighter sociables and phaetons. We liked to stand at the kerb as the teams went by with a flash of gold or silver studded harness, and pick out the liveries of people we knew. . . .[5]

In 1904 the Earl of Strathmore took a lease on No. 20 St James's Square, now the headquarters of the Distillers' Company. This house, in the south-west corner of the square, was more comfortably situated than the older and more run-down Norfolk House in the south-east corner where the premier duke and earl of England had his London home. The Earl liked the house because, he said, it was "handy for the Carlton Club". The Countess liked it, in spite of the vast amount of wasted space. Built by Robert Adam, its palatial stone façade of huge pilasters and pedimented windows is still an outstanding feature. Inside, its beauty was enhanced by the Adam alcoves, fireplaces, staircase and huge drawing-room on the first floor. Even the stables across the back courtyard had an Adam façade.

The family took up residence in St James's Square in May of each year, for that London season which formed an almost obligatory part of fashionable life. For the children there were outings to parks and to friends' houses, to music and dancing classes, to exhibitions and concerts and to junior dances in the larger houses such as Lansdowne House which occupied the land between Berkeley Square and Piccadilly. The family also stayed at St James's for shorter holidays at Christmas time. David Lyon, the younger of "the two Benjamins" recalled: "Once a year we were taken to the Drury Lane pantomine, where we sat enthralled from start to finish. . . . During the holidays my sister and I used to go to the theatre as often as we were allowed – usually to the cheaper seats as our purses never bulged. She had a wide taste in plays, but I think Barrie's were her favourites. . . ."[6] J. M. Barrie was almost 'a local boy', having been born at Kirriemuir, only twelve miles from Glamis.

When she was five years old, Lady Elizabeth Bowes-Lyon was driven from St James's Square to a children's party where she met, for the first time, Prince Albert. Lady Asquith assures us that ". . . it was at Lady Leicester's party that [Prince Albert] first saw his future wife, and amid all the distractions of crackers and iced cakes the little girl made so deep an impression that at their first grown up meeting, about thirteen years later, he immediately recognized her."[7] One can almost forgive the "Crawfie"-like authors who have given us 'factionalized' and so-called 'eye-witness' accounts of that first meeting at which, we are told, the young Lady Elizabeth picked the cherries from her cake and gave them to the thin, stammering boy next to her. Like other myths and legends, such as those concerning Alfred and Canute, this story ought to be true even if it isn't.

So much for what we might describe as the physical or material nature of the homes in which the Queen Mother spent her formative years. At the heart of each of these homes was the Countess of Strathmore, described by Robert Lacey in *Majesty* as "the great fly-wheel maintaining the momentum and balance of the household".[8] "Fly-wheel" has a connotation of physical efficiency, relentless power and an endless grinding away. Lady Strathmore was, by all accounts, the most pleasant, feminine and considerate of people. An active gardener, an accomplished needlewoman and a talented musician, she was described by Lady Asquith as: ". . . noted for her charm. From all accounts no mother can ever have been more loving and more loved. Of her it was said, 'If there be a genius for family life, she has it.'"[9] Lord Gorell, a frequent visitor to Glamis, wrote: "It was all so friendly and so kind, days of such whole-hearted, delightful youth under the gracious guidance of Lady Strathmore, kindest and most understanding of hostesses, and the old castle re-echoed with fun and laughter."[10] One of her older daughters has been quoted as saying: "I never heard her say a harsh word in my life. But we had to obey her, we knew that. We were brought up with very definite principles."[11]

In 1978 I had a series of interviews at Clarence House, during one of which a member of the Queen Mother's staff used, unconsciously, the very same words about Queen Elizabeth. He had been on her Staff for many years and claimed that in all that time he had never seen her angry or heard her say a harsh word – although there had been occasions when staff had made serious mistakes and might have expected to have been 'told off'. "But she just smiles and gets on with it." In this we can see how the behaviour of Lady Strathmore has been repeated in that of her youngest daughter.

Like many mothers of large families, Lady Strathmore tended to be less strict with "the two Benjamins" than with the older children. However, they were not spoilt. As the older sister recalled:

> As Elizabeth was the youngest daughter, she was very much with our mother. She was such an attractive little thing that an old friend asked my mother, "What *can* you do to punish Elizabeth?" My mother said, "It is quite enough just to say '*Elizabeth!*' in a very sad way; then she will hang her head and be sorry." It is quite true; I have heard her myself. My father adored her too, but it was really my mother who brought her up.[12]

Indeed, Lady Strathmore "brought her up" in every way. As David Lyon wrote: "My mother taught us to read and write. At the ages of six and seven we could each of us have written a fairly detailed account of all the Bible stories. This was entirely due to our mother's teaching. She also taught us the rudiments of music, dancing and drawing, at all of which my sister became fairly proficient."[13]

It was Lady Strathmore who engaged the French governesses with whom the children had always to speak French, so that when she was ten the Queen Mother could speak it fluently. She also learned German from the one German governess whose appointment broke the 'tradition' of having a Mademoiselle in the schoolroom.

From her mother, she learned her love of gardening, her consideration for and empathy with people from widely differing social circles and a seemingly effortless ability to give pleasure to other people. Enveloped but not swamped by her mother's love, her own character blossomed, so that no one would disagree with Lady Asquith's verdict written for the Coronation of 1937, when she noted the then Queen's ". . . indefinable charm. In all true charm there is, of course, much that remains elusive, but surely in this case there is also a sufficiency of quite definable charm. 'Oh, what a polite lady!' was the delighted comment of a little boy after he had been introduced to the young Duchess of York. For a child to be able to distinguish what it was that pleased him shows a very definite quality."[14]

From the father who "adored her too", she learned a devotion to the duty of one's position. He was much quieter than Lady Strathmore and does not figure much in the memoirs or biographies of friends and relations. He was an active Lieutenant of the county of Angus, a conscientious landowner who took great care of all those who worked on his estates. His daughter has shown the same sense of acceptance of the responsibilities of power and position. Indeed, as we shall see in Chapter 15, her dislike of the Duke of Windsor stemmed largely from her belief that he had failed to accept the duties which devolved on him as heir to the throne. But this devotion to duty has not been merely an intellectual exercise nor has it led to the mere acting out of an accepted and expected role. As Lady Asquith pointed out in 1937: "Had the Queen's manner while Duchess of York ever begun to appear mechanical, had she ever seemed to be merely acting a part, reaction would soon have set in. But since she still genuinely finds her own happiness in giving it to others, the world-famous smile still shows as spontaneous, as unconscripted, as sunshine. And that is why people still flock to see her passing by."[15] And over forty years later these words still ring true.

A major influence on the development of the Queen Mother's early years was religion. At Glamis, the chapel was used for daily prayers, and guests were expected to share these prayers with the family and the household. At St Paul's, the family said morning prayers together while the children were young. When all the boys had gone away to school, Lady Elizabeth and her mother read a chapter of the Bible together each morning. At St Paul's and while in residence in London, the family attended church every Sunday, acknowledging the part played by God in the lives of a family whose motto is "In thou, my God, I place my trust without change to the end." The Lady Elizabeth helped her mother through the grief at the sudden death of Alec in 1911. She also helped to lessen the grief at the death of Fergus during the Battle of Loos in 1915. On both occasions she learned from her mother that the family motto had a real meaning for those who had sorrows to bear.

There, then, is something of the family framework within which the Queen Mother spent her early years. A loving and loved member of a happy family, it is not surprising that she became a loving and successful wife to King George VI. His childhood had been spent in an entirely different atmosphere, in which, according to John Gore, the father (later King George V) ". . . regarded his family as a ship's company of whom he was the master and the martinet and adopted towards them a boisterous manner which, however suited to the quarterdeck, appeared intimidating . . . harsh. . . ."[16]

From a very early age Lady Elizabeth was nicknamed "Princess Elizabeth". In 1903 the Duchess of Atholl visited Glamis and wrote: "I was very impressed by the charm and dignity of a little daughter, two or three years old, who came into the room [looking] as if a little princess had stepped out of an eighteenth-century picture. . . ."[17]

The Reverend James Stirton, minister of Glamis, was at the castle for a party given by Lady Strathmore for the ladies of the district in 1909, during which Lady Elizabeth and her younger brother danced to the music provided by Lady Strathmore at the piano and by Mr Neal, the family's music master, on his violin. Mr Stirton remembered asking the little girl, "And who are you supposed to be, my dear?" To which came the reply, "I call myself the Princess Elizabeth."[18]

But this assumption of regality did not bring with it any precocious bumptiousness. Indeed, the young girl was the essence of kindness and tact. When she was only five, she overheard one of her mother's friends comment on "poor X [who] will only be married for his money". She broke into the adult conversation with the sentence, "Perhaps someone will marry him 'cos she loves him." And when she was seven, other children paid tribute to her tact, according to a frequent visitor quoted in Lady Asquith's biography: "Elizabeth was always the most astonishing child for knowing the right thing to say. One day, when she was seven, my daughters were consulting as to the best method of dealing with a very difficult guest. 'Oh! I know!' exclaimed one at last. 'Let's ask Elizabeth. She can talk to anyone.'"[19] And memoirs and biographies agree that this was so. Older people were delighted with her: "Shall us sit and talk?"; children accepted her as a pleasant leader. David wrote of her as being a most unselfish person and a most enchanting companion, while Mr Stirton remembered her at the age of eight looking as if she had just stepped out of a painting by van Dyck. This impression of her resemblance to one of the royal Stewarts was heightened by the fact that her mother had made for her a party frock copied from a van Dyck painting.

In 1908 she was bridesmaid at the wedding of her eldest brother, Lord (Patrick) Glamis, to Lady Dorothy Osborne, daughter of the Duke of Leeds. Her first 'public' appearance at this wedding at the Guards' Chapel at Wellington Barracks took place across the park from Buckingham Palace and Clarence House, her future homes. In July 1910 her eldest sister, Lady Mary, married Lord Elphinstone, and once again Lady Elizabeth was a bridesmaid.

The year 1910 was marred by the death of King Edward VII but somewhat cheered by the accession of King George V and Queen Mary. Mademoiselle Lang, the French governess, wrote an account of an incident that took place at a garden party at Glamis during the summer of 1910, when kings and queens were fairly commonplace topics of conversation. It seems that Lady Elizabeth went to the palmist in her tent. Mademoiselle Lang asked, "What did she say?" "She was silly. She said I am going to be a queen when I grow up." "That is not possible unless they change the laws of England for you," said the governess. "Who wants to be Queen anyway?" asked the young "Princess Elizabeth", who danced away singing a song she had been taught by the governess, "*S'il fleurisse, je serai reine.*"[20]

Certainly she had no idea of being queen when, on 22nd June 1911, she watched her father and mother leave 20 St James's Square to take their places in Westminster Abbey for the coronation of King George V and Queen

Mary. She saw the coronation procession from the windows of a family friend whose London house overlooked the route. Little did she or her friends realize that she would play a leading role in the next coronation procession.

3

Lady Elizabeth and the First World War

BETWEEN 1912 AND 1919 Lady Elizabeth's life went through three distinct phases, each of which in its own way helped her to mature.

In September 1912 David, the younger "Benjamin", left home to go to boarding-school. Lady Elizabeth wrote: "David went to school for the first time on Friday last. I believe he is quite enjoying it. I miss him horribly." This brought the twelve-year-old girl and her mother even closer together.

There were boarding-schools to which some, very forward-looking, parents sent their girls, so that they would have the same educational opportunities as their brothers. However, the majority of middle- and upper-class parents were concerned only with the education of their sons. As L. E. Jones pointed out in *An Edwardian Youth*: "We were a family of six, two girls and four boys, all four being expensively educated. But next to nothing was spent upon the girls. They were neither educated to support themselves nor given opportunities of meeting young men who might have worked to support them."[1] Lady Strathmore was not 'fashionable' enough to send Lady Elizabeth away to school. She did, however, send her to a private day-school for girls. (The Queen Mother claims not to remember the name of the school, although Margaret, Duchess of Argyll, in her autobiography, is emphatic in claiming that both she and the Queen had been pupils at Miss Wolff's school in South Audley Street.[2]) This experiment lasted only two terms. Lady Elizabeth left the school at Easter 1913, having won the prize for literature. She was never happy at school, where she missed the constant companionship of older people.

In April 1913 Lady Strathmore engaged a German governess, Kathie Kuebler, to look after "the two Benjamins" during the Easter vacation. Lady Elizabeth managed to persuade her mother to allow Fräulein Kuebler to stay on as a permanent governess and not to send her back to the London day-school. The twenty-one-year-old Fräulein remembered her as "charming to look at ... she had a small delicate figure, a sensitive, somewhat pale little face, dark hair and very beautiful violet-blue eyes . . . a child far more mature and understanding than her years warranted". X She proved to be a willing and able pupil, prepared to follow a rigid time-table which began with piano lessons at 8 am and went on until 4 pm with lessons in a variety of subjects including French, German, history, geography, mathematics, drawing, nature study, needlework and gymnastics. After a year of this Teutonic regularity, Lady Elizabeth was able to sit and pass her Junior Oxford Examination.

In May 1913 she enjoyed the pleasures of the London season. Her governess, who acted as chaperone at the junior dances, wrote about her meeting "the children of the King" and recorded that she danced with Prince Albert. He was then a naval cadet who, on a ship's visit to Canada, had refused to take part in a dance in Quebec. However, in the autumn of 1913 he danced every dance at a ball for the fleet in Alexandria.[4] The romantic 'factionalizers' like to believe that this change of attitude was inspired by the dances he enjoyed with Lady Elizabeth during the London season which intervened between visits to Canada and Alexandria. X

During this 1913 season, she was allowed to have luncheon with her parents in the dining-room of 20 St James's Square, a very unusual privilege for a thirteen-year-old girl at a time when children were expected to be rarely seen and never heard. At the family dining-table she met many eminent statesmen and politicians. One visitor was Goschen, son of a Chancellor of the Exchequer in Salisbury's government in 1886 and destined to be a Viceroy of India. Lord Curzon and Lord Lansdowne, former Viceroys and eminent politicians, were also guests. During this Season the King, George V, was trying to help the politicians to find a solution to the Irish problem. Among those he called in to advise him were Lord George Hamilton, who had been a member of Disraeli's government (1874–80), and Lord Rosebery, who had been leader of the Liberal Party and Prime Minister after Gladstone's retirement in 1893. These two elder statesmen were frequent visitors at 20 St James's Square. There is no record of the conversations which took place at the dining-table, but it is difficult to imagine that politics were not discussed, in front of a child who was already "far more mature and understanding than her years warranted".[5]

On 4th August 1914 Lady Elizabeth woke up to enjoy the pleasures of her fourteenth birthday. She looked forward in particular to the treat promised by her mother, who had taken a box at the Coliseum, then one of London's largest theatres. However, that was also the day on which Prime Minister Asquith told Parliament that Britain had given Germany until midnight to take all her troops out of Belgium; failure to do so would mean that Britain would have to declare war on Germany. So, as Lady Elizabeth was taken, by car, to the theatre, she saw the crowds in the streets waiting for the expected announcement. In the theatre itself there was a buzz of excitement among the audience which gave a special cheer to the Russian ballerina Federovna – for Russia was already at war with Germany. And while the fourteen-year-old girl was making her way to bed, King George V was still at work. He wrote:

> Tuesday Aug. 4th. I held a Council at 10.45 [pm] to declare war with Germany. It is a terrible catastrophe, but it is not our fault. An enormous crowd collected outside the Palace; we went on to the balcony both before and after dinner. When they heard that war had been declared, the excitement increased and May and I with David went on to the balcony; the cheering was terrific. Please God it may soon be over and that He will protect dear Bertie's life. Bed at 12.0.[6]

On 4th August the Foreign Secretary, Sir Edward Grey, said to a friend: "The lamps are going out all over Europe; we shall not see them lit again in our lifetime."[7]

This sombre view of the probable effects of a European war was not shared by the vast majority who enthusiastically cheered outside Buckingham Palace and who wandered through the streets, gardens, parks and squares – including St James's Square – during that fateful night. Their spokesman was to be the young poet Rupert Brooke with his: "Now God be thanked who has matched us with this hour", which was typical of the welcome given to the outbreak of war.

Within the first few days of the declaration of war, four of the Bowes-Lyon boys joined the army. Patrick, John and Fergus served in the Black Watch, and Michael enlisted in the Royal Scots. Their father, who was sixty, also put on uniform, and their sister Lady Rose went to train as a nurse in a London hospital. Lady Elizabeth and her mother went to Glamis in the second week in August and helped convert the castle into a hospital. The fourteen-year-old girl found herself running errands to the village, knitting and making shirts for the local battalion, the 5th Black Watch. She rumpled tissue paper as lining for sleeping-bags and generally helped her mother turn their holiday home into a reception-centre and hospital.

There was some relief from this more serious work. On 17th September Fergus married Lady Christian Dawson-Damer, a daughter of the Earl of Portarlington. The newly-weds spent their honeymoon at St Paul's Walden Bury while the rest of the family trekked to Scotland for Jock's marriage on 29th September to Fenella Hepburn-Stuart-Forbes-Trefusis. But this slight relaxation was short-lived. By December 1914 the first of the wounded had arrived. Between then and 1919 over fifteen hundred officers and men spent some time at Glamis, where Lady Elizabeth worked under the supervision of her sister Lady Rose, who had returned to Glamis once her training had been completed. Lady Strathmore made it a point to meet each man as he arrived at the door of the castle and saw to it that everyone was supplied with the cigarettes or tobacco that they wanted. Lady Elizabeth was responsible for collecting the mail from the post-office, for helping men to write letters home and for going to the village to buy things for them. Mother and daughter organized concerts, in which they and the soldiers took part. There were jig-saws to be done, games of cards to be played, films to be seen, parties to organize for Christmas and birthdays and every effort made to help speed the men's recovery.

There are a vast number of memoirs, anecdotes and stories about life at Glamis during this period. There was the sergeant who wrote: "My three weeks at Glamis have been the happiest I ever struck. I love Lady Strathmore so very much on account of her being so very like my dear mother, as was; and as for Lady Elizabeth, why, she and my fiancay are as like as two peas."[8] There were those who remembered her singing to them; others remembered the gifts they received when they left Glamis to her "Soldier, I wish you well!" Many men remember her constant care for them: "How is your shoulder?" "Did you sleep well?" "Does it pain you?" "Have you no tobacco?"

Lady Asquith quotes the long account given by one soldier of his stay at Glamis. Part of his story was concerned with his parents' fears that he might have to have an arm amputated. This fear was unwittingly increased by a photograph, taken by Lady Elizabeth. The soldier's right arm in its sling was hidden in the side-on photograph. A friend wrote to tell him how upset his parents were because of this loss of his arm. His story goes on: "I couldn't fathom the thing at all and I showed the letter to Lady Elizabeth, and she was very sorry that my parents were worried unnecessarily, and said somthing must be done to put their minds at rest. So she wrote off straight to them saying exactly how my arm was progressing and how sorry she was to think that they'd been in such a taking."[9] The letter was accompanied by another photograph – this time taken front-on – so that the worried parents could see that their son had not lost an arm.

It would be easy to write a number of such panegyries and to lapse into bathos. But it is worthwhile recalling that Lady Elizabeth spent four important years working at Glamis. In peacetime she would have spent these teenage years as a member of a privileged class – dancing, holidaying, visiting and being visited. In fact she went through those formative years being compelled to mature at an unusual pace, thrown into contact with men from widely differing social backgrounds. She also helped nurse many officers and men from Australia and New Zealand – and was reminded of that when, as Duchess of York, she toured those countries in the 1920s.

But the war had other maturing effects also. In September 1915 Fergus came home for a few hours' leave before rejoining his regiment, the Black Watch, in France. He left Glamis on the Monday night before the Battle of

Loos, which started on Thursday 25th September. On Friday a telegram was received at Glamis. Fergus had been killed in the taking of the Hohenzollern Redoubt. For a time Lady Elizabeth took her mother's place in welcoming newcomers and saying goodbye to those who were leaving to rejoin their regiments.

In May 1916 her sister Rose was married to William Spencer Leveson-Gower, heir to Earl Granville. The wedding was held at the family parish church of St James, Piccadilly, and the reception held at No. 20. After the wedding Lady Elizabeth went back to Glamis with her mother – to whom she was even closer than ever now that Rose had left home. She was also forced to take on more responsibilities in her sister's absence and to try to help her mother recover from the shock of Fergus's death. Each morning they went to the chapel, and, as this became known to the soldier-inmates, many would join them there.

Early in 1917 the younger brother, Michael, was reported killed in action, a further blow to Lord and Lady Strathmore, just beginning to get over the effects of Fergus's death. Lady Elizabeth arranged for David to come home from Eton to share with her the burden of trying to help their parents through this crisis. David refused to wear any mourning, insisting that Michael was alive and that he had seen him in a dream. Three months later came the news that Michael was indeed a prisoner-of-war. He had been too ill to write. It was only after the war that Lord Strathmore learned that his son, though badly wounded, ill and a prisoner in one of the worst camps, had given up his chance to be repatriated in an exchange in favour of another badly wounded officer. The Strathmore sense of duty ran deep.

And so at long last the war ended, although Glamis remained full of patients until late in 1919 and the family had to wait until February 1919 for the repatriation of Michael. Meanwhile Lady Elizabeth, while nursing at Glamis, was also actively involved in helping some of her former patients through the problems of demobilization and finding employment. Later in February the family gathered in London for the wedding of Princess Patricia of Connaught to Commander Alexander Ramsay – a neighbour of the Strathmores in Forfarshire. This was a popular marriage of a royal Princess to a commoner, a "democratization of the throne". In June 1919 the Treaty of Versailles was signed, and in July Lady Elizabeth watched the Victory March through London. Slowly life returned to normal. She attended Royal Ascot a few weeks before her nineteenth birthday. Once again there were the pleasures of St Paul's Walden Bury and the expectation of holidays at Glamis and visits to Streatlam Castle.

But in fact life was never going to be 'normal' again, not if, by 'normal', we mean a return to life as it had been before 1914. This was true for the world as a whole, for Britain in general and for the upper class in particular. For Lady

Elizabeth the period of the war had been one during which she had lived her life rather than, as she would have, merely prepared for life. For some of her age-group the return to peace meant a dash for wild living, an attempt to cram into a few months all the experiences they might have had if they had grown up in normal peacetime. For some, such as Anthony Eden, Harold Macmillan and Oswald Mosley, the war led to the deepening of social consciousness and a resolution that they would try to build a better world. For Lady Elizabeth the experiences of the war and the sorrow she had seen both at first hand and vicariously had been a maturing process. As Lady Asquith commented: "Her natural sense of responsibility – a cheerful and not a self-righteous one – was fostered both by her upbringing and the War. A sense of responsibility is undeniably a burden, and the fact that she never tried to shift any weight from her young shoulders explains why, at the age of eighteen, for all its gaiety, the observant saw on her face a look of experience beyond her years. . . ."[10]

PART II: 1920–1935

4

Prince Albert, 1895–1920

THE CHILDHOOD OF Prince Albert was completely different from that of Lady Elizabeth Bowes-Lyon. The tone for his upbringing seems to have been set by the very date of his birth – 14th December. This was the anniversary of the deaths of the Prince Consort in 1861 and of Princess Alice in 1878. Queen Victoria maintained this day as one of mourning and, as her son (later Edward VII) and the newly born child's grandfather, wrote to the proud father (later George V): "Grandmama was rather distressed that this happy event should have taken place on a darkly sad anniversary for us."[1] The fearful father, then Duke of York, wrote to his ageing grandmother: "I am afraid dear Grandmama you were rather distressed that he was born on the 14th, that doubly sad day to you and all our family, but we hope that his having been born on that day may be the means of making it a little less sad to you. Dear Grandmama, we propose with your permission to call him *Albert* after dear Grandpapa and we also hope that you will be his Godmother. . . ."[2] Queen Victoria agreed to act as godmother, and, the family hoped, the first crisis in the child's life had been surmounted.

Unlike Lady Elizabeth, Prince Albert did not grow up in a loving, caring, outgoing family. The dominant partner in his parents' marriage was his father, then Duke of York.[3] In Lady Elizabeth's childhood, the dominant figure was her mother who had, as we have seen "a genius for family life". The Duke of York, on the other hand, "remained a distant figure inspiring reverence, reserved affection and sometimes genuine fear",[4] and the Duchess of York, ever anxious to support her husband, the future 'Majesty', seemed unable to cope with the problems of being a mother.[5]

Lady Elizabeth was fortunate in that as the elder of "the two Benjamins", she was a favoured daughter, very much thrown into the company of her mother, who was less strict with the younger children than she had been with the older ones. Prince Albert was unfortunate in that he was the middle of three children born within three years. He was only eighteen months younger than his eldest brother, David (later Edward VIII and Duke of Windsor), and sixteen months older than his sister, Mary (later Princess Royal). These three children made up a group of their own in the family. It is not unusual for the middle child of a family – or the middle child of a group of three within a larger family – to be the least regarded. In her diary Queen Victoria noted: "The dear little York children came, looking very well. David [the eldest] is a delightful child, so intelligent, nice and friendly. The baby [Mary] is a sweet pretty little thing."[6] The fond grandmother made no comment on the least-regarded middle child.

Lady Elizabeth and the rest of the Bowes-Lyon children had been fortunate in the quality of their nursemaids. The York children were less fortunate. In *The Rise and Fall of the British Nanny*, Gathorne-Hardy details the ways in which some nannies came between parents and their children, trying to assert their own position as the loving one and undermining the position of the parents *vis-à-vis* their children. As one claimed: "The parents didn't know how to look after children."[7] The nanny to the York children used to twist infant David's arm before bringing him in to see his parents – who were glad to return the crying infant to his nanny, who then soothed him and so confirmed her position in his life. This sadistic woman followed Queen Victoria's example – considering David the best of the children and ignoring Albert.[8]

Nurtured in the loving atmosphere of the Strathmore family, it is not surprising that Lady Elizabeth developed a generous, considerate and sympathetic character. It is not surprising that Prince Albert's development was different. He reacted to the way in which he was treated by becoming stubbornly disobedient and showing the quick temper which was to be one of his adult traits. On his fifth birthday his father wrote to him: "Now that you are five years old, I hope that you will always try to be obedient and do at once what you are told, as you will find it come much easier to you the sooner you begin."[9] This letter to a five-year-old is at once a reflection on the father and on the character of the child.

In 1902 the Duke of York appointed a Mr Hansell to act as tutor to his two older sons, until they were old enough to enter the Royal Navy when they were thirteen years old. The unfortunate Prince Albert had as little good fortune with Mr Hansell as he had had with his nanny and with the date of his birth. There were constant reports to the Duke of York of the Prince's bad temper and of his lack of "readier obedience". Such reports led to painful interviews with an angry father which further frightened the already shy, sensitive and stammering Prince. His stammer seems to have been, in part at least, the result of his being forced to change from writing with his left hand. Certainly he did not stammer until he was almost eight years old, when his tutor compelled him to write with his right hand.

This stammer further increased the Prince's apparent inability – particularly in languages. He found it hard enough to express himself properly in English let alone in French and German. His failure in languages led to more angry scenes with his father where the stammering child was made to feel even more of a failure than he had appeared in the schoolroom. And, as if to further add to his burdens, there was the painful experiment undertaken to try to cure the Prince of knock-knees – a failing common to all the York children except the "so intelligent, nice and friendly" eldest son. Prince Albert was forced to wear splints during the day and, for a long period, through the night as well.

The one bright spot in the young Prince's life was the annual visit to Abergeldie, a few miles from Balmoral. Like the Bowes-Lyon children, the royal children travelled by train to Scotland and enjoyed the fishing, grouse-shooting, cycling and deer-stalking. But the summer holiday was all too short before the Princes were thrown back into the traumas of the schoolroom each autumn. In the spring of 1907 the eldest son went off as a cadet at the Junior Royal Naval College at Osborne on the Isle of Wight. For the next year Prince Albert was drilled by Mr Hansell who was anxious that the younger brother should do well in the Osborne entrance examinations in November and December 1908. Unfortunately he was woefully weak at mathematics – a compulsory subject in the examination. The harder he tried, the more he failed; the more frequent the failure, the quicker the childish temper, so that his father wrote: "You must really give up losing your temper when you make a mistake in a sum . . . remember you are nearly twelve years old . . .",[10] but to Mr Hansell the royal command went out: "You must be very strict and make him stick to it and do many papers."[11]

The unfortunate Albert managed to pass the oral examination in November 1908, overcoming his stammer sufficiently to answer "brightly and well". He was also successful in the written examinations in December, a tribute, says his biographer, to his determination.[12]

On 15th January 1909 "Cadet H.R.H. Prince Albert of Wales" entered the new world of Osborne, along with other thirteen-year-olds. Unlike them, he had never been away from home before, had never played a game of football or cricket with other boys or been taught in a normal classroom. Unlike the others, he stammered – and was quickly the butt of derision among those who "could not resist the temptation to boast that they had once kicked a Prince of the Blood Royal".[13]

But away from his parents and Mr Hansell the Prince quickly settled down. He made friends because of his easy-going personality – (a trait which may surprise us with our knowledge of the crippling nature of his early upbringing) – friends with whom he was at ease, among whom he rarely stammered and whose friendship he retained for the rest of his life. He never enjoyed rugby or cricket but proved to be a good athlete. He also showed a determination, as the Captain of the College noted: "He shows the grit and 'never say I'm beaten' spirit which is strong in him – a grand trait in anybody's character...."[14] However, he was no more successful at academic studies here than he had been with Mr Hansell. In the passing-out examinations in December 1910 he came sixty-eighth out of sixty-eight, to the expectation of his angry father. (We ought, however, to note that George V himself was not all that intelligent. When Lloyd George stayed with the royal family at Balmoral in the autumn of 1910, he wrote to his wife: "The King is a very jolly chap but thank God there is not much in his head. They're very simple, very, very, ordinary people and perhaps on the whole that's how it should be."[15])

In January 1911 Prince Albert entered the Royal Naval College, Dartmouth, where he had to spend three years before passing out as a midshipman. Here he enjoyed some aspects of College life; in particular he was able to foster his love for riding, to become a proficient cross-country runner and an excellent left-handed tennis player. Here too he worked hard at his studies but managed only to move up six places in class, where he finished as sixty-first out of sixty-seven.

His period at Dartmouth was punctuated by a break to take part in his parents' coronation on 22nd June 1911 and by the pleasure of being with his father at the review of the fleet off Weymouth between 7th and 11th May 1912. Perhaps the most significant event of his Dartmouth days was his confirmation on 18th April 1912, an event which obviously affected him because in 1914 he wrote to the confirming Bishop: "It is just two years ago tomorrow that you confirmed me in that small church in Sandringham. I have always remembered that day as one on which I took a great step in life."[16] He was to continue to find religion a strengthening influence during later periods of his life.

On 17th January 1913 the Prince boarded the cruiser *Cumberland* at Devonport for the final training cruise in foreign waters. This cruise gave the trainee-cadet a chance to put into practice many of the things he had learned in the classrooms at Osborne and Dartmouth. In spite of his father's orders, the visit of the *Cumberland* to various foreign ports became the opportunity for peoples in different parts of the Empire and the rest of the world to fête the young Prince. This was the case in the West Indian islands and Canada where "nothing would tempt him on to the dance floor". He returned to Plymouth on 8th July 1913 for a few weeks' leave, during which, it is claimed, he met and danced with Lady Elizabeth. Whatever the truth of that claim, there is no doubt that, when the *Cumberland* visited Alexandria in November 1913, "I went to bed at 3.0 am having danced nearly every dance."[17]

On 17th and 18th July 1914 Prince Albert, now stationed on the battleship *Collingwood*, accompanied his father during a grand review of the Navy before putting out to sea on exercises. Father and son hoped that these would be followed by a period of leave. Unfortunately the First World War broke out, and on 28th July the fleet was ordered to its war station by the First Lord of the Admiralty, Winston Churchill; on 4th August Britain was at war with Germany and her ally, Austria. The King who prayed for "Bertie's life" wrote to his son on board *Collingwood*: "Always do your duty. May God bless and protect you my dear boy is the earnest prayer of your very devoted Papa. . . . You can be sure that you are constantly in my thoughts."[18]

The Prince-midshipman served on *Collingwood* throughout 1914 and 1915, as the battleship undertook the role of watchdog, ensuring the safe passage of British merchant shipping and blockading the German coast. He was on duty during the Battle of Jutland in May–June 1916. His Captain wrote: "Prince Albert was in bed on sick list when we prepared for action but got up and went to his turret, where he remained until we finally secured guns next day."[19] The Prince wrote his own long account of the Battle which he ended with the words: "It was certainly a great experience to have been through."[20] Unfortunately for him the gastric troubles which had put him into the sick bay on *Collingwood* worsened; in July 1917 he was taken to hospital and in August forced to resign from the Navy. He was operated on in November 1917 and it was hoped that his troubles were over.

Prince Albert then persuaded the King to allow him to join the Royal Naval Air Squadron. On 1st February 1918 he reported for duty at HMS *Daedalus*, a stretch of land near Cranwell in Lincolnshire where he was appointed to take charge of a Boy Wing and where he proved to be a popular and efficient disciplinarian. On 11th April 1918 the King and Queen visited Cranwell to mark the formation of the Royal Air Force. Flight Lieutenant Prince Albert was with his parents as his 2,500 cadets paraded before them.

In July 1918 the Prince left Cranwell to report to RAF Headquarters at St Leonard's, where he was in charge of a squadron, helping to train the young men in the new Force. On 30th August his father inspected the camp and wrote a long letter of praise to the delighted Albert, who had found that he had a natural ability to lead, guide and inspire younger people.

He was stationed in France when the Armistice was signed on 11th November 1918 and along with his elder brother enjoyed the festivities in Paris in November and December 1918. However, the eager Albert persuaded his father to allow him to return to England so that he could learn to fly. He did his training at the Waddon Lane Aerodrome, Croydon (later absorbed into the larger Croydon Airport, which proved too small for post-1945 aeroplanes and has now been developed as a residential area). On 31st July 1919 he gained his wings and became a fully qualified pilot, the first member of the royal family to do so and the only British sovereign to be a qualified pilot.

Almost as soon as he had gained his wings, the Prince had to give up his service career because his father thought it time that he prepared himself to become an active member of the 'royal firm'. The Prince of Wales was about to undertake those tours of the Empire which won him so much fame, and Albert would be needed to take his place at home. As part of his training for this 'royal' career the Prince spent two terms at Trinity College, Cambridge, in the autumn of 1919 and spring 1920. His father was not willing to allow him to live in College, where he might have enjoyed the full life of an undergraduate even if only for two terms. He lived out of College with his life-long friend Louis Greig, an excellent tennis player, with whom Prince Albert played in the All-England Tennis Championships at Wimbledon. Greig played a great part in helping to form the young Prince's character. He helped him face the problems of his poor health and hesitant speech and also to overcome his natural tendency to fly off into a temper when he played a game badly, and taught him not to be discouraged by defeat. Greig himself claimed that, "My principal contribution was to put steel into him." His success may be judged by the way in which the future King overcame many adversities in his future life.[21]

Prince Albert had to undertake a number of public engagements while an undergraduate and, though his stammer sometimes afflicted him, it was noticeable that when he was relaxed he was able to speak without any hesitation. At this time he was being helped by an Italian professor who hoped to be able to cure him of the stammer completely. King George seemed to be pleased with his work at Cambridge and with his attempts to take the place of the Prince of Wales. As a mark of his pleasure and as an encouragement to the young Prince, he announced in the Birthday Honours List of 3rd June 1920 that he accorded to his second son the title of Baron Killarney, Earl of Inverness and Duke of York. In 1892 he himself had become the first Duke of York since the ill-fated Duke "who had ten thousand men". Albert wrote to tell his father that he was "very proud to bear the name that you did for many years . . ." and in reply George V wrote:

Dearest Bertie,

I was delighted to get your letter this morning and to know that you appreciate that I have given you that fine old title of Duke of York which I bore for more than nine years and is the oldest dukedom in this country. I know that you have behaved very well, in a difficult situation for a young man and that you have done what I asked you to do. I feel that this splendid title will be safe in your hands and that you will never do anything which could in any way tarnish it. I hope you will always look upon me as yr. best friend and always tell me everything and you will find me ever ready to help you and give you good advice.

Looking forward to seeing you tomorrow

Ever my dear boy

Yr. very devoted Papa

G.R.I.[22]

In 1919 Prince Albert had become the very active and involved President of the newly formed Industrial Welfare Society (IWS), whose aims were "the formulation and development of the many activities, industrial, educational and recreational, indicated in the word 'Welfare' for the benefit of all those engaged in industry". He visited factories, went down coal mines, drove trains and lorries, poured molten iron from crucibles in an ironworks, to try to learn at first hand some of the problems of industry. In his presidential address in 1920 he warned the country of the danger that lay ahead if industrial relations did not improve and invited industrialists to see if they could not help the "worker to free himself from the grip of the machine . . . to make fuller use of his leisure".[23] He became known, and deservedly, as "the Industrial Prince". The King was delighted with the success of his work in this field. When the Prime Minister brought up the question of industrial relations, the King chuckled and declared that that was "my second son's department". This may not have been as glamorous as touring the Empire, as the Prince of Wales was doing, but it did bring the royal family much closer to people in Great Britain.

In March 1921 the Industrial Welfare Society sponsored a series of football games between boys from the Briton Ferry Steelworks in South Wales and teams in London. The Duke of York was at the game at Westminster School along with Sir Alexander Grant, Chairman of the McVitie and Price Biscuit Company and a close friend of the leader of the Labour Party, Ramsay MacDonald. They agreed that the games had been a good idea, in that they allowed boys from industrial Wales and public schools to meet each other and to learn a little about their different lives. But they had too little time to find out much about each other. What was needed was a longer time together.

Further discussions followed with other interested people, and the idea of a summer camp was born. In August 1921 the first of the Duke of York's Camps was held at New Romney. The success of this first of "my camps" ensured that the venture would continue. In time it became an established part of the social life of hundreds of boys from different walks of life and from widely varying schools. It was another, very vivid and welcome proof of the Duke's involvement in people's lives and his desire to ensure that the community should not be riven into 'them' and 'us' as appeared all too likely in the 1920s when on one side there was a fear of Bolshevism and on the other a suspicion that the "hard-faced men who had done well out of the war" were trying to turn back the industrial, social, economic and political clocks. The Duke of York showed that such a division was not inevitable, provided that people of good will involved themselves in industrial and social affairs. That he was prepared to do so was a welcome boost to the reformers. That he felt able to do so and that he showed himself an efficient and enthusiastic leader was an indication of the way in which the shy, stammering youth had matured and was prepared to be his own man.

5

A royal marriage, 1923

IN THE 1960S AND 1970S newspapers have devoted thousands of column-inches to the private lives of members of the royal family, and photographers have earned vast sums for particular 'snaps' of royalty off-guard. It is a matter of judgement as to whether the episode of Prince Charles's cherry brandy was more or less newsworthy and tasteless than a photograph of Princess Margaret sunbathing on a Greek island. But the female reporter responsible for the first and the photographer with his long-range lens responsible for the second earned themselves an ephemeral notoriety in the newspaper world. Editors, reporters and photographers have considered it part of their task to dog the footsteps of royalty and to report every step taken on a ski-slope, every vault into a saddle and every dive into a pool – as well as every word spoken in anger and every misdemeanour.

It was not always so. In Chapter 12 we shall see that for a long time the British Press carefully avoided references to Edward VIII's relationship with Mrs Simpson – unlike the foreign Press. And even earlier, the publicity-seeking Alfred Harmsworth did not send reporters to sniff out the comings and goings of Edward VII and Mrs Keppel. There was a reticence on the part of newspaper proprietors and editors when dealing with the private lives of the royal family. So it was that George V's sons were able to enjoy themselves in public without fear that a report or a photograph would appear in a newspaper or magazine. In Lady Cynthia Asquith's *Diaries, 1915–18* we read: "*Tuesday* 12 March 1918 . . . Just before leaving [a dance] at 12.30 am saw the Prince of Wales dancing around with Mrs Dudley Ward, a pretty little fluff, with whom he is said to be rather in love. He is a dapper little fellow – too small – but really a pretty face. He looked as pleased as Punch and chattered away the whole time. He obviously means to have fun. . . ."[1] In Chapter 12 we shall examine the significance of this relationship between the young Prince of Wales and the much older Mrs Ward. Here it is pertinent to point out that there was little, if any, Press comment on this relationship, which went on for almost twenty years, although the couple frequently appeared together in public and their friends were well aware of the intimate nature of their 'friendship'.

Prince Albert, like his elder brother, went to dances at the homes of aristocratic friends. At one such dance, given by Lord and Lady Farquhar at 6 Grosvenor Square in May 1920, the twenty-four-year-old Prince met, once again, the twenty-year-old Lady Elizabeth Bowes-Lyon. But Lady Elizabeth was no "pretty little fluff", nor was the Prince merely out to "have fun" as his elder brother understood the word. Robert Lacey quotes Lady Elizabeth's friends of the early twenties in comparing the behaviour of the Prince of Wales's lady friends and that of the girl friends of the Duke of York. For the latter, "Holding hands in a boat, *that* was courting. . . ."[2]

We have seen that Lady Elizabeth had stayed on at Glamis long after the official end to the War. She had not been part of the London scene during the first post-war seasons. Nor, when she came south, was she as mindless as so many others of her age seem to have been. The experience of nursing the sick and wounded, the effects of the death of one brother and the grief shared with a loved mother seemed to have matured her. So she was able to cope with the "host of admirers" she attracted when she came south and "took London by storm".[3] On the other hand friends and admirers have also paid tribute to her ability to withdraw from the tinsel and glamour of the feverish season, and noted the frequent occasions on which a more serious look would cloud her face as if she were thinking of that 'lost generation' which lay in France and Flanders and wondering whether the gaiety of the season was an apt memorial to these dead.

Lady Airlie, a lady-in-waiting to Queen Mary, knew the Bowes-Lyon family as neighbours in Scotland and acquaintances in London. In *Thatched with Gold*, she wrote: "Lady Elizabeth was very unlike the cocktail-drinking, chain-smoking girls who came to be regarded as typical of the 1920s. Her radiant vitality and a blending of gaiety, kindness and sincerity made her irresistible to men. One knew instinctively that she was a girl who would find real happiness only in marriage and motherhood. A born homemaker."[4] And of the meeting at the Farquhar dance Lady Airlie notes: "The Duke [as he became two weeks after the dance] told me long afterwards that he had fallen in love that evening, although he did not realize it until later."[5]

During the 1920 Season Lady Elizabeth widened the circle of her admirers and friends. Old men were taken with her thoughtful charm, younger men with her beauty and vitality. Lady Cynthia Colville, a close friend of Lady Mary Bowes-Lyon, the second of the Strathmores' children, was a frequent visitor to Glamis Castle and had known "the two Benjamins" since Lady Elizabeth was five years old. We might expect from an older woman a more realistic view of Lady Elizabeth's successes during this season. In *Crowded Life*, she writes: "I was amused to find that [she] at a very youthful age kept up a correspondence with more than one young man who found her intelligent exuberance quite irresistible . . . the unusually attractive and popular Elizabeth had so many devoted admirers that she found it difficult to decide upon which to bestow her favour; not because she was flirtatious but . . . because she felt that marriage was desperately important and irrevocable."[6]

The lease of the family's London home in St James's Square ended in the summer of 1920 and Lord Strathmore leased another large and beautiful house at 17 Bruton Street, a few doors from Berkeley Square (since demolished and now the site of an office of the Lombard Bank). While this house was being redecorated during the summer of 1920, the family followed its usual practice and went to Glamis for their long holiday. Lady Airlie was also on holiday in her Scottish home, Cortachy Castle, where Princess Mary was a guest. Prince Albert, now Duke of York, came to stay with Lady Airlie and his sister, and Lord Strathmore, ever eager to play host at Glamis, invited the party across from Cortachy. Here, in the relaxed family atmosphere that was so essentially a part of life at Glamis, the Duke had another chance to discover if he had "fallen in love".

In *Thatched with Gold*, Lady Airlie, commenting on the Duke's behaviour after this visit to Glamis, writes:

> Someone else had realized it [that he had fallen in love] – his mother. When I was driving with her one afternoon in the winter of 1920 she told me that the Prime Minister [Lloyd George] had advised the King that the country would not tolerate an alliance with a foreigner for the Prince of Wales and that the Duke of York should also look for a bride among the British aristocracy. "I don't think Bertie will be sorry to hear that," the Queen added. "I have discovered that he is very much attracted to Lady Elizabeth Bowes-Lyon. He's always talking about her. She seems a charming girl, but I don't know her very well." I replied that I had known her all her life and could say nothing but good of her.[7]

The Duke and Lady Elizabeth both, but separately, realized that they had a friend in the influential and knowledgeable Lady Airlie: "[They] started dropping in at my flat, on various pretexts, always separately but each talked of the other. She was frankly doubtful, uncertain of her feelings and afraid of the public life which would lie ahead of her as the King's daughter-in-law. The Duke's humility was touching. He was deeply in love but so humble."[8]

By the spring of 1921 the Duke had told his mother and father that he intended to ask Lady Elizabeth to marry him. We can gauge the royal opinion of "the Glamis girl" from the note which King George V sent his son: "You will be a lucky fellow if she accepts you."[9] The Duke did propose and was refused by a Lady Elizabeth who was unwilling to become a member of the royal family. Lady Airlie wrote of "my disappointment". She went on: "Lady Strathmore too was sorry; she was the soul of kindness and the Duke looked so disconsolate. 'I do hope he will find a nice wife who will make him happy,' she wrote to me. 'I like him so much and he is a man who will be made or marred by his wife. . . .'"[10]

However, the young couple continued to meet – inevitably, because of Lady Elizabeth's friendship with Princess Mary and because of the fairly close circle within which each of them moved, in and out of London. During the summer of 1921 Queen Mary went to stay with Lady Airlie at Cortachy, along with Princess Mary and the Duke of York. The Queen asked that they be invited to Glamis. Of this visit Lady Airlie writes:

> In the summer of 1921 when Lady Strathmore was ill, she [Lady Elizabeth] not only helped to nurse her but ran the household at Glamis and entertained the usual number of guests who were invited every year for the shooting. The Queen and the Duke of York had arranged to visit Glamis that summer, and they arrived there to find Lady Strathmore ill in bed and her youngest daughter deputising for her. . . . Queen Mary was by then her son's ally. I always felt that the visit to Glamis was inspired by her desire to help him, although she was much too tactful to let this be apparent.
>
> In the setting of the grim old castle . . . Lady Elizabeth filled her mother's place as hostess so charmingly that the Queen was more than ever convinced that this was "the one girl who could make Bertie happy", as she told me afterwards. "But I shall say nothing to either of them," she added. "Mothers should never meddle in their children's love affairs."[11]

During that visit the Duke of York wrote: "It is delightful here and Elizabeth is very kind to me. The more I see her, the more I like her."[12]

On their return to St Paul's in the autumn of 1921, the Strathmore family had to prepare not only for Christmas but for the wedding of Princess Mary to Lord Lascelles. Their engagement was announced in late November and the wedding day fixed for 28th February 1922. Lady Elizabeth was invited to be one of the bridesmaids at the first post-war royal wedding. It was accorded the status of a State ceremonial, so she rode in procession through the streets of London to and from Westminster Abbey along with her bridesmaid friends Lady Mary Cambridge and Lady May Cambridge, Lady Mary Thynne and Miss Diamond Hardinge, all of whom were to be bridesmaids at her own wedding.

In the spring of 1922 Lady Elizabeth went to stay with Diamond Hardinge in Paris. Lord Hardinge, Diamond's father, was British Ambassador to France and a widower, so his daughter was the official hostess at the imposing mansion in the Rue de Faubourg St Honoré. There were any number of young officials at the Embassy willing to take the charming and lively Lady Elizabeth to theatres, cafés and balls as well as on long drives to Fontainebleau and Malmaison. She was always "absolutely charming and lovely" as Molly, Lady Berkeley, remembered her on that visit.[13]

In September 1922 Lady Elizabeth once more acted as hostess at Glamis, and again the Duke of York was one of the guests. For a second time he enjoyed the pleasures of that family life which was the distinctive feature of the Strathmores. At first he found it strange that a family should be so closely knit. However, he quickly learned to enjoy the teasing and affection of the large family. Before long he felt fully at home and, at ease with these kindly people, he 'blossomed'.[14]

Back in London Lady Airlie continued to play the part of matchmaker. If Queen Mary did not think it right to meddle in her children's love affairs, Lady Airlie thought that "as the Duke was not my son, I might be permitted a little discreet meddling. Although the romance seemed at an end I continued to plead his cause from time to time – and Lady Elizabeth continued to visit me. . . ."[15]

One of London's leading hostesses, Mrs Ronnie Greville, included the Duke and Lady Elizabeth in her dinner-parties and theatre-parties. She was the daughter of a Scottish whisky millionaire who had played a major part in bringing together Edwina Ashley and Lord Louis Mountbatten (later Earl and Countess Mountbatten of Burma). She was anxious to play a similar matchmaking role for the Duke and Lady Elizabeth.

The couple met frequently at St Paul's Walden Bury, where the Duke enjoyed the peaceful calm of the English countryside along with the girl to whom St Paul's was very much 'home'. That he continued to fall more deeply in love was obvious to friends and family. That the Lady Elizabeth was aware of this and that she baulked at the prospect of a royal marriage was also obvious, particularly to her family. Her mother wrote: "That winter [1922–3] was the first time I have ever known Elizabeth really worried. I think she was torn between her longing to make Bertie happy and her reluctance to take on the big responsibilities which this marriage must bring. . . ."[16]

On Saturday 13th January 1923 the young couple went for a walk in the woods at Walden Bury, where Lady Elizabeth at last accepted the Duke's proposal of marriage. He immediately sent a telegram to his mother and father, "ALL RIGHT BERTIE". On the Sunday he rushed off to Sandringham, arriving just after tea. In his diary, King George noted: "Bertie with Greig arrived after tea and informed us that he was engaged to Elizabeth Bowes-Lyon, to which we gladly gave our consent. I trust they will be very happy."[17] Queen Mary noted: "We are delighted and he looks beaming."

On Monday the Duke was in London. From here he wrote to Queen Mary: "You and Papa were both so charming to me yesterday about my engagement, and I can never really thank you properly for giving your constant to it. I am very very happy and I can only hope that Elizabeth feels the same as I do. I know I am very lucky to have won her over at last."[18]

Lady Airlie had sent her notes of congratulation to the young couple. In reply the Duke wrote: "How can I thank you enough for your charming letter to me about the wonderful happening in my life which has come to pass, and my dream which has at last been realized. It seems too marvellous to me that my darling Elizabeth will one day be my wife. We are both very, very happy and I am sure always will be. I owe so much to you and can only bless you for what you did."[19]

The world at large was informed of the engagement through the Court Circular –

COURT CIRCULAR

YORK COTTAGE, SANDRINGHAM

MONDAY

The Duke of York, attended by Wing Commander Louis Greig, has arrived at York Cottage.

It is with the greatest pleasure that the King and Queen announce the betrothal of their beloved son the Duke of York to the Lady Elizabeth Bowes-Lyon, daughter of the Earl and Countess of Strathmore, to which union the King has gladly given his consent.[20]

For the first time Lady Elizabeth found that she was a household name; thousands of letters poured into her home at Walden Bury; every newspaper and magazine had long articles on her and the engagement. When, a few days later, she went up to London and Bruton Street, she saw the newspaper posters emblazoned with her name. Many of the reports about her, her family and the engagement were based on little but the gleanings which reporters had brought back after interviewing servants and friends. In one newspaper her father was quoted as saying: "We are quite pleased, as HRH has a high sense of duty, is a fine type of the young Englishman, and has been a devoted suitor for two or three years."[21] This realistic approach to the marriage of the youngest daughter of this family with its own long and distinguished history was common throughout the family. One of them was quoted as saying, "Thank God, she has married a good man."[22]

In those hectic days following the announcement of their engagement, the Bruton Street house was besieged by reporters and photographers. A reporter from *The Star* managed to get a personal interview with Lady Elizabeth, and that evening Londoners were able to read:

"I suppose," Lady Elizabeth began, "you have come to congratulate me? How very kind of you. I am so happy, as you can see for yourself." A pause, and then: "You ask where is the Duke? Well, Bertie – you know everyone calls him

Prince Bertie – has gone out hunting and he won't be back until this evening, when, I've no doubt [smiling] I shall see him."

Lady Elizabeth was seated at a little writing-desk, pen in hand and a pile of letters and telegrams before her. "I never imagined our engagement meant so much hard work. I think cablegrams must have come from all parts of the world, and I have been trying to answer them. I hadn't the remotest idea everybody would be so interested or so kind."

Asked about her reported hesitation before accepting the proposal, she replied with the greatest composure. "It is true he proposed in the garden at Walden on Sunday. The story that he asked me two or three times amused me. It was just news. Now look at me. Do you think I am the sort of person Bertie would have to ask twice?"[23]

It is not surprising that a few days later a royal secretary was sent from Buckingham Palace with instructions that there were to be no more interviews.

On Saturday 20th January 1923 Lady Elizabeth, accompanied by her mother and father, went to Sandringham to meet King George V and Queen Mary. They were living in York Cottage while the ageing Queen Alexandra lived in the big house. Every biographer of George V, Queen Mary and their children has written about the astonishment which York Cottage inevitably provokes. In *King George V* Harold Nicolson described the royal house:

It was, and remains, a glum little villa, encompassed by thickets of laurel and rhododendron, shadowed by huge Wellingtonias and separated by an abrupt rim of lawn from a pond, at the edge of which a leaden pelican gazes in dejection upon the water-lilies and bamboos. The local brown stone in which the house was constructed is concealed by roughcast which in its turn is enlivened by very imitation Tudor beams. The rooms inside, with their fumed oak surrounds, their white overmantels framing oval mirrors, their Doulton tiles and stained glass fanlights, are indistinguishable from those of any Surbiton or Upper Norwood home.[24]

The Strathmores were not overawed by the interview with the King and Queen. Their families had been intimate with kings and queens long before the Hanoverians were brought to the throne of Great Britain and Ireland. Indeed, as we have seen, the Bentincks had played no small part in paving the way for this accession, helping to unmake the last of the Stewarts whom the Glamis family had served and to enthrone William III. Nor were they overawed by the royal dwelling, the drawing-room of which reminded Lady Strathmore of a room in her father-in-law's old house in Belgrave Mansions.

Supported by these confident parents, Lady Elizabeth was the better able to be her natural self. Her future in-laws were impressed: "Elizabeth is charming, so pretty and engaging and natural. Bertie is supremely happy," Queen Mary wrote that night, and the King's comment was no less enthusiastic: "She is a pretty and charming girl and Bertie is a very lucky fellow."[25]

This was the first of the royal sons to become engaged. King George V had a constant worry that his sons would marry 'badly' so that he would have to suffer flighty, thoughtless, gauche daughters-in-law. We know that one reason for these fears, which he continually expressed in letters and diaries, was the behaviour of his eldest son, with his penchant for married women, members of the 'fast set' which lived up to the 'gay' in 'the gay twenties'. It is more than likely that in any circumstance the King would have been won over by the natural charm, urbanity, thoughtful yet vivacious Lady Elizabeth. Most other men had been. What made it absolutely certain that he would welcome this "Glamis girl" into the royal circle was the thought that here was one daughter-in-law who would not cause him any worry. As Sir John Wheeler-Bennett writes in *George VI*: "Indeed, from the first moment, King George took Lady Elizabeth into his heart. He admired her fearlessness, her beauty and her wit, and even his stern insistence on punctuality was not proof against her charm. To no one else would he have said – as he did when his son and daughter-in-law arrived two minutes late for dinner and she apologized – 'You are not late my dear, I think we must have sat down two minutes too early.'"[26]

She, for her part, gave him an affection and love which his own children seemed unable or unwilling to give him. In *Dawson of Penn*, Francis Watson quotes a letter which she wrote after George V's death: "I miss him dreadfully. Unlike his own children, I was never afraid of him, and in all the twelve years of having me as a daughter-in-law he never spoke one unkind or abrupt word to me, and was always ready to listen and give advice on one's own silly little affairs. He was so kind and so *dependable*. And when he was in the mood, he could be deliciously funny too! Don't you think so?"[27]

In 1772 King George III had persuaded Parliament to pass the Royal Marriages Act. This decreed that ". . . no descendant of His late Majesty George II (other than the issue of princesses married or who may marry into foreign families) shall be capable of contracting matrimony without the previous consent of His Majesty, his heirs and successors, signified under the great seal."[28] This explains why there was a special meeting of the Privy Council on 12th February 1923 at which the King signed the following document: "Now know ye that we have consented and by these Presents signify Our Consent to the contracting of Matrimony between His Royal Highness Albert Frederick Arthur George, Duke of York, and the Lady Elizabeth Angela Margaret Bowes-Lyon, youngest daughter of the Right Honourable Claude George, Earl of Strathmore and Kinghorne."[29]

Public welcome to the news of the engagement was typified by the headline "Linked again with Royalty as When a Lyon Wedded Robert II's daughter." There was an equal public welcome to the announcement that the wedding would take place at Westminster Abbey. The last royal prince married in the Abbey had been young Richard II in 1383 – when Robert II was King of Scotland and a Lyon girl Queen.

The period between the announcement of the engagement and the wedding day – 26th April 1923 – was filled with what one might describe as the 'normal' lead-in to a royal wedding. There were thousands of letters and telegrams, thousands of unsolicited gifts – many of which had to be returned lest the senders use an acceptance as a means of gaining cheap publicity and an advertising gimmick. There were visits to institutions and societies, hospitals and homes, and, particularly relevant to the Duke's personal interests, correspondence with the secretary of the Council of the Industrial Welfare Society of which he was President: "I wish with all my heart for a large increase in the membership of the Society. If I am able to propose for membership at the next Council the names of many firms who at present stand aloof, I shall feel that the Industrial Welfare Society has honoured the occasion of my marriage and my personal happiness in a manner which I deeply appreciate."[30]

Lady Elizabeth chose to have her wedding-dress made of Nottingham lace, in the hope that this would not only provide temporary employment for a small number of people in the lace trade but be an advertisement for British products. She, like her husband-to-be, was aware of the effects of the depression which had already settled down on British industry so that there were about one and a half million men without work. Of the Nottingham lace trade *The Times* wrote: "For the past three years seventy-five per cent of the machinery of this great and beautiful industry has been lying idle owing to the state of the Continental exchanges which worked a double injury, preventing our exports and making it worth retailers' while to import cheap Continental laces. In 1906 there were 37,500 people employed in the trade, of whom over 22,000 were women; in 1914 there were 50,000 and today only part-time work can be found for 17,000."[31]

Just after 11 am on Thursday 26th April 1923 Lady Elizabeth left her home in Bruton Street to drive to the Abbey. Because she was still a private citizen and not yet a member of the royal family, she rode in a state landau with an escort of four mounted policemen; the troops lining the route did not present arms to her as she made her way to the Abbey. All along the route the crowds packed the pavements and hung out of windows of houses and offices overlooking the road. The British love of pageantry had been starved during the war, whetted by the marriages of the two Princesses in 1919 and 1922 and now had a chance to give of its best in the marriage of the Prince. As *The Times* pointed out in an editorial: "There is but one wedding to which the people look forward with still deeper interest – the wedding which will give a wife to the Heir to the Throne and, in the course of nature, a future Queen to England and the British peoples."[32]

According to George V, "It stopped raining at about 9.30, and the sun actually came out as the bride entered the Abbey"[33] with her six bridesmaids. She paused on her entry into the Abbey, left her father and went to lay her bouquet of White York roses on the Tomb of the Unknown Warrior. Perhaps, in the moment of great personal happiness, she was remembering not only her own brother Fergus but also the many others whom she had nursed back to health before they returned to France and death.

The Archbishop of Canterbury read the service; the Archbishop of York gave an address in which he paid tribute to the personal work of the Duke and the family life of the bride. He also asked that they remember the special attention which would be paid to the way in which they lived their married lives:

> Will you take and keep this gift of wedded life as a sacred trust? . . . with all our hearts we wish that it may be happy. You can and will resolve that it will be noble. You will not think so much of enjoyment as of achievement. You will have a great ambition to make this one life now given to you something rich and true and beautiful.
>
> And you, dear bride, in your Scottish home, have grown up from childhood among country folk and friendship with them has been your native air. So have you both been fitted for your place in the people's life. The nations and classes which make up our Commonwealth too often live their lives apart. It is . . . a great thing that there should be in our midst one family which, regarded by all as in a true sense their own, makes the whole Empire kin and helps to give it the spirit of family life.[34]

After the ceremony there was the slow drive through the crowded streets back to Buckingham Palace. As one newspaper recorded: "She drove to the Abbey in the simplest possible manner. On her return all was changed. From a commoner she became as if by magic the fourth lady in the land, and she returned to the same spot which she had passed with such little ostentation an hour before, in the gorgeous royal scarlet and gold coach and with an imposing escort of cavalry. The large crowds cheered them heartily, the Scots among them vociferously."[35]

Almost every newspaper referred to the bride's smile as, sitting beside her husband, she rode back to the Palace. More than one sub-editor hit on the sub-title of "the smiling Duchess", catching the "brightest jewel of the day", the smile for which the former Lady Elizabeth was to become so well known.

6

A learner-member of 'the royal firm'

THEY SPENT THE FIRST part of their honeymoon at Mrs Ronnie Greville's house at Polesden Lacey in Great Bookham, Surrey. This Regency house had been built in 1824 on the site of an eighteenth-century building which had belonged to the famous actor-playwright Richard Brinsley Sheridan.

On the third day they allowed the Press to take photographs to accompany the announcement in the *London Gazette* that the Duke of York's wife would take "the title, style or attribute of Royal Highness in accordance with the settled general rule that a wife takes the status of her husband". By this announcement the King put an end to speculation as to whether the 'commoner' Lady Elizabeth was, in fact, to become a 'royal'. From the time of the appearance of the short paragraph in the *London Gazette* she was known as "Her Royal Highness, the Duchess of York". She was now, in truth and not merely in play, a princess.

On 27th April the Duke wrote to his mother: "I do hope you will not miss me very much, though I believe you will as I have stayed with you so much longer really than the brothers."[1] We have no record of Queen Mary's reply to her newly married son. We do, however, have a letter written about this time by King George V:

Dearest Bertie
. . . You are indeed a lucky man to have such a charming and delightful wife as Elizabeth and I am sure you will both be very happy together and I trust you both will have many many years of happiness before you and that you will be as happy as Mama and I are after you have been married for thirty years, I can't wish you more. . . . It must have been with a pang that you left your home after twenty-seven years. I miss you very much and regret your having left us, but now you will have your own home which I hope will be as happy as the one you have left. You have always been so sensible and easy to work with and you have always been ready to listen to any advice and to agree with my opinions about people and things, that I feel that we have always got on very well

together (very different to dear David). I trust that this state of affairs will always remain the same between us and that you will come to me for advice whenever you want it. . . . By your quiet useful work you have endeared yrself to the people, as shown on Thursday by the splendid reception they gave you. I am quite certain that Elizabeth will be a splendid partner in your work and share with you and help you in all you have to do.

Wishing you and Elizabeth every good luck and a very happy honeymoon.

Ever my dear boy

Yr. most devoted Papa

G.R.I.[2]

It is a matter of regret that the King had not shown the same understanding and sympathy, appreciation and warmth towards the Prince when he was living at home. If he had, it is at least possible that the Duke of York would not have been so lacking in confidence and might not have had his painful stammer. On the other hand, if that had not been the case, one would not have been able to appreciate so fully the extent of the contribution made by the Duchess of York to the development of her husband's character and public image. For, as we shall see, George V's hope that "Elizabeth will be a splendid partner in your work . . . and help you in all you have to do" was more than amply fulfilled.

On 7th May the young couple were back in London on their way to Glamis. They visited the Strathmores in Bruton Street, and in the evening the Prince of Wales drove with them to Euston to see them off. Unfortunately the weather in Scotland was appalling, a mixture of snow, rain and cold winds. To add further to their misery, the Duchess went down with a sharp attack of whooping cough – "so unromantic", she wrote to Queen Mary. On 19th May they came south again. Because their intended home at White Lodge, Richmond Park, was not quite ready for occupation, they went to stay at Frogmore in the shadow of Windsor Castle. The Duke had lived here when he was a child and seems to have had only happy memories of the place, writing to his former tutor, Mr Hansell: "So funny being here again. Nothing has changed at all except that it has been lent to us!! Old memories come rushing back all the time, and our old schoolroom is just the same, even to the ink-stains on the writing table. . . . It makes me feel so much older."[3] No recalling, it seems, of the splints, the childish temper, the failures at mathematics and the slog for enough marks to get into Osborne. Nor does he mention his childish fear of Queen Victoria, although he must have shown the Duchess the private mausoleum at Frogmore where Victoria was buried beside Prince Albert, her Prince Consort.[4]

Before the wedding the King had announced that their home was to be White Lodge in Richmond Park, one of the royal grace-and-favour houses. The Lodge had been built in 1727 by King George II as "a place of refreshment after the chase" in the nearby Deer Park. His wife, Queen Caroline, often used the Lodge, and Sir Walter Scott used it in *The Heart of Midlothian* as the scene for the interview between the Queen, the Duke of Argyll and Jennie Deans, when the Scots girl pleaded for the pardon of her sister Effie, then under sentence of death for child murder.

In 1805 the tenant of White Lodge was Viscount Sidmouth (Henry Addington), who had been Prime Minister between Pitt's resignation in 1801 and his recall to office in 1804. This replacement of the greater by the lesser had led someone to pen the rhyme:

> Pitt is to Addington
> As London is to Paddington.

On 10th September 1805 Horatio Nelson drove from Merton to visit his old friend at White Lodge before going to Portsmouth to embark on the *Victory*. Here, with his finger dipped in wine, he drew upon "a little round study table" the plan of battle he hoped to follow should he manage to bring the combined fleets of Spain and France to action: "Rodney broke the enemy's line in one place, I will break it in two." At the Battle of Trafalgar he and Collingwood led two lines of assault on the enemy fleet, and Britain's supremacy at sea was assured by the victory.

After Sidmouth's death in 1844 various members of the royal family lived at White Lodge. After the death of her mother in 1861 Queen Victoria and Prince Albert spent part of their last summer there, then, in 1869, Queen Victoria gave the Lodge to the Duke and Duchess of Teck. The Duchess, born in 1833, was the daughter of Adolphus, Duke of Cambridge (1774–1850), son of George III, and it was her daughter, Princess May of Teck, who in 1923 shared the throne of England as Queen Mary. For her White Lodge had very special childhood memories. It was also the home from which she had left to be married to the future King of England and to which she had returned for the birth of her first son, the future Edward VIII. Here, too, her parents had died. So it was a mark of her special regard for the couple she called "the Yorks" that they were given the tenancy of the White Lodge. Queen Mary also supervised the work of redecoration and modernization of the old house during the spring and early summer of 1923 while they were on their honeymoon and when they were at Frogmore. Kitchens and bathrooms had to be brought up to date, electricity installed and the stables converted to accommodate cars and chauffeurs instead of horses and grooms. By the beginning of June the house was declared fit for occupation, and the young couple moved in.

On the Thursday of Ascot Week, 28th June, the King and Queen came for lunch – the first visit of the 'in-laws'. The Duke had written to his mother: "I had better warn you that our cook is not very good, but she can do the plain dishes well and I know you like that sort." The visit was a great success; Queen Mary wrote that the Yorks had made the house "very nice", while the King noted in his diary: "May and I paid a visit to Bertie and Elizabeth at White Lodge and had luncheon with them. They have made the house so nice with all their presents."[5]

But for the young Duchess it was not merely a case of moving into a new home, nor of coping with her in-laws. She had also to learn to play a number of new roles, for the royal family was short of women to undertake royal engagements. We have seen that in 1922 the then Lady Elizabeth had been a bridesmaid at the wedding of the King's only daughter, Princess Mary, to Viscount Lascelles. Since her marriage she had gone to live in Yorkshire with her husband and her young family and was not available for royal engagements. On 9th June 1923 the Court had gone into a four-week period of mourning following the death of Princess Christian, fifth child and third daughter of Queen Victoria. She had played a leading role as an active member of 'the royal firm'. Now, the organizers of the societies and institutions with which Princess Christian had been connected turned to the Duchess of York to ask her to become their new patron or President. Among these were the North Islington Welfare Centre and Wards, the Young Women's Christian Association, the Mothercraft Training Society, the National Society for the Prevention of Cruelty to Children, the Royal Hospital and Home for Incurables at Putney and the Princess Christian Nursery Training College in Manchester.

The young Duchess found that she had little time to spend on the conversion of the White Lodge into a comfortable home. Every post brought in requests for her to visit this hospital, lay that foundation stone, become patron of a society, open a new ward, attend a bazaar or a fête. There are the jaundiced cynics who question the value of royal patronage; they are the same people who, in 1977, questioned the celebrating of the Silver Jubilee of Queen Elizabeth II. The extent of those celebrations and the evident warmth of the welcome given to the Queen during her tour of the country provided, one hopes, sufficient answer to such questionings. And those who organize and run the hundreds of voluntary organizations up and down the country have given a similar warmth of welcome to their royal patrons. In particular they have welcomed the ones who have given so freely of their time to furthering the work of various societies and institutions.

In addition to this side of her public work there were also more formal, official royal engagements, though King George V wanted to "break her in slowly". On 30th June 1923 she made her first public appearance as a member of the royal family when she went with the King, the Queen and the Duke to the Royal Air Force Pageant at Hendon. Over eighty thousand people were present, and the very latest aircraft were on view, including the new De

Glamis Castle, the ancestral home of the Strathmore family where Elizabeth Bowes-Lyon enjoyed so much of her childhood. During the First World War it was a military hospital and she helped her mother and sister run it – as many ex-soldiers remembered when she became Duchess of York and, later, Queen.

Lord and Lady Strathmore with their children at St Paul's Walden Bury, their English country home. *Standing, left to right:* Fergus, Jock, Lord Strathmore, May, Patrick and Alec. *Seated:* Rose, Lady Strathmore holding the infant David, Elizabeth and Michael.

St Paul's Walden Bury, the country house where Lady Elizabeth Bowes-Lyon was born. About thirty miles from London, this Hertfordshire home was one which she and her brother remembered with great pleasure.

Lady Elizabeth aged seven, a photograph which shows why she earned the nickname of "Princess".

Lady Elizabeth, aged nine, mounted on a pony at St Paul's Walden Bury.

In this photograph taken at Glamis, Lady Elizabeth, aged nine, poses with her brother David, the youngest in the family, in fancy dress.

One of the official engagement photographs of Lady Elizabeth Bowes-Lyon and "Bertie", Prince Albert, the Duke of York, later King George VI.

Lady Elizabeth with her father, the Earl of Strathmore, and her eldest brother, Lord Glamis, just before her marriage to the Duke of York.

A studio portrait taken at the time of her engagement to the Duke of York in 1923.

Lady Elizabeth Bowes-Lyon leaving her parents' home, 17 Bruton Street, for her marriage to the Duke of York in Westminster Abbey.

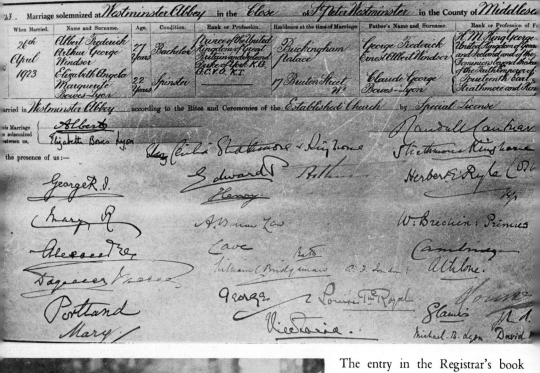

23. Marriage solemnized at *Westminster Abbey* in the *Close* of *St Peter Westminster* in the County of *Middlesex*

When Married.	Name and Surname.	Age.	Condition.	Rank or Profession.	Residence at the time of Marriage.	Father's Name and Surname.	Rank or Profession of Father.
26th April 1923	Albert Frederick Arthur George Windsor	27 Years	Bachelor	Prince of the United Kingdom of Great Britain and Ireland Duke of York K.G. G.C.V.O. K.T.	Buckingham Palace	George Frederick Ernest Albert Windsor	H.M. King George V United Kingdom of Great Britain and Ireland and of the Dominions beyond the Seas of the South Emperor of India
	Elizabeth Angela Marguerite Bowes-Lyon	22 Years	Spinster		17 Bruton Street W.1	Claude George Bowes-Lyon	Fourteenth Earl of Strathmore and Kinghorne

Married in *Westminster Abbey* according to the Rites and Ceremonies of the *Established Church* by *Special License*

This Marriage was solemnized between us, — *Albert* / *Elizabeth Bowes Lyon*

in the presence of us:—

George R.I.
Mary R
Alexander
Portland
Mary

Mary Cecilia Strathmore & Kinghorne
Edward P.
Henry.
A. Bonar Law
Cave
William Bridgeman

George
Victoria.

Randall Cantuar
Strathmore Kinghorne
Herbert E. Ryle
W. Brechin: Primus
Cambridge
Athlone.
Louise, The Royal
Maud
Glamis
Michael B. Lyon
David

The entry in the Registrar's book with its mass of important signatures – led by that of King George V and his Queen, Mary.

A photograph taken at Polesden Lacey on the first part of their honeymoon.

The new Duchess of York makes her first public appearance as a member of the royal family at the Royal Air Force Pageant at Hendon, June 1923.

The Duchess of York tries her hand at the coconut shy during a visit to a Charity Fair in Loughton, Essex, July 1923.

Balmoral Castle where the
new Duchess of York spent
the first of many holidays in
September 1923. It is not far
from Glamis and the scenes
served to remind her of her
own ancestral home.

With Queen Mary and the
Duke of York at Balmoral,
September 1923.

Havilland 9 which, it was claimed, could travel at 150 miles per hour and reach an altitude of two miles.

In July the Yorks were sent on an official visit to Liverpool, which included an afternoon at the Aintree Races. Later in July the King and Queen took them to Scotland and drew them into the ceremonies of the official visit to the Palace of Holyroodhouse. Throughout the week of that visit the young Duke and his Scottish Duchess took an active part in the ceremonies, a preview perhaps for the fuller part which they were to play in Scotland during 1929.

And all the time there was the less formal work of attending horse shows, visiting working-men's clubs and boys' clubs, hospitals and colleges, sales of work and fêtes, flower shows and balls. There were towns to be visited, such as Brighton and Manchester, Hatfield and Guildford, Alton and Glasgow, which involved a good deal of travelling as well as a seemingly endless shaking of hands. And "the smiling Duchess" appeared to have a special gift for these duties and for the more formal ceremonies. As *The Times* said in its Coronation Supplement, 1937: "She lays a foundation stone as though she has just discovered a new and delightful way of spending an afternoon."[6]

The young Duchess quickly, efficiently and cheerfully learned to play the role of an active young 'royal'. But she had another role to learn – that of a member of a royal Court, where life was quite unlike the freer, relaxed and happy atmosphere of Glamis and St Paul's Walden Bury. One of the things she had to try to cope with was the King's insistence on time-tabling and time-keeping. The young Duchess never really managed to be on time, but as we have seen, the King learned to excuse her. Someone once complained to him about the Duchess's unpunctuality. "Ah, but if she weren't late," replied the King, "she would be perfect, and how horrible that would be."[7] He had come to have a high regard for Bertie's wife.

And life at Court was different to life at Glamis in that dress was always very formal. During the day the King and all the men in his Household wore frock-coats. The ladies wore tailored clothes and always wore or carried gloves. When the King and Queen dined at Buckingham Palace, he always wore tails and she a full evening dress with a tiara – even when they dined alone without any members of their Household. When the family was at Windsor, the King, his sons and senior members of the Household wore the Windsor uniform, which consisted of a dark-blue evening-dress coat with collar and cuffs of scarlet, and knee breeches. Other men wore black evening-dress coats with knee breeches. The ladies wore long gloves with their full evening dress. Dinner was served by pages in blue and footmen in scarlet livery. Music was provided by a string band from one of the Regiments of Guards. When the ladies withdrew to leave the men free to take their port, each faced the King and dropped a deep curtsey.

All this was so different from life among the Strathmores. It is a sign of the strength of the Duchess's character that she did not break under the strain of trying to come to terms with the rigid formality of Court life. Indeed, she managed to soften it, to warm the atmosphere and to bring some relaxed joy into the lives of the King and Queen. In *A King's Story* the Duke of Windsor described her impact on the family as that of "a refreshing spirit".[8] As at Glamis, she would sit at the piano and sing and draw others around her to join in the singing. She taught her in-laws to play charades and, in the foolish play-acting, to relax and laugh a little – at themselves as well as at others. It is a mark of the high regard in which she was held by the King and Queen that she was able to play this role in the family.

She also had to learn another role with regard to men and women who had been her equals before her marriage and some of whom now served as members of her Household. It is a sign of her confidence that she was able to have a relaxed and friendly yet dignified relationship with her attendants. She insisted that when they were at home with their Household there was to be none of the rigid formality that was a feature of life at the Palace. They called their staff by their Christian names. It was on the insistence of senior members of the Household that the staff addressed the Duke and Duchess as "Your Royal Highness", and later as "Your Majesty" or, more generally as "Sir" or "Ma'am", frightened that if they were allowed to use Christian names in informal situations they might at some time let the name drop on a more formal occasion.

But the most important role which the Duchess had to learn to play – and which she continued to play until 1952 – was as the supporter and mainstay of her shy, reserved and sometimes frightened husband. It was somewhat easier for her to play that role because of the strength of her own character and because of the nature of his regard for her. But she had to nurture their relationship in the intimacy of their private lives. Indeed, when one reads of the many public calls on her time and his, of the many official and semi-official duties that they undertook, it comes as a surprise that they had any sort of private life at all. But there were garden-parties at White Lodge, private dinner-parties at Claridge's and outings to the theatre. In *The Light of Common Day*, Lady Diana Cooper quotes from a letter written by her husband Duff Cooper (Lord Norwich):

Did I tell you that I . . . went to a play. The Duke and Duchess of York were there. They are such a sweet little couple and so fond of one another. They reminded me of us sitting together in the box having private jokes, and in the interval when we were all sitting in the room behind the box they slipped out, and I found them standing together in a dark corner of the passage talking happily as we might. She affects no shadow of airs or graces.[9]

It was because they were "so fond of one another" that the Duchess was able to exercise such an influence in her husband's life and development. It was because she had "no shadows or airs or graces" that no one resented that influence. On the contrary, people were grateful that she did so.

Their home at White Lodge was the base in which they lived their private life and from which they sallied forth to undertake their public duties. Although Queen Mary had considered it a mark of her favour that "the Yorks" had been given this house, they soon realized that it was not a very suitable place in which to live. It was too far out of London for a couple who often had to go to an engagement in the day and return to Richmond to change for another engagement in the evening. Indeed, the Duchess often used her mother's home in Bruton Street as a place in which to change dresses between engagements. And it was not only distance. It was, and still is, all too easy to get lost in the Park, as anyone who has been there knows. On more than one occasion the Yorks' chauffeur drove, in fog, around and around the Park searching in vain for the road to the Lodge. When, as sometimes happened, they were in a rush to get to an engagement, they were held up by traffic and, on one occasion, by an accident in which the Duke only narrowly missed serious injury.

During the summer time the Park became a haven for crowds looking for a taste of the countryside and trying to get a glimpse of the Yorks and their home. It became increasingly difficult for them to enjoy much privacy. And the Duchess and her staff found the Lodge a difficult house to run. Certainly the Duke had an allowance of £25,000 from the Civil List, and the Duchess had more money to spend than she had ever enjoyed before, but the cost of heating the sprawling Lodge with its long, wasteful corridors, proved too much.

Yet they could not ask for a new home without risking offending the King and Queen, who thought that they had done them a special favour by giving them White Lodge. Nor, when they had managed to get over that hurdle, could they persuade the Crown Commissioners and the Ministry of Works to find them a new home. It is justifiable to move ahead of our story to 1927 when White Lodge passed to Viscount Lee of Fareham. He had given Chequers to be a country home for the incumbent Prime Minister and was offered White Lodge in return. In *A Good Innings*, the private papers of Lee of Fareham, we read an extract from his wife's diary:

> Augs. 25/1926. Some time ago A. [her husband] asked me, as a joke, if I would like to live at White Lodge in Richmond Park, and it has now actually been offered to us! It appears that the Duke and Duchess of York, who were almost forced by the King and Queen to make their home there after they were married, now want to give it up, as being too far from London and inconvenient for the sort of life which they have to live, and the question is

whether the Crown can find a suitable tenant who will take it over at a rent which would enable the Yorks to be provided with an adequate house in the West End not too far from Buckingham Palace.[10]

And so to a consideration of the most important of the roles which the young Duchess was to fill, that of supporter and guide to her husband. His biographer calls his marriage "the first great climacteric of his life". He had, as we have seen, an unfortunate upbringing, bullied by his father, ignored by his mother, overshadowed by a more brilliant and popular brother. It is not surprising that he was an introspective and highly strung man who was handicapped by his nervousness, "greatly cut off by his stammer". Yet those who knew him well – in the services – write and speak of his high qualities, his individual thinking and his personal convictions. His work with the Industrial Welfare Society and with the Boys' Camps showed him at his best. But he was all too rarely at his best; too frequently he lived down to his parents' low expectations of him. He needed someone who would provide him with a warmth, a love, and these he found in his wife. She provided the sympathy which he needed to enable his fine qualities to mature and to flower. The Duchess was aware of these qualities before they were married; the world would come to appreciate them long before his early death in 1952. She did not create the qualities or plant them, but she did nurture them as no one had done before. She gave him a confidence in himself and in his work which enabled him to rise to become a greatly loved King.

George VI's biographer wrote: "The Duchess was not only to be the partner of his happiness but his inspiration of encouragement in the face of adversity, his enduring strength in joy and sadness. Hers was the ability to sustain or reward him by a single smile or gesture in the public battles which he waged with his stammer, . . . to calm that passionate temper which ever and anon would burst its bounds."[11]

The stammer was both a sign of his nervousness and a cause of his belief in his inabilities. He was constantly frustrated as he struggled to get out the next word. He had gone to several specialists for treatment; their failure to cure him seemed only to confirm his own failings and even to lead to the unworthy suggestion that his incapacity in speech was a sign of an affliction of the mind rather than of tongue.

It was the Duchess who persuaded him, reluctantly, to see a Mr Logue, an Australian speech-therapist who had lived in London since 1924. On 19th October 1926 Logue recommended a series of exercises to develop the diaphragm and a new method of breathing. The Duchess went with her husband to some of his sessions with Logue so that she could learn what had to be done. The therapist insisted that she had a major part to play – in helping the Duke appreciate that he had a problem with his breathing and not with his speech and certainly not with his mind. It was the Duchess who had to ensure that the exercises were faithfully carried out at home, and the Duchess who shared the Duke's obvious pleasure in the rapid improvement that took place after only a month's treatment, when he wrote to his father: "I have been seeing Logue every day, & I have noticed a great improvement in my talking, & also in making speeches which I did this week. I am sure I am going to get quite all right in time, but twenty-four years of talking in the wrong way cannot be cured in a month. I wish I could have found him before, as now that I know the right way to breathe my fear of talking will vanish."[12]

The Duke never lost his dislike of public speaking, but he lost his fears as to his capacity to lead a public life and to be a respected member of 'the royal firm'. In Chapter 8 we shall see that the success of the tour of Australia and New Zealand was due in no small part to the Duke's newly discovered pleasure in being able to speak without embarrassing himself and his audience. For this pleasure, as for most others, he was indebted to his wife.

7

Going abroad –
but home for a baby's birth, 1926

DURING THE IMPERIAL CONFERENCE in the summer of 1923, the Duke of
York hinted to one of the Dominion Prime Ministers that he and the Duchess
would like to be invited to tour his country. But the King declared that "the
young people had just been married and must settle down".[1] However, in the
autumn of 1923 the Foreign Office decided that they had to attend two events
in Belgrade where, on 21st October, the infant son of King Alexander was to
be christened and, on 22nd October, the King's cousin, Prince Paul, was to
wed Princess Olga of Greece. At the first of these ceremonies the Yorks were
to stand as godparents; at the second the Duke was to be the official
representative of King George V.

One of the aims of the twin ceremonies was to celebrate the birth (and
baptism) of an heir to the throne of what was still known as 'the kingdom of
the Serbs, Croats and Slovenes' – soon to be simplified into 'Yugoslavia'. A
second aim was to help strengthen the ties which bound the Balkan royal
families together. This was the particular ambition of Queen Marie of
Rumania, the daughter of Queen Victoria's second son and the mother of
future queens of Greece and Yugoslavia. Queen Marie was affectionately
known as "Cousin Missy" in the British royal family, and the twin
ceremonies were used for a third purpose – to help her show off and confirm
the family link with the British monarchy. For the Duchess, the Balkan trip
was an opportunity to get to know some of the members of the wider family
descended from Queen Victoria – a family which was closely, if confusedly,
interlinked through royal marriages.

During the baptism ceremony on 21st October, the Duke, as godfather
(*Koom*), had to carry the infant on a cushion while his grandmother undressed
him, after which he was handed over to the aged Patriarch of Serbia for total
immersion according to the rites of the Greek Orthodox Church. The old
priest lost his grip on the infant, who slipped into the font. The quick-
thinking Duke scooped him up and handed him back to the frightened

Patriarch. The child was christened Peter. Eleven years later he came to the throne of Yugoslavia after the assassination of his father. During the Second World War, when his country was invaded by the Germans, King Peter was rescued by the RAF and later took refuge in this country, where his *Koom* acted as friend and adviser to a king who never recovered his throne.

The Duchess as godmother (*Koomitsa*) played little part in the baptism ceremony, apart from admiring her husband's dexterity. On the following day she attended the wedding of Prince Paul of Yugoslavia and Princess Olga of Greece, when she had a chance to get to know the members of the family a little better. They, for their part, were won over by her charm; as the Duke wrote to his father: "They were all enchanted with Elizabeth especially Cousin Missy. She was wonderful with all of them."[2] But she would have a chance in the future to get to know this branch of the family even better. In November 1934, just a month after the boy-King Peter had come to the throne of Yugoslavia, Princess Marina of Greece, Olga's sister, married the Duke of York's younger brother, Prince George, Duke of Kent.

During the winter season 1923–4 the Yorks rented a house at Guilsborough, in Northamptonshire, which enabled the Duke to hunt with both the Pytchley and the Whaddon Chase. For the summer season of 1924 there were plans for the couple to become increasingly involved in public life. White Lodge was still not fully renovated and would be obviously unsuitable as a base for the busy couple. They were very relieved when Princess Mary allowed them to use the Lascelles' London house, since she was expecting her second child and would not be coming to London. So the Yorks moved into Chesterfield House, which then stood on the corner of South Audley and Curzon Streets, but which has now been demolished to make way for a block of flats. The Yorks entertained at Chesterfield House and altogether they enjoyed the "brilliant and crowded season . . . a gay social life of their own . . . among their friends". There were also the State functions associated with the visits of the King and Queen of Rumania, the King and Queen of Italy, and the heir to the throne of Ethiopia. During this season the Duchess attended her first Court assemblies as a member of the royal family and the balls associated with the State visits. She was also busily involved in her role of "the leading young female of the royal firm". Hospitals and orphanages, nurses' homes and schools, factories and welfare centres had to be opened or visited. There were speeches to be made, hands to be shaken, awards to be handed out and congratulations to be offered. And always, as one ex-soldier remembered, "How she laughed and was so sympathetic and nice that it put you at your ease, and made you feel it was a shared adventure."[3]

On 19th July 1924 the Yorks were sent on an official visit to Northern Ireland. The Government of Ireland Act, 1920, had set up a separate Parliament and government of the six counties of Northern Ireland. On

22nd June 1921 the first session of the Northern Irish Parliament was opened in person by King George V. The Yorks' visit was the first by members of the royal family since that momentous opening – a sign perhaps of the King's increasing confidence in his son's capacity.

This official visit followed what has become "the usual pattern". There was the unveiling of a War Memorial at the Queen's University, which granted honorary degrees to both the Duke and the Duchess. There were visits to Belfast and Londonderry, both of which awarded the Duke the Freedom of their cities. Foundation stones were laid, industrial centres visited and, always, there were crowds of Ulstermen to cheer them on their way. The Duke was aware of the way in which people admired his wife and of the ease with which she, with her sense of humour and simple dignity, was helping him overcome his inferiority complex. Before leaving Ulster he wrote to his father: "Our reception has been quite astounding. . . . Elizabeth has been marvellous as usual and the people simply love her already. I am very lucky indeed to have her help me as she knows exactly what to do and say to all the people we meet. . . ."[4]

During the autumn the Yorks kept up their active public life, the Duke playing a leading part in the work of his Industrial Welfare Society, the Duchess confirming the opinion that she was now very much *the* royal female. As if as a reward for their work at home and in Ulster, King George V agreed that in the winter they could go on a visit to East Africa and the Sudan. While part of their time would be spent on official duties, there would be time for them to enjoy a much-needed holiday.

They left London on 1st December 1924 for Marseilles, where they boarded the liner *Mulbera*. Before the ship sailed the Duke wrote to his father: "I don't think I really thanked you properly for allowing Elizabeth and me to go. I am sure we shall enjoy the trip . . . besides being interesting, we shall gain a great deal of experience through what we shall see and do."[5] They sailed from Marseilles on 5th December and arrived in Mombasa on 22nd December. Immediately they were thrown into a whirl of activity. First there was a garden-party given by the Governor. Then there was a native dance festival in their honour in which five thousand men and women took part. In the evening the Duke held a long consultation with the Governor, Sir Robert Coryndon, so that he could become familiar with the problems involved in the development of Kenya.

They travelled 325 miles by train from Mombasa to Nairobi, where the Duchess spent her first-ever Christmas away from the Strathmore family-clan. After a round of official duties in Nairobi, the Yorks set out for a six-week safari, during which they enjoyed some success at shooting game, lived under canvas by night and travelled long distances by car or on mules by day. They ploughed through undergrowth and suffered when the rains came. The

Duchess wore slacks, a belted bush-shirt and a big felt bush-hat. The young couple enjoyed the freedom even if it involved some physical discomfort and hardship. In return the people of Kenya welcomed the enthusiasm and the interest which the Yorks showed in their young country. Unfortunately the visit had to be cut short because of the death of the Governor following an operation for pancreatitis. They then made their way to Uganda, where their official duties involved a visit to the Kubaka of Buganda, attendance at a tribal gathering of some twelve thousand spearmen and a journey along the Nile on their way to Khartoum, the capital of the Sudan. Here they stayed at the great palace which Kitchener had built on the site of a smaller palace where Gordon had been killed by the Mahdi's men in 1885.

After a short stay here, they embarked at Port Sudan on 9th April and ten days later arrived back in London. There were large crowds waiting when they reached Victoria Station. Since MCC cricketers were returning on the same train, there was some humorous debate as to whether the crowd had come to meet the Yorks or the cricketers. But there could be no doubt that the young couple who met the King were more mature, more experienced and more 'aware' because of their travels in East Africa.

On 23rd April 1924 King George V had opened the British Empire Exhibition at Wembley. The opening, including the King's speech, was broadcast, the first time that the monarch's voice had been heard over the radio. In 1925 the Duke of York succeeded his brother, the Prince of Wales, as President of the Exhibition. The date chosen for the second opening was 10th May 1925, the fifteenth anniversary of the accession of George V. The Duke managed to get through the ordeal of making a public speech on that day, although, as his father wrote: "There were some rather long pauses."[6]

As President of the Exhibition the Duke had to do a good deal of entertaining, and the Yorks rented Curzon House as a London home. The Duke and Duchess were kept busy throughout 1925, largely because of the Duke's association with the Exhibition. But there were many other calls on their time – to attend the Cup Final and Sheep Dog Trials and to visit towns up and down the country. On 24th June the Duchess was at York Minster for the restoration of the medieval glass windows in the north transept, the cost of which was borne by the women of this country.[7] The *Yorkshire Herald* noted: "She most certainly captivated us all at York yesterday, and there is no one who is not proud to think that she bears the name of our historic and wonderful city."[8]

Princess Mary (Lascelles) was expecting her second child that summer when the Duchess of York told her mother that she too was pregnant. The Duke of York was delighted. As he wrote to his mother: "We had always wanted a child to make our happiness complete."[9] He used the word "child" in an acknowledgement that his wife very much wanted to have a daughter.

The Yorks spent the autumn at Glamis and Balmoral. On their return south the Duchess insisted that they had to have a London home in which the baby could be born. She was not going to risk a birth at White Lodge, where doctors might get lost while on their way to treat her. So they arranged to lease 40 Grosvenor Square. But after their return from a Christmas holiday at Sandringham, they agreed with Lady Strathmore's suggestion that they should move into the Strathmore home at 17 Bruton Street. This they did at the end of January. For a short while the Duchess was able to enjoy meetings with her friends in London and was also free to get out to St Paul's Walden Bury with the Duke. Perhaps it was being at St Paul's that reminded the Duchess of her own nursery days under Alah (Mrs Knight). It was arranged that Alah should transfer from her sister's household to her own to serve as nanny to the new baby.

On 19th April 1926 the Yorks drove through incessant rain to have lunch with the King and Queen at Windsor Castle. On the following day the doctors were called to 17 Bruton Street. The Home Secretary, Sir William Joynson-Hicks, was also summoned. His presence was the result of an almost barbarous custom which had begun because of rumours that a boy-baby had been substituted for a dead child during the confinement of Queen Mary of Modena, the Catholic wife of James II. To ensure that no 'knavish' or 'Papist' tricks were ever again practised, it was decreed that the Home Secretary should be personally present during the birth of each royal child born in line of succession.

However, Joynson-Hicks's journey was in vain. There were complications which indicated that the baby was not going to be born as early as had been hoped. Joynson-Hicks was sent back home, and the obstetric surgeon, Sir Henry Simpson, was called in. During the night he telephoned to tell Joynson-Hicks that he could go to bed, since there was no likelihood of a birth taking place. However, during the night, the three gynaecologists in attendance on the Duchess decided that they had to "take a certain line of treatment". It is likely that the Duchess underwent a Caesarean operation. Be that as it may, Joynson-Hicks's sleep was interrupted, and he was asked to go to Bruton Street, where the Duke met him at the door. They talked together in the library for three hours before the doctors called both of them upstairs. Joynson-Hicks later wrote; "The Duke and I went into a room adjoining that of the Duchess, and in a minute or two Sir Henry Simson (sic) brought the Princess out to us. I congratulated His Royal Highness – but I cannot say that I made a deep obeisance to the baby – and then went home to bed. In due course the announcement was issued from the Home Office and the great bell of St Paul's was rung. . . . It may well be that the Princess Elizabeth may become Queen of England."[10]

The grandparents at Windsor were informed of the baby's birth, as Queen

Mary noted in her diary: "We were awakened at 4 am by Reggie Seymour who informed us that darling Elizabeth had got a daughter at 2.40. Such a relief and joy."[11]

The first editions of the national Press were already on their way to the newsagents. They missed the story, and the nation first heard of the Princess's birth through the new medium, the "wireless". London papers carried the news of the child's birth in their midday editions, by which time crowds had begun to gather outside the house. The King and Queen travelled from Windsor "to 17 Bruton Street to congratulate Bertie and we found Celia Strathmore there, saw the baby who is a little darling with a lovely complexion and pretty fair hair".[12]

Another early visitor was Lady Airlie, friend of Queen Mary and, as we have seen, matchmaker to the Yorks. She wrote: "I called at 17 Bruton Street on 22nd April, the day after the birth; though I little thought then that I was paying homage to the future Queen of England. . . ."[13]

The Times pointed out: "The birth of the little Princess . . . affects the position of her uncles, Prince Henry and Prince George, in the succession to the throne."[14] But the Dukes and Duchess had no such constitutional niceties in mind. The Duke wrote: "You don't know what a tremendous joy it is to Elizabeth and me to have our little girl . . . it seems so wonderful and so strange. I am so proud of Elizabeth at this moment after all she has gone through during the last few days and I am so thankful that everything has happened as it should and so successfully."[15] Rather than consideration of lines of succession, the Yorks were more concerned with finding a name for their baby. The Duke wrote to ask his father's consent to their choice:

Elizabeth and I have been thinking over names for our little girl and we should like to call her –   Elizabeth Alexandra Mary
I hope you will approve of these names and I am sure there will be no muddle over two Elizabeths in the family. We are so anxious for her first name to be Elizabeth as it is such a nice name and there has been no one of that name in our family for a long time. Elizabeth of York sounds nice, too.

The King readily agreed to the choice of names which honoured his mother and his wife as well as his daughter Mary, who had been the first visitor to Bruton Street on the morning of the 21st.

Princess Mary, true friend of the Duchess and daughter of the King, was one of the six godparents at the christening which took place in the private chapel of Buckingham Palace on 29th May. One of those present was the Duke of Connaught, seventh child of Queen Victoria, who had been born in 1850. He turned to Lady Elphinstone, the baby's aunt, and said sadly, "You'll see her grow up: I shan't." Here was a baptism which took the memory back to a christening in 1850 and looked to a future of which we ourselves are the living present.

8

The World Tour, 1927

IT IS DIFFICULT TODAY, even for older people, to recall the intangible yet real meaning that the words 'British Empire' once had for people living in this country. For younger readers, brought up in the years since the Second World War, it must be almost impossible to begin to understand the pride expressed in Kipling's

> Never was isle so little, never was sea so lone,
> But over the scud and the palm-trees an English flag has flown.[1]

For some, the term 'Empire' led to the assumption that there was a master-race lording it over subject races; for others, the term implied a brotherhood of peoples living in different parts of the world. For the practical-minded there was the thought that in the 1920s the countries of the Empire played an important role in the Mother Country's economy: Canada and Australia sold just over half of all their exports to Britain, while for New Zealand and South Africa the figures were eighty-four and seventy-seven per cent respectively. For their part these countries took about half of all Britain's exports and so ensured employment for a large section of British workers. And yet there was no formal, constitutional link binding these countries together. In 1926 the government had set up a committee under Lord Balfour to examine the nature of the relationship between the Mother Country and the self-governing Dominions of Australia, Canada, New Zealand and South Africa. In its report the Committee noted: "They [the Dominions] are autonomous communities within the British Empire, equal in status, in no way subordinate one to another in any aspect of their domestic or external affairs, though united by a common allegiance to the Crown and freely associated as members of the British Commonwealth of Nations."[2]

As if to confirm that "allegiance to the Crown" King George V had sent his eldest son and heir on a series of goodwill missions. He was in Canada in 1919, the West Indies, Australia and New Zealand in 1920, India in 1922 and South Africa in 1925. These official visits served to remind peoples in far-distant countries that they shared, at least, the Crown in common.

The Yorks had wanted to play their part in this cementing of relationships between the Dominions and the Crown. As we have seen, they might have gone on a tour in 1923, but the King thought that they had to be given time to "settle down". During the Imperial Conference of 1926, the Prime Minister of Australia asked the King to send one of his elder sons to Australia in 1927 for the official opening of the Federal Parliament in the new capital, Canberra. This was a project close to the King's heart. He had, as Duke of York, opened the first session of the new Dominion's Parliament in Melbourne in 1901. Shortly after gaining its right to self-government, the Australian government decided to build a new Federal capital in Canberra. The foundation stones had been laid in 1913; in 1920 another foundation stone, that of the Capitol, was laid by the Prince of Wales. The work of building had been completed by 1926, and it was intended that the seat of government should be transferred to Canberra in 1927, when Parliament would meet for the first time in the new buildings.

The King fully understood Albert's wish to have a chance to play a part in the development of the ties between the Crown and Australia. But he had serious doubts as to his son's ability to carry off the role. Would his stammer mar the dignity of the official Opening of Parliament? Would it not embarrass both him and the Australians? Then there was the question of his son's own confidence. It was all very well for him to protest, in Buckingham Palace, that he could perform all the duties which would be involved in a State visit and the official opening of Parliament. But would he maintain that confidence when he was on his own, in a strange country, surrounded by strangers some of whom might be hostile to him, while others would be waiting for him to reveal some inability? And was he physically fit, stammer apart, to carry out the arduous tasks that would lie ahead? Could he cope with the long hours of travel, the hours of standing to meet official guests at parties, balls and other functions? Would he be hampered by the stomach complaint which had forced him to leave the Navy?

In spite of his doubts, the King suggested to Prime Minister Bruce of Australia that he was considering sending his second son to represent him at the official opening. Bruce had heard the Duke speak on several occasions during the Imperial Conference. He was "appalled at the prospect of the King's representative being so gravely inhibited".[3] And, at the last moment, the Duke himself had his doubts as to his fitness for the task.

It was the Duchess who undertook to speak to the King, who "never spoke one unkind or abrupt word to me. He was always ready to listen and give advice."[4] She used her influence with him and Queen Mary to show them that it would be unfair and maybe psychologically damaging to pass over the Duke of York once again. And it was she who took him to Mr Logue in the hope that the stammer would be cured. We have already seen that Logue's success was due, in no small part, to her persistent encouragement of her afflicted husband. By October 1926 Logue had done his work and the Duke had been able to assure his father that he could now speak without much hesitation. When the King agreed to let the Yorks go to Australia, the Duke wrote to Logue: "I must send you a line to tell you how grateful I am to you for all that you have done in helping me with my speech defect. I really do think you have given me a good start in the way of getting over it and I am sure if I carry on your exercises and instructions that I shall not go back. I am full of confidence for this trip now."5 The Duchess had played an essential part in all this – in finding Logue, persuading an unwilling and doubting husband to undertake the course of treatment and helping him through the initial weeks of exercises.

Australians were lukewarm when they heard that the Yorks were to represent the King. They had hoped for the return of the Prince of Wales, who had won their devotion and had drawn fantastic crowds when he toured the country in 1920. The Yorks had, as yet, no public-image to match that of the glamorous 'Wales', and there were exaggerated rumours about the Duke's stammer.

In spite of her determination that her husband should not be passed over, the Duchess prepared for the trip with very mixed feelings, for her baby was not yet a year old, and they would be apart for six months. She arranged that, under Alah's care, the baby would stay alternately with the King and Queen and with the Strathmore grandparents. But, as she later wrote to Queen Mary: "I felt very much leaving on Thursday, and the baby was so sweet playing with the buttons on Bertie's uniform that it quite broke me up."6 Indeed, when they left Bruton Street to be driven to Victoria Station the Duchess was so upset that the car had to be driven twice around Grosvenor Gardens to give her time to regain her composure before she was able to face the crowds and the official farewells at the station.

The Yorks sailed on board the battleship *Renown*, which left Portsmouth on 6th January 1927. Although their main aim was to take part in the official opening of the Australian Parliament, their route had to be organized to take account of the wishes of the people of New Zealand that the Yorks visit their country, too. So it was that the *Renown* sailed via Jamaica, the Panama Canal and the Pacific Ocean on its way to the southern continent. The Duke was determined that his visit should succeed. On board ship he held daily conferences with his staff of advisers so that he would be the better prepared for what lay ahead.

On 27th February 1927 the *Renown* dropped anchor in Auckland and the visit to New Zealand had begun – in a sudden rainstorm which, fortunately, had stopped by the time the Yorks embarked on the royal barge to make their passage to the quayside. The Duchess made an immediate impact on the crowds on the quay as well as on those who formed the "enthusiastic crowd of small boats all crowding in for an unexpected long view of the Duke and Duchess motionless in the barge". The New Zealand newspapers approved of ". . . the way the little Duchess waved to the daring and soaked boys on the top of the wharf buildings . . ." and of ". . . her lovely colouring, the swift, upward, smiling glance, the steady eyes, blue as the forget-me-nots in her little blue hat." They appreciated that, "Never once during the formality of the morning functions did her face lose the look of alert interest. She smiled her way straight into the hearts of the people."[7]

Two days before the Yorks had landed, King George had sent them a telegram: "There is a strenuous time before you but we know that you both will do everything to secure the success which has already attended your efforts."[8]

It was indeed a strenuous tour that they had undertaken. There were dinners, receptions, garden-parties, balls and other official duties – and a little time for fishing. There were speeches to be made, hospitals, schools and other institutions to be visited – and everywhere cheering crowds. The Duke proved to be a great success. He wrote to his father: "I had to make three speeches the first morning. The last one in the Town Hall quite a long one, and I can tell you that I was really pleased with the way I made it, as I had perfect confidence in myself and I did not hesitate at all. Logue's teaching is still working well, but of course if I get tired it still worries me."[9]

One of the features of his speeches was his call to the people to take care of the young of their new nation. "Take care of the children and the country will take care of itself." This was a more human Prince than the almost film-star-like 'Wales'. The New Zealanders also liked the fact that the Duke was a keen and competent sportsman – riding, fishing and playing tennis were paths into the affections of the sportsmen of New Zealand.

But a major factor in the success of the tour was the impact made by the Duchess of York. She was less shy than the Duke, more able to make easy contact with crowds and individuals. It proved to be good public relations when, on her journey through the North Island, she met men who had been at Glamis during the war years. Some of them wrote to let her know where they would be standing in a crowd at various stopping-places. One was too shy, and although he had travelled hundreds of miles, he was content to stand in the front row of a crowd as she passed. But she saw him and called him over to talk about the time they had spent in Glamis. One young man wrote: "She shines and warms like sunlight. I never used to believe the stories one reads about people swearing themselves 'ready to die' for Mary, Queen of Scots, or Maria Theresa. But if they were anything like the Duchess of York, I can easily understand it."[10]

At a more official level was the report from the Governor-General to the King:

I want to tell Your Majesty of an incident. On the second day of the visit, Mr Coates [Prime Minister of New Zealand] met by chance a man who is a noted Communist agitator in Auckland. He said to Mr Coates, "I've done with this – Communism." Mr Coates asked why this sudden conversion had taken place. The man said: "Why, they're human! Yesterday I was in the crowd with the wife and one of the children waved his hand, and I'm blessed if the Duchess didn't wave back and smile right into my face not two yards away. I'll never say a word against them again. I've done with it for good and all."[11]

When they started their visit to the South Island, the Duchess had an attack of tonsillitis and was forced to return to Wellington to rest at Government House. The Duke's first thought was to cancel the rest of the tour. He did not think that, "deprived of his wife's encouragement and support at this moment", he could carry on. He believed, says Wheeler-Bennett, that it was the Duchess whom the crowds were really cheering and that it was "she whom they really wanted to see".[12] But she persuaded him that the tour had to go on – without her. And this proved to be a mixed blessing. The initial effect of the Duchess's absence was a drop in public interest – evidenced by the falling sales of tickets to functions which the Duke and Duchess had originally promised to attend. However, as the tour went on, the Duke seemed to call on inner reserves and with great success. In towns and in country districts he was met by enthusiastic crowds so that he finished the tour with a new confidence in himself. As one of those with him noted: ". . . In my view it was the [warmth of the people on his] arrival in Christchurch and the reception there and in Dunedin which opened the Duke of York's eyes to his popularity. I really believe that in his humble way he thought no one would bother to turn out to see him alone, and when the streets were crowded with enthusiastic, happy people throwing streamers and obviously delighted to see him he was quite overwhelmed and from that moment grew in confidence and stature."[13]

As a footnote to this memorable trip is the comment of a young New Zealander with whom I was discussing the writing of this book. When I told him that I had to write about the Yorks' trip to his country, he asked: "Were they the ones who made the famous visit? All the old people still talk about them." This tribute from a thirty-year-old is a comment not only on the success of this visit but on the value of the monarchy as the major link uniting the countries of the Commonwealth.

It was a happy Duke who met a fully recovered wife on board the *Renown* on 22nd March at Invercargill on the Foveaux Strait at the southern tip of South Island. The first lap of their tour had been a great success. Now they were better fitted to undertake the visit to Australia.

On 26th March the *Renown* sailed into Sydney Harbour, "filled with craft of all sorts", and to an enthusiastic welcome which served as a harbinger for the success of the two-month-long tour. Lord Stonehaven, the Governor-General, reported: "To say that they instantly made the best possible impression seems almost an impertinence, and it only faintly expresses the real pride and joy to which their presence gave rise. . . . I don't believe that such a scene could have been reproduced anywhere outside the Empire, and I am certain that nothing could have given rise to it except a Royal Visit."[14]

The tour of Australia involved travelling vast distances over that great but largely uninhabited country. The visit to Queensland comprised a trip to the Blue Mountains and 'stop-overs' at sheep stations. Then on to Tasmania, 'the Garden State', before going on to Melbourne for the celebrations of Anzac Day, 25th April, when twenty-five thousand ex-servicemen marched past the Duke. In Melbourne the Duchess met several people who had been patients at Glamis. Then it was on to South Australia before they made their way to Canberra for the original purpose of the visit.

On 9th May 1901 another Duke of York had opened the first Parliament of the new Commonwealth of Australia. Now, twenty-six years later, his son was to perform the same function for the Parliament in its new home. Originally it had been proposed that the Duke should make only one speech, inside the Parliament building. It was he who insisted on making a speech to the vast crowds assembled outside to see the opening. This was a sign of his newly won confidence in his own ability. And the speech was a great success, "the most moving and successful of the long series which he delivered on the tour". His speech to the people inside the Senate Chamber was another which was "perfectly admirable in delivery" in spite of the heat from the lights needed by the cameras.[15] One reason for this success was the Duchess's insistence throughout the tour that every day there were to be hours set aside for speech practices. During these she helped her nervous husband. She sat by his side as he made his important speeches and is reported to have said "Darling, how splendid. I am so proud of you!" It may be that people had been able to see how important a part she played in her husband's success; it might be that she won affections for more personal reasons. Be that as it may, there was no doubt that she had made a great impact. The Governor of South Australia must have been speaking for millions when he wrote to King George V: "The Duchess has had a tremendous ovation and leaves us with the responsibility of having a continent in love with her."[16]

The Yorks had won a special place in the affections of the Australians, one of whom noted: " We in Australia don't only take credit for the Yorks. Queen Mary once told me, 'Australia also made King George and me, when we went out as Duke and Duchess of York to open the first parliament.'"[17] And this tour had helped 'make' the younger Yorks. They sailed from Melbourne on 12th May to visit Western Australia, where enthusiastic crowds filled theatres in Perth and streets in Fremantle as well as roads along the route they had to follow. Then on 23rd May the *Renown* set sail for the long journey back to the Mother Country. On their return trip the Yorks visited Mauritius and had a few days' relaxation in Malta and Gibraltar.

They arrived back in England on 27th June, a young couple who had done their job well. The Duke, under the promptings and encouragement of his wife, had become more confident.[18] She, for her part, had received the final polish of royal training. She had done all that was expected of royalty on a long and arduous tour. Londoners provided them with an unexpected loyal demonstration on 27th June, calling for them outside the gates of Buckingham Palace and cheering as they appeared on the balcony, the Duchess holding her fourteen-month-old baby, Elizabeth.

The newly won confidence and the ability to speak properly gave the Duke a greater sense of security in his relationship with his father. After his return from Australia he went to stay at Balmoral from where the King wrote to Queen Mary: "Delighted to have Bertie with me; he came yesterday evening, have had several talks with him and find him very sensible, very different to David [the Prince of Wales]."[19] And behind this successful, "very sensible" Duke was the supportive figure of the "smiling Duchess" who shared her husband's pleasure in his continued development. Some people may still have thought more highly of his brother,[20] but the Australians had already given their verdict, as reported by an experienced political observer: "I made a special point of finding out how the Duke of York had gone down. The Prince of Wales had been phenomenally fêted and popular, yet almost everywhere people had liked the Duke of York better. This was not the opinion I had expected, so that I cross-questioned them closely on this. 'This fellow's trying to do his job better than the other,' was the reply."[21]

9

The Scottish link, 1929–30

IN 1924 THE DUCHESS OF YORK heard that 145 Piccadilly was to be vacated. She asked the Commissioners of Crown Lands if she and her husband could become the new tenants of this former Rothschild home, which was only two doors away from Apsley House. (Along with a row of other similar mansions, it has since been demolished to make way for the new exit from Park Lane at Hyde Park Corner. The towering Intercontinental Hotel now stands on the site of the Yorks' home.)

When it had become vacant in 1921, the *Financial News* had described the four-storeyed house as: "This important mansion, situate at Hyde Park Corner . . . approached by a carriage drive used jointly with 144 Piccadilly. [It] contains spacious and well lighted accommodation, including entrance hall, principal staircase hall, a secondary staircase with electric passenger-lift, drawing-room, dining-room, ballroom, study, library, about twenty-five bedrooms. . . ." The Duchess realized that this would make an ideal London base. But it took three years of protracted negotiations before the Commissioners finally agreed to grant them a yearly tenancy. The house was made ready for occupation while the Yorks were still in Australia.

They were, at last, free of White Lodge, whose new tenant was Sir Arthur Lee (p. 67). He wrote:

> There was practically no central heating, and the rooms in winter were desperately cold; the electric light was inadequate and unsafely installed; the drains were of uncertain date and apparently without system, and there was nothing to show how they were planned or where they went to. Inside the house, conditions were equally primitive, and the only downstairs lavatory, which must have been installed at least a hundred years ago, was located in the window-seat of what is now the Secretary's office! In the Duke of Teck's time, he had no dressing-room at all upstairs and had to come down in his dressing-gown to this ground floor room to shave and perform his toilet.[1]

No. 145 Piccadilly was to be the Yorks' home for the next nine and a half years. It was here that they settled into a pattern of family-cum-public life that was to do so much for the development of both the Duke and our present Queen. In making 145 into a home and creating an atmosphere in which the Duke and the children could 'grow', the Duchess played a dominant role.

The centre of family life was her own sitting-room, which had a desk at which she worked but where the children came to play when their mother was relaxing. Each morning they were brought to see their parents before being whisked away to nursery or, later, schoolroom. The parents were then free to get on with their work; for the Duchess this usually meant helping to make household decisions before getting down to her desk work – letters which had to be answered, arrangements for visits to be made or speeches to be prepared.

The parents took luncheon on their own, the children joining them towards the end of the meal. In the afternoons the Duchess may have had time for an afternoon's shopping, a visit to or from personal friends. Very often there was a public engagement of some sort – while the children were taken in a royal carriage for an afternoon's drive through Hyde Park or Battersea Park.

The Duchess's evenings were normally taken up by some public function when she was in London. Charity balls, gala nights at theatres, or, later, cinemas, official dinners of one or other of the many societies, institutions and regiments with which she was associated, all took up her time. There was, however, time for private entertaining of friends and relations, semi-private entertaining of politicians and their families and official entertaining of visiting princes and foreign statesmen, as well as the more homely entertainment provided for touring cricket teams and the officers and wives of various regiments.

The main objectives of the Duchess's life were to make her husband happy and to provide for him that warmth and affection in which his innate qualities would have opportunity to flower. Her success was evident as he steadily emerged as a strong personality who became, in time, a respected monarch. And it is a measure of her skill that she managed to do this without in any way making him appear dependent, or herself obtruding too evidently on to the scene. Indeed, one of their friends has said: "That was the measure of her greatness as a woman. She drew him out and made him a man so strong that she could lean upon him."[2]

King George V and Queen Mary were well aware of the way in which their daughter-in-law was proving to be not only an admirable partner for their diffident son but a valuable member of 'the royal firm'. Just after their return from Australia the King created the Duchess a Grand Dame of the Order of the British Empire. In August 1927 he approved her appointment as Colonel-in-Chief of the King's Own Yorkshire Light Infantry, her first regiment. Subsequently she was appointed Colonel-in-Chief to other regiments, which increased her public duties. She visited her regiments, received their colonels on appointment and on retirement, presented colours, attended receptions and frequently paid official as well as less publicized visits to 'her' regiments. She continues to do so even now; during one of my visits to Clarence House in July 1978, she was driven away to present new colours to the King's Own at Colchester.

Both she and the Duke continued to show an informed and involved interest in social conditions. They gave their support to schemes for slum clearance, for providing holidays for poor children and the elderly and for work in the field of public health. In September 1927 she was made a Burgess of the City of Glasgow, which was trying to cope with a massive housing problem. In reply to the Lord Provost's welcome, the Duke said: "Your kind words regarding the interest which is taken by my wife in movements for social and educational advancement are specially gratifying, for no one knows better than I do how great is the help which she has given me in my public duties. The exhibition which is to be opened by her this afternoon is concerned with subjects [Health and Housing] in which we are both intensely interested. . . ."[3]

In November 1928 the even tenor of their lives was broken by the King's serious illness, arising from a lung infection. There seemed at least the possibility that George V might not recover from his operation because of his "weakening heart condition". The newspapers drew public attention to the fact that although the Prince of Wales was heir, he might not marry, which made the baby Princess Elizabeth the heiress-presumptive to the throne after her father the Duke of York. During the autumn and winter there was an increase in the size of the crowds gathered outside 145 each afternoon to see the Princess being taken for her daily airing.

For the parents this was a period of anxiety, not only on account of the illness of the Duke's father but because of their legitimate concern for the burdens which might fall on the shoulders of their baby. Little did they know then of the burden that was to fall on their own unwitting shoulders in 1936.

The King spent the winter and spring convalescing at Bognor, but in May his condition worsened and in July a second operation was required. George V recovered from this during the summer so that at the end of August he was fit to go to Sandringham and "walk about at once, so glad to be home again".

The King's illness meant an increase in the public duties of the young Yorks. In March 1929 they were sent as official representatives at the wedding of Prince Olav of Norway and Princess Martha of Sweden. The Swedish newspapers, reporting their visit to the National Theatre, commented on the Duchess's "little fringe, her intensely blue eyes and her friendly smile".[4]

The Duchess was pleased on religious and historical grounds that her husband was chosen to be the Lord High Commissioner to the General Assembly of the Church of Scotland for 1929. In 1561 the Assembly had voted to ask Queen Mary of Scotland to appoint a representative who would keep her informed of its work. Ever since then this has been a royal appointment, but no member of the royal family had held office since 1679, so it was a mark of the King's regard for his son that the Duke should have been chosen.

And to have been appointed for 1929 was a mark of a very special favour, for in May 1929 the two Churches of Scotland were finally to reunite. In May 1843 there had been a dispute between the Assembly and the London government over the Church's claim to control the appointment of ministers to local churches. Two hundred members had walked out of the Assembly to form the Free Church of Scotland. Since 1920 there had been discussions on the question of reuniting the two Churches, and by 1928 the Moderators of both Churches were able to tell the Prime Minister, Stanley Baldwin, that reunion would be complete within a year. It was agreed by the Moderators, the Prime Minister and the King that some royal recognition should be granted to this historic coming-together of the once-divided Churches. So it was agreed that the Duke should act as Lord High Commissioner to the last independent Assembly of the larger Church of Scotland in May, while the King would attend the first session of the United Assembly in Edinburgh in October. However, the King did not recover sufficiently to go to Scotland in the autumn so that the Duke of York was asked to act as his father's representative for the second ceremony as well.

As Lord High Commissioner, the King's representative, the Duke of York opened the session of the Assembly 'in the King's name' and speaking from the throne. He stayed at the King's official residence, Holyroodhouse, from which he rode in state, with a mounted escort, a guard of honour and a salute of twenty-one guns. The people of Edinburgh were delighted to welcome "the girl from Glamis" and her husband. The *Scotsman* reported:

> Sunshine and cheers were blended in the great welcome which Edinburgh gave her royal visitors when they rode through the streets in the State procession from the Palace to St Giles. . . .
>
> The Duke and Duchess had an ovation infused with an extraordinary interest and enthusiasm. The association of the King's son and the little Duchess who had become the popular darling of the people transformed the routine of welcome into rapture. . . .
>
> The Duke's salute was naturally the more formal acceptance of the great welcome, the smile of the Duchess was to her hosts of admirers the more intimate and less official expression. Her Royal Highness waved freely to the crowds, took special notice of the children, of whom there were many, and did not forget to bestow frequent acknowledgment to spectators in high windows.[5]

On the great day of the Union, 2nd October 1929, the Duke was again his father's representative at a memorable ceremony where ten thousand people gathered to watch the two Moderators shake hands before going on to take part in a service of union. The Duke made a speech in which he spoke of the King's regret at not being present at this historic ceremony and of his own pleasure in being allowed to play a part in this reunion. From Sandringham the King wrote to congratulate him on his speeches. The Duchess, who had played her part in the public ceremonies, had good reason to be proud of her husband who had shown in Scotland, as he had in New Zealand and Australia, a capacity for doing the right thing in the royal way.

But if all was well with the Yorks, things were far from bright elsewhere. By the time they had returned from their Scottish triumph, unemployment had reached a record level. On 24th October there began the collapse of the stock market on Wall Street which led to massive unemployment in the USA. This, in turn, led to a rise in the level of unemployment in Britain – to two million in 1930 and to three million in 1931. Welsh miners sang and begged in London's streets. Lady Airlie wrote:

> In July 1931 I motored with friends through the north of England. The drive was a terrible eye-opener. We passed through towns and villages dead and deserted except for knots of men out of work, standing at the street corners or besieging the Labour Exchanges. Everywhere factory chimneys were smokeless; pitheads were still, village shops were without customers. Now and then we saw a lonely woman, leaning her elbows listlessly on her gate, without the heart even to chat to her neighbours.
>
> Between Chester-le-Street and Durham there was scarcely a sign of life. The great houses themselves were tenantless, their windows staring blankly, like eyeless sockets in a skeleton face. Many of the owners had let their lodges to people catering for passing motorists. The gates were placarded with 'Teas served' signs; tables were laid out in the gardens, but no one was sitting at them. It was as though a blight had swept over the whole countryside.[6]

And inside the royal family there were growing tensions from the Prince of Wales's life-style. His biographer wrote of his being "madly, passionately, *abjectly* in love with" Mrs Dudley Ward.[7] He went to see her every day when he was in London, stayed at her house whenever he could, followed her around the country when she went on holidays. He also had "brief affairs with other women, notably the much publicized one with Lady Furness".[8] There is good reason for thinking that anger and concern at his son's irresponsible life was one cause of the King's slow recovery. Certainly the state of the King's health and the behaviour of the Prince of Wales were two factors which made life for the Yorks less bright than they might have expected.

In January 1930 the Duke of York went to Italy for the wedding of the Crown Prince Umberto of Italy to Princess Marie José of Belgium. The

Duchess was unable to go because she was suffering from bronchitis. On his return she was able to tell him that the doctors had confirmed their hopes: she was expecting another baby. Princess Elizabeth had arrived almost on their wedding anniversary; the new baby might be born on the Duchess's birthday, 4th August.

It is not surprising that the parents hoped that their second child might be a boy. This was a reasonable assumption on simple averages and because there tended to be more boys than girls born into both the Windsor and Strathmore families. Nor is it surprising that the Duchess was determined that the baby should be born in her father's home, Glamis Castle. Her streak of Scottish romanticism may have helped her decide to enhance the family home with the birth of a future king.

Inside the royal family the wish for a "boy of York" grew stronger as it seemed increasingly unlikely that the Prince of Wales would settle down to marriage. A "boy of York" would provide the country with a future king – and remove the shadow of the burden of sovereignty from the Yorks' daughter.

Other people had come to the same conclusion, including the Ceremonial Secretary to the Home Office, Mr Harry Boyd. He was obsessed with the fear that, because the Duchess of York had decided to have her baby at Glamis, there might be some impression that the affair was going to be conducted in "an irregular, hole and corner way". He told Lady Airlie: "This child will be in direct succession to the throne, and if its birth is not properly witnessed its legal right might be questioned. It has happened before in history" – a reference to the birth of the son of James II and Mary of Modena and the controversy that had arisen over the supposed substitution. "We must not risk anything of that sort."9

It had originally been arranged that J. R. Clynes, the Home Secretary, and Mr Boyd should take rooms in a hotel in Perth and that two sleepers should be reserved for them on every night train until the birth. Mr Boyd was horrified at the thought of this: "Just imagine if it should occur in the early hours of the morning and the Home Secretary could not get to Glamis in time."10 Lady Airlie came to his rescue. He and the Home Secretary were invited to stay at Airlie Castle, near Glamis.

The baby was expected to be born between 6th and 12th August. On the morning of 5th August Boyd and Clynes arrived at Airlie. The Post Office rigged up a special line from Airlie to Glamis for telephone calls, and a motor cyclist was kept on stand-by at Glamis in case the wire broke down. Lady Airlie gives an account of the almost farcical events of the next two weeks:

> Mr Clynes was a small man, very quiet and shy, dressed in a rather ill-fitting suit and a grey Homburg hat. He talked very little, in contrast to Mr Boyd,

who fidgeted incessantly and seemed still preoccupied with the fear of some plot. . . .

On the 10th we met Sir Henry Simpson, the Royal accoucheur, by appointment at the gate of Glamis – Mr Clynes being too afraid of embarrassing the Duchess of York to go inside. On hearing from Sir Henry that the event could not be later than the 11th, we sat up all night, sustained by frequent cups of coffee, but there was no further communication.

By the 14th Mr Boyd was in a panic and reminded the Home Secretary so severely of his duty when he was on the point of going out for a drive with me, that we returned to the house to sit making conversation and waiting for the telephone to ring. As nothing happened we breathed more freely and the next day resumed our excursions to neighbouring houses, though within a restricted radius.

On the morning of the 21st, Mr Boyd, wild-eyed and haggard after sitting up all night, telephoned to Glamis once again, only to hear from Admiral Brooke that there was still no news. He wandered out dejectedly into the gardens – by then none of us dared to go further afield.

That evening as I was dressing for dinner the telephone bell rang in my room. The agitated voice of Admiral Brooke asked for Mr Boyd. I ran in my dressing-gown to Mr Boyd's door and banged on it . . . "A telephone call for you from Glamis."

I heard . . . a wail of anguish through the closed door . . . "I can't go downstairs, I'm not dressed and I can't find my suit."

"Then put on your dressing-gown and take the call in my room," I shouted back. "I'm not dressed either but it doesn't matter."

Mr Boyd dashed out of his bedroom in a dark blue kimono and into mine. I heard him spluttering into the telephone . . . "What! in an hour? You haven't given us much time. We must start at once."

Fortunately all was well. They arrived at Glamis with nearly half an hour to spare.[11]

It is little wonder that when he was King, George VI did away with the need for the Home Secretary to be in attendance at the birth of his first grandchild in 1948.

The little Princess was the first member of the royal family to be born in Scotland since Prince Robert, younger brother of King Charles I, who was born at Dunfermline in 1602. The Scottish people, and in particular the people from the neighbourhood of Glamis, were delighted. So too were the King and Queen, who left Sandringham for Balmoral on the day after the baby's birth. They visited their latest granddaughter at Glamis on 30th August.

There was a problem with finding names for the Princess. On 27th August the Duchess wrote to Queen Mary at Balmoral: "I am very anxious to call her Ann Margaret as I think Ann of York sounds pretty, and Elizabeth and Ann go so well together. I wonder what you think? Lots of people have suggested Margaret, but it has no family links really on either side."[12] But the King would not allow the use of the name 'Ann' so the Duchess wrote: "Bertie and I have decided now to call our little daughter 'Margaret Rose', instead of 'Margaret Ann', as Papa does not like 'Ann' – I hope that you like it. I think that it is very pretty together."[13]

'Papa' agreed to the names which honoured three Scottish queens of the name Margaret, and the 'Rose' which was a tribute both to the Duchess's sister and to the White Rose of York. On 30th October, the baby was christened 'Margaret Rose' by the Archbishop of Canterbury at Buckingham Palace.

So, while the economic crisis deepened and the behaviour of the errant Prince of Wales gave cause for concern, the Yorks with their two little daughters returned to 145 for the start of what proved to be their happiest years.

10

The happiest period, 1930–5

THE DUKE AND DUCHESS OF YORK were delighted with the success of their public work, particularly in New Zealand, Canada and Scotland. This bred a new self-confidence on the part of the Duke and a wish to be allowed to get more closely involved in public affairs. He asked his father if he might see the reports which came in from British representatives in foreign countries and in the Dominions. King George V refused him this privilege and even advised him to have nothing to do with Britain's political leaders.

In 1930 he was given another and more public slight. When the Governor-General of Canada, Lord Willingdon, was due to retire in 1931, R. B. Bennet, the Prime Minister of Canada, suggested that the Duke of York would be a very good substitute for the position. This idea was put to the British government. J. H. Thomas, Colonial Secretary, who had once been "insistent that the Princes should go to the Dominions as G.C.s or even as Governors of the Australian States", refused to agree that the Duke of York should be sent to Canada.[1] The Duke and Duchess must have known that Thomas, a rough-spoken ex-engine driver, and the King were very great personal friends. Thomas's refusal might have been taken as an indication that the King believed his son was unfit to take up the Canadian post. If so, it merely drove the Duke more firmly back into his sheltered family life. Here, at least, he was valued for himself, and here too he could find that love which would allow his character to grow free from the warps inflicted on it by his upbringing.

It was fortunate for the young couple that just about this time they were given a new home and a fresh interest on which to centre their joint activities. In 1929 the Prince of Wales had acquired Fort Belvedere, near Virginia Water, as a 'grace-and-favour' residence. In September 1931 the King thought it right that his second son should have his own country home at Royal Lodge in Windsor Great Park, another grace-and-favour house. Built in 1811 by the Prince Regent who, as George IV, had continued to use it as his home, after his death it had housed a number of members of the royal family and friends and former servants of the sovereign. By the time the Yorks went to see it, it was very much run down and dilapidated.

And the autumn of 1931 was hardly the best of time for members of the royal family to be seen spending money on yet another home. In August the Labour government had split over the methods to be used to solve Britain's financial problems, and the National Government formed under Ramsay MacDonald had instituted a series of cuts in public expenditure – the salaries of judges, teachers and others were cut, along with the weekly benefit paid to the three million unemployed. The King, seeking to give added point to the need for financial stringency, had told the Prime Minister that he wanted a cut of £50,000 in the Civil List (the money granted each year to the sovereign out of taxation). The Duke of York's income of £25,000 a year was also cut, which meant that he could not afford to lay out money on rehabilitating Royal Lodge.

However, by the middle of 1933 there were the beginnings of an economic recovery, and the number of unemployed started to fall. The Yorks set about restoring the grand salon which a previous owner had divided into five narrow rooms. This room, measuring forty-eight by twenty-nine feet, was twenty feet high and dominated the Lodge. They had brand-new wings built on to either flank of the existing house to accommodate the nursery and staff.

Even before this work had started, the Yorks had begun to tackle the wilderness of the garden, which in 1931 covered fifteen acres but which they extended to ninety acres. Much of the work of clearing and planting was done by the young couple. One afternoon when the King and Queen had driven over from Windsor Castle to Royal Lodge, they found the Duchess of York raking leaves and Princess Elizabeth pushing a barrow full of rubbish towards a fire tended by a chauffeur. "But where is the Duke?" asked the King. "There he is, Grandpa," said the Princess, pointing to her father's feet. He was lying at full length under a mass of tangled rhododendrons, hacking away at the branches. Queen Mary made them all line up, with their dirty faces, and photographed them.[2]

The restoration of the garden was a joint venture, as a former Deputy Ranger of Windsor Great Park has said: "The gardens [of Royal Lodge] are the inspiration and the work of the Duke and Duchess of York themselves. . . . *They were so close together that they always thought alike.*"[3]

Just outside the garden hedges is a small chapel where the York family used to worship when they were at the Lodge, except on major feasts such as Easter Sunday when they went across to St George's Chapel at the castle. The Duchess felt that it was like old times to have a chapel of her own; it brought back memories of life at Glamis, with its chapel inside the castle and the morning prayers with her family – and during the war with many wounded soldiers.

Living at Royal Lodge gave the Yorks a chance to see more of the Prince of Wales whenever he was in residence at Fort Belvedere. Lady Furness was present during one visit on a very wintry afternoon when the four of them went skating on the frozen Virginia Water. She wrote: "The lovely face of the Duchess, her superb colouring heightened by the cold, her eyes wrinkled with the sense of fun never far below the surface, made a picture I shall never forget."[4]

But, above all, the Lodge was a family home. A member of the royal household, who often stayed with them as an extra guest during Ascot Week, wrote: "It was the most charming, comfortable and simple home you can imagine. I can honestly say that never in my whole life have I seen a family so happy." And as with the Strathmore family so with the Yorks: the centre, "the flywheel", of this family life was the mother.

In April 1932 the little Princess Elizabeth had her sixth birthday, and the parents began to give thought to their daughter's education. The Duchess's sister, Lady Rose Leveson-Gower, who lived in Rosyth, told them about a young Dunfermline governess, Marion Crawford, who taught the Leveson-Gower children for a short session each day. Miss Crawford walked miles every week, making her way to pupils in various aristocratic homes in the Scottish hills. The Yorks liked the sound of this energetic teacher. In the summer they drove from Glamis to meet her, and two weeks later the Duchess wrote: "Why not come for a month and see how you like us and we like you?"[5]

"Crawfie" stayed with the family for fifteen years. When she left to get married, she wrote a series of memoirs of her life with what had become by then the royal family. A good deal of what she wrote comes under the heading of Annan's "inconceivable banality", and one wonders who was interested in the colour of the royal bedspreads and sheets, but hidden among the saccharine, over-sweet and over-intimate accounts of royal life there are nuggets of information which are of some significance. In *The Little Princesses* Miss Crawford wrote: "No one ever had employers who interfered so little. I had often the feeling that the Duke and Duchess, most happy in their own married life, were not over concerned with the higher education of their daughters. They wanted most for them a really happy childhood, with lots of pleasant memories stored up against the days that might come and, later, happy marriages."[6]

It is from Miss Crawford's writings that we learn of the way in which the Yorks divided their day and tried to give their children as much attention as was possible. Every morning, "no matter how busy the day, how early the start", the children romped into their parents' bedroom and had "high jinks". After their morning lessons the Princesses were taken to have lunch with their parents – a privilege not accorded to most other children whose parents were members of London society. The afternoon was spent in lessons or outings. After tea there was always a long period of nursery games in which the children were joined by their parents and, whenever he could manage it, their Uncle David, the Prince of Wales. The Duchess taught her children various card games; Uncle David enjoyed reading to them, and almost always there was a game of charades. One evening as he left, the Prince turned to the Duchess and remarked, "You make family life so much fun."[7] In this we might see admiration of the Duchess, regret for his own childhood as well as envy for the younger brother's good fortune in having found such a pleasant and helpful wife whereas he, David, seemed to be able to get along only with older and already-married women.

"Crawfie" also wrote of the high spot of the day, bath time, when the Duke and Duchess would go to join in the fun. We know from other, later, biographies that this bath-time ritual was repeated in the lives of the children of Queen Elizabeth II. She remembered the pleasure she had derived from the mutual splashing of parents and children and was determined to give her own children some of the same. So it was that the happy childhood of "the girl from Glamis" was repeated not only in the lives of her children but in those of her grandchildren.

By the time that Miss Crawford came to teach the little Princess, she had already been taught to read by her mother. According to Lady Cynthia Asquith, the Duchess used to read Bible stories aloud each Sunday morning and chose "the right sort of books" for winter evenings, "fairy stories, *Alice*, *Black Beauty*, *At the Back of the North Wind*, *Peter Pan* and anything we can find about horses and dogs...".[8] It was the Duchess who taught the children their prayers and formed in them the same trusting faith on which her own life had been based.

During weekends at Royal Lodge the children carried on with their lessons, but there was also a chance to ride or to play in the garden or the park. If it was their father who gave them an interest in riding, it was the Duchess who was responsible for introducing him and them to the pleasure of owning house dogs. In the summer of 1933 the children admired a corgi puppy belonging to some friends. The Duchess bought one, and the fame of the Welsh corgi was assured.

"Crawfie" did not write her articles and books until the 1950s, but even in the 1930s knowledge of the Yorks' happy family life was widespread. One newspaper referred to 145 Piccadilly as "the home at the heart of the Empire". There were always small groups of sightseers gathered around the gates of the mansion, while passengers on London buses going down Piccadilly would crane their necks to try to catch a glimpse of the house, the gardens and, perhaps, the children.

But royal life was not all pleasure for the Duchess of York, nor was it all spent in the happy family atmosphere. There was the almost incessant call of public duty, involving hours at the desk, answering letters from the charities and societies with which she was linked. These included Dr Barnardo's, the Middlesex Hospital, Moorfields Eye Hospital, West Ham Central Mission, the National Society for Maternity and Child Welfare, Croydon General Hospital, St Mary's Hospital Paddington, to name but a few around London. But many of her interests meant engagements involving long travel. There were official visits to towns as far apart as Plymouth and Middlesbrough; there was a library to be opened in Sheffield and a Service of Thanksgiving for the restoration of Lincoln Cathedral. And almost always there were crowds, as at the Aldershot Tattoo, the Richmond Horse Show, the Highland Games, the Circus at Olympia and a long, arduous tour of South Wales.

So it was that a good part of every morning was spent with her secretarial staff in the office at 145. And after so many public engagements it must have been a relaxation for the Yorks to stay at home in the evening. Unlike the Prince of Wales, they did not enjoy the club life of London's Mayfair. The Duchess liked reading and playing the piano or a game of patience. Sometimes one of the staff would be sent to get tickets, and the couple would slip unrecognized into the cinema at Marble Arch. Sometimes, but rarely, there were dinner-parties at their home or at the home of one of their close friends. In his diary Harold Nicolson noted:

> 20th February 1936
> 4 King's Bench Walk, EC4
>
> My new pal Maureen Stanley asked me to come round and meet her father [Lord Londonderry] who is just back from hob-nobbing with Hitler. When I got in, there was a dear little woman in black sitting on the sofa, and she said to me, "We have not met since Berlin." I sat down beside her and chattered away all friendly, thinking meanwhile, "Berlin? Berlin? How odd. Obviously she is English, yet I do not remember her at all. Yet there is something about her which is vaguely familiar." While thus thinking, another woman came in and curtsied low to her and I realized that it was the Duchess of York. Did I show by the tremor of an eye-lid that I had not recognized her from the first? I did not. I steered my conversation onward in the same course as before but with different sails; the dear old jib of comradeship was lowered and very gently the spinnaker of "Yes, Ma'am" was hoisted in its place. I do not believe that she can have noticed the transition. She is charm personified.[9]

✗The Yorks followed a royal pattern for their holidays. Along with all the other members of the royal family, they spent Christmas at Sandringham. The autumn was almost always passed in Scotland.✗At first they had stayed at Glamis, but as Lady Strathmore became older and less vigorous, their visits tended to shorten and more time was spent at Birkhall on the Balmoral estate.

Birkhall, with its six thousand acres and charming Georgian mansion, had been bought by Prince Albert, the Prince Consort, as a Scottish home for the then Prince of Wales, later King Edward VII. It was Albert who was responsible for the purchase of Balmoral and for the building of the 'Scottish baronial' mansion in which he and Queen Victoria spent much of their time. Balmoral remains a favourite holiday home for the royal family, and Birkhall a convenient house for such members of 'the royal firm' as do not choose to stay at Balmoral itself.[10]

At the centre of the Yorks' Birkhall home was the Duchess, of whom "Crawfie" wrote: "The little Duchess had the nicest, easiest, most friendly of manners. My whole impression was of someone small and quite perfect."[11]

The ageing George V was fully aware of the vast difference between the life-styles of his two eldest sons. He told his Prime Minister, Stanley Baldwin, "After I am dead the boy [his heir] will ruin himself in twelve months." According to Lady Airlie, the King had discussed the Prince of Wales's behaviour only a few weeks before his death, when he told Lady Blanche Lennox, "I pray to God that my eldest son will never marry and have children, and that nothing will come between Bertie and Lilibet and the throne."[12]

The old King had a high regard for the way in which the Duchess of York had helped his second son develop and mature. He approved of the happy family atmosphere which she had created in their homes at Windsor, Birkhall and 145. He had discovered that from the window of his study and with the help of field glasses he could see part of the Yorks' house at 145 Piccadilly. Each morning he would train his glasses on that house, and each morning would come the wave of a handkerchief as "Lilibet" waved good morning to her "Grandpa England". Little did anyone realize how quickly the lives of the Yorks would be changed by the events of 1936.

The Duke of York (*extreme left*) and the Duchess (*centre*) on a visit to Makwar Dam during their tour of East Africa in 1925.

London, 1926. The Duke of York stands proudly behind his Duchess and their first child, Princess Elizabeth, now Queen Elizabeth II.

The Duke and Duchess of York driving through Queen Street, Auckland, on their way to a civic reception during their first major Tour, 1927.

The Duchess of York charming the Australians during a drive on their Tour in 1927.

A word of encouragement to the Duke during the opening of the new Parliament Building, Canberra, 1927. This was the most important public task he had undertaken to that date and his success during this Tour helped make him more confident.

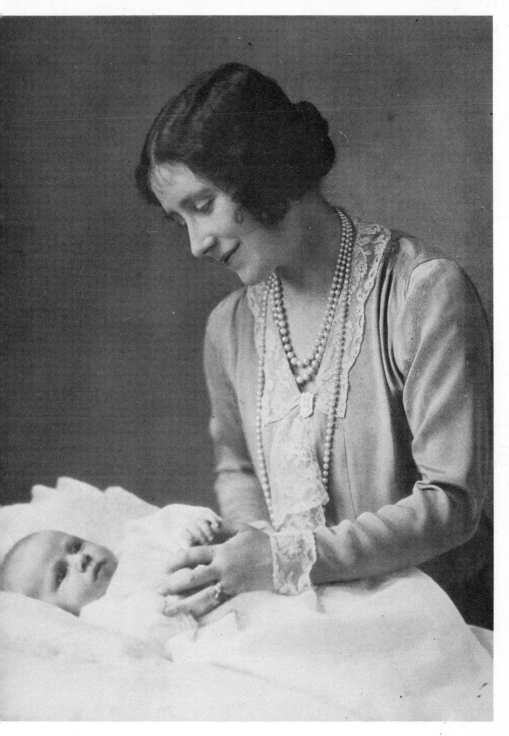

The Duchess of York with the infant Princess Margaret Rose, 1930.

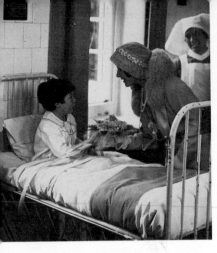

The Duchess of York in one of her "smiling Duchess" poses during a visit to the children's ward after opening an extension to the Harrow and Wealdstone Hospital, 1931.

Opening new buildings at the Middlesex Hospital, 1935.

The Duke and Duchess of York leaving St Paul's Cathedral after the service held to celebrate the Silver Jubilee of King George V and Queen Mary, 1935. The two Princesses, Elizabeth (the inquisitive one) and Margaret (standing in front of her father) had begun to take a small part in public life by this time.

his is the only known
otograph of the
uchess of York in
iform – she was never
wear one again,
guing that she didn't
ve the figure for it.
ere, in 1936, she was
her way to award
zes at the St John
mbulance and
rsing Competition
als.

e Duchess of York
h the two Princesses
d the royal corgis –
he garden at Royal
lge, Windsor, then
ow her favourite
ntry home which she
the Duke of York
almost created.

King George V's
coffin on its last sad
journey, 1936.

The interment of
King George V's
body in St George's
Chapel, Windsor.

King George VI and Queen
Elizabeth drive through the
crowded and decorated streets
on their way to the Coronation
Service.

The new King, his Queen, his
mother Queen Mary, and the
two Princesses come on to the
balcony of Buckingham Palace
to accept the cheers of the
crowds which filled the Mall
and the space around the
Victoria Memorial.

In Paris, July 1938, Queen Elizabeth's clothes were widely admired. This was the first foreign visit made by their Majesties and the first State Visit to Paris since 1914.

On the porch of Hyde Park, the Roosevelt home, the King and Queen chat with the President, Franklin D. Roosevelt, his wife and his mother. The Queen "captured" America while the visit, she declared, had "made us".

PART III: 1936

11

The death of King George V, 1936

IN 1934 THE DUKE OF KENT, the youngest of the King's surviving sons, married Princess Marina of Greece in Westminster Abbey. The Duchess of York now had a glamorous sister-in-law to share some of the burdens imposed on the females of the royal family. In 1935, the Duke of Gloucester married Lady Alice Montagu-Douglas-Scott, daughter of the Scottish Duke of Buccleuch. "The girl from Glamis" had a fellow-countrywoman at Court, and there were now three daughters-in-law upon whom the King could call when there was a job to be done. Only the Prince of Wales remained a bachelor.

On 6th May 1935 King George V was given the unprecedented honour of a Jubilee to celebrate the twenty-fifth anniversary of his accession. This was seen by some as a government's attempt to revive memories of Queen Victoria's Diamond and Golden Jubilees and as a means of undoing the harm that might have been done to the nation's reputation by the notorious debate at the Oxford Union in February 1933, when the undergraduates had voted that they "would not fight for King and Country".

There were many who questioned the holding of a Jubilee and the spending of public money on festivities at a time when there were still over one and a half million men out of work. The public welcome for the Jubilee was then, as in 1977, the best answer to these cynical doubters. On 6th May the King and Queen drove to St Paul's Cathedral to attend a Thanksgiving Service. The King noted in his diary: "A never to be forgotten day.... The greatest number of people in the streets that I have ever seen in my life. The enthusiasm was indeed most touching."[1] And this "enthusiasm" was maintained throughout the following week when, every night, the King and Queen appeared on the floodlit balcony of Buckingham Palace to be cheered by the crowds who had waited all day. And similar "enthusiasm" was seen when they drove through the poorer parts of London – Battersea, Kennington, Lambeth, Limehouse, Whitechapel and the slums around the docks. Everywhere they were greeted by hordes of cheering children, the applause of older people and the sight of banners, flags and streamers even in the poorest streets. Sister Catherine Black, who had been appointed to look after the King ever since his illness, wrote: "His pleasure at the wonderful evidence of the people's love and regard during the Jubilee was touching. I can remember him coming back from a drive through the East End, very tired but radiantly happy. 'I'd no idea they felt like that about me,' he said with his usual frankness. 'I am beginning to think that they must really like me for myself.'"[2]

Tom Jones, the Prime Minister's secretary, had his own explanation for this wave of popularity: "It is surely due to the people realizing the contrast between the homely ways of the King and the bullying of the Continental despots [Hitler and Mussolini]."[3] Harold Nicolson, the royal biographer had another explanation: "Yet behind it all . . . there was another sentiment. In those twenty-five years his subjects had come to recognize that King George represented and enhanced those domestic virtues that they regarded as specifically British virtues. . . . In him they saw, reflected and magnified, what they cherished as their own individual ideals – faith, duty, honesty, courage, common sense, tolerance, decency and truth."[4]

The Duke and Duchess of York were sent to represent the King and Queen at the Jubilee celebrations in Edinburgh and later shared in the state drives through parts of London. Little did they or the cheering crowds realize that before long it would be the Yorks themselves who would be welcomed because of those "domestic virtues" of which Nicolson had written.

On 3rd June the King had his seventieth birthday. He had stood up to the strains of his Jubilee celebrations, but now, without warning, he collapsed, and the doctors ordered a complete rest. During the Court balls and the festivities associated with Ascot Week, the Duchess of York was very much the Queen's right-hand, supporting her in the way she would have to support and help her husband.

On 3rd December the King's sister, Princess Victoria, died at her home, Coppins, in Iver, Buckinghamshire. She was sixty-seven years old. To many in the immediate family, including the Duchess of York, this death of the King's favourite sister was a shattering blow. In his diary George V noted: "How I shall miss her and our daily talks on the telephone. No one ever had a sister like her."[5] He was supposed to have presided at the State Opening of Parliament on the afternoon of Princess Victoria's death, but he cancelled it – and never appeared in public again.

Stanley Baldwin believed that, having had his Jubilee and suffered the death of his sister, the King spent the last days of 1935 "packing up his luggage and getting ready to depart".[6] On 21st December the Court went, as usual, to Sandringham for the Christmas holiday. From here the King broadcast his Christmas message to the people of the Empire. But even that broadcast lacked the sparkle which people had come to expect from the man who had captured their imagination when he first used the medium in 1932. And his family could see that he was unable to walk upright, easily tired and frequently vague about what he wanted them to do for him.

During this Christmas holiday the Duchess of York suffered an attack of influenza which developed into pneumonia. The Duke was with her at Royal Lodge on 15th January, the day on which George V went for a short ride on his white pony, with Queen Mary walking alongside him. Next day the King complained of a cold. Queen Mary noted in her diary: "Most worrying. I sent for Bertie to help me with the party" [which had come for the shooting].[7] Although the Duchess was still very ill, she insisted that "Bertie" had to go across to Norfolk to be with his mother.

When the Duke returned from Sandringham on 19th January, he had to tell the convalescing Duchess that the King was gravely ill and might not recover. By this time the little Princesses had been sent back from Sandringham to Windsor, and Miss Crawford had been recalled from her holiday. The Duchess warned her: "Don't let all this depress them more than is absolutely necessary, Crawfie. They are so young."[8]

The Prince of Wales went to London on 19th January to tell the Prime Minister that his father was dying. On Monday 20th January a few chosen members of the Privy Council gathered in the King's bedroom at Sandringham for the purpose of appointing Counsellors of State. Wheeler-Bennett wrote: "Weak and dying, the King sat propped up in a chair, just visible to the Privy Councillors through the open door of his sitting-room." And then, quoting from Queen Mary's diary, he goes on: "Lord Dawson managed to get G to say 'Approved', and he was able to sign two little crosses, as he was unable to sign his name, which distressed him. . . . David and Bertie returned at 2.30 in D's airplane. . . . G became weaker during the evening and we realized the end was approaching. We family dined alone and then went to G's room at intervals and at five to twelve my darling husband passed peacefully away – my children were angelic."[9]

The public had been kept informed of the King's condition through Press releases and regular reports on the BBC, the most famous of which was the penultimate message: "The King's life is moving peacefully towards its close." Over at Royal Lodge the Duchess listened to these broadcasts. Just after midnight the Duke telephoned her to tell her of the King's death. It was she who had to tell the little Princesses that their grandfather was dead. The *Daily Express* reminded the nation – and the Yorks – of the significance of this death. Its headline ran:

NINE-YEAR-OLD PRINCESS ELIZABETH, ELDEST DAUGHTER OF THE DUKE AND DUCHESS OF YORK, IS NOW SECOND IN THE LINE OF SUCCESSION TO THE THRONE. ONE DAY SHE MAY BE QUEEN ELIZABETH OF ENGLAND.[10]

Only the lives of the new King and her father stood between the little Princess and the throne.

The Duke returned from Sandringham to Royal Lodge, and on 22nd January the Yorks travelled together to Sandringham so that the Duchess might give what comfort she could to her mother-in-law. Since they first met, fifteen years before, a strong bond of friendship had grown between them. It is not surprising that the Queen tended to lean on her eldest daughter-in-law rather than on the much younger Duchesses of Kent and Gloucester who had been in the royal family for only fifteen months and three months respectively.

There was a short family service at the little church at Sandringham, where the coffin rested for thirty-six hours. Queen Mary noted in her diary: "Went to the Church after luncheon. It all looked very peaceful – but so sad. My sons returned, also Harry [of Gloucester] and Alice [his wife] and Elizabeth [of York]."[11] On Thursday 23rd January the coffin was taken on a gun-carriage to Wolferton Station. The King, his brothers and his brother-in-law walked behind. With Queen Mary in her carriage were the Princess Royal and the Duchess of York.

At the station the coffin was placed aboard a special funeral-train. At King's Cross Station, London, another gun-carriage was waiting, as well as the Imperial Crown, which was then fixed on top of the draped coffin. The royal family travelled in the funeral-train and made their way from King's Cross to Buckingham Palace. Meanwhile the coffin was taken in a simple family procession through London to Westminster Hall for a Lying-in-State.

Tom Jones watched this "mournful little procession" and wrote in his diary:

> ... Went to the Strand and from the window of my second-hand bookseller, Gaston, I saw the mournful little procession pass on its way from King's Cross to Westminster Hall – perhaps forty men in all counting mounted and on foot. The King plodded heavily along weighed down by a thick long overcoat, looking utterly done. The only patch of colour was the Royal Standard on the coffin. The absence of the military and of music, the walking of the King and the Dukes, the fewness of those taking part, the intense quiet of a thronged street, made the sight a moving one. I suppose it could happen in this simple way nowhere but in London. [12]

The body lay in state for four days. During this time there was a demonstration of popular affection even more marked than that which had made the Silver Jubilee such a splendid occasion. Dense crowds waited, sometimes all night, to take their place in the long lines around the Parliament buildings. There was a continuous procession of people through the Hall, where about a million people filed past the coffin at which officers of the Household stood on guard.

On the last evening, 27th January, the King and his three brothers took the place of the officers keeping vigil. Queen Mary noted: "At midnight my four sons stood guard over their father's coffin for twenty minutes, a very touching thought."[13]

After four days, on the morning of Tuesday 28th January, the dead King's body was taken to Windsor. Violet Markham, a close friend of Tom Jones, wrote to him on 30th January to describe the procession from Westminster Hall:

> I went to London on Monday and saw what I wanted to see very comfortably. The Chairman took me into Westminster Hall for the Lying-in-State, and I had a superb view of what you truly call that solemn and splendid procession, from the Devonshires' house overlooking the Mall. We shall never see anything like it again. If our Army is only a remnant, it's a very fine remnant in discipline and drill. But the palm nevertheless went to the sailors. I thought that the phalanx drawing the carriage which looked like a mechanized tractor the most amazing example of time and step ever seen in London. I can't describe the scene going along the Mall and the wan sunshine that fell on the coffin as it passed. And the lament of the pipes. From the same spot I and my great-nephew Tim Tallents, who was with me again on Tuesday, had cheered the King and Queen a few brief months ago on their return home from St Paul's. The contrast was indeed poignant.[14]

The Duchess of York rode in the Glass Coach along with Queen Mary, Queen Maud of Norway (King George V's sister) and the Princess Royal. When the procession reached Paddington Station, it was already two hours late because of the crush of the crowds, some of whom had waited all night to pay their last respects to the dead monarch and to show their support for the widowed Queen. Princess Elizabeth and "Crawfie" were waiting at the station. The child went across to her mother and stayed with her throughout the rest of the day, as the train took the family and the coffin to Windsor. The official ceremony was held in St George's Chapel where the little Princess and her mother stood together with other members of the royal family as the body was committed to the vault below the Chapel.

Various explanations have been offered for the nation's mourning for the death of the old King. C. L. Mowat, an academic historian, notes:

> The familiar post-war world was fast vanishing; the new order [of Hitler, Stalin and Mussolini] was cold and empty, modern and menacing. Hence the nation's mourning for King George was partly a mourning for the past. . . . The public outpouring of grief was increased by the . . . silence on the air, save for the sound of the ticking of a clock and every quarter of an hour the silken tones of the BBC's chief announcer, Stuart Hibberd, repeating the words "The King's life is moving peacefully towards its close."[15]

Violet Markham noted on 30th January 1936:

It must be difficult to resist the universal feeling at such times. In one's sorrow – and it's really a personal sorrow – one cannot but feel that the King was happy in his passing – to be swept without suffering on to the further shore by that great high tide of the nation's love and loyalty which had known no ebb since the Jubilee. And he has left us a great legacy – the greatest proof ever given in history, that in the end it is character not cleverness that counts; goodness and simplicity, not analytical subtlety and the power to spin verbal webs.[16]

An old order had passed away. The Queen let it be known that she wished to be called 'Queen Mary' and not 'the Queen Mother'. Londoners read the headline: "Edward VIII flies to London" on 21st January, and, as Tom Jones noted: "In a month we shall all be used to the new title." And the Yorks had to get used to the idea that the father's death and the accession of the popular bachelor King had altered their place in the line of succession. By how much their position had been changed did not become clear until later in the fateful year during which Britain had three kings.

12

The gathering storm

THE DEATH OF GEORGE V and the accession of Edward VIII seemed to many people at that time a case of 'off with the old and on with new'. There was a good deal of newspaper comment on the new 'young' King, which tended to overlook the fact that he was forty-one years old. He had been the subject of a generally favourable critique in 1926 when A. G. Gardiner, in *Certain People of Importance*, wrote:

> We do not ask for a brilliant king, and we should not tolerate an ambitious king, but we need a king whose character we can respect, whose loyalty to his office is above suspicion, and whose capacity is adequate. We have such a king today, and it is because we hope the country will have such a king in the future that we scrutinise a little closely the promise of the Prince.
>
> He has now passed through that phase in which it was sufficient to regard him as the Prince Charming of romance, a sort of visitor out of a fairy tale, whose engaging ways won all hearts and from whom nothing was asked except that he should appear and be acclaimed. . . . He is now a man of thirty-two. He has served his apprenticeship and has reached an age when the character is formed and when responsibilities must be assumed.[1]

The new King was praised by the leaders of the major political parties. Prime Minister Baldwin, speaking in the House of Commons after the death of George V, said:

> He brings to the altar of national service a personality richly endowed with experience in public affairs; he has the secret of youth in the prime of age; he has a wider and more intimate knowledge of all classes of his subjects, not only at home but throughout the Dominions and India, than any of his predecessors. . . . We look forward with confidence and assurance to the new reign, believing that under God's Providence he will establish the throne more firmly than ever on its surest and only foundation, the hearts of the people.[2]

Even people who were aware of the serious defects in the new King's

character were prepared to hope that all would be well. One such was Tom
Jones. Baldwin told Jones that the new King was weak-willed and stubborn
and went on – "Nor is there any man who can handle him." Jones noted in
his diary: "I pressed my view that he'll rise to the new responsibilities though
he may discharge them in his own way."[3]

But we know that none of the initial hopes was realized. It was the tragic
failure of the new King which brought the Yorks to the throne. For this
reason his failure is pertinent to this study of the Queen Mother's life, which
would have taken a different shape if it had not been for the Abdication.

There is evidence to suggest that Edward VIII had long been aware of his
own inability to live up to other people's high expectations. Arthur Lee (later
Viscount Lee of Fareham) served with him on the Western Front in 1915
and in his memoirs wrote:

> While on my daily rounds at this time, I frequently came across the little Prince
> of Wales. He seemed incorrigibly self-effacing, and his main desire appeared to
> be to get either killed or wounded. . . . It was current gossip in those days that
> one reason why he exposed himself so heedlessly was that he had a morbid
> dread of succeeding to the throne and, when begged to be more careful, his reply
> always was "But why should I?; my brother would love the job and would
> make a much better King.[4]"

In *Majesty* Robert Lacey quotes some of the new King's close friends on his
reaction to the death of George V. Lady Hardinge called it "frantic and
unreasonable . . . far exceeded that of his mother and three brothers".[5]
According to Lacey the death of the King had taken him by surprise.[6] His
friends had become persuaded that, during the last months of his father's life,
the Prince was seriously considering renouncing his claim to the throne in
favour of Bertie. His "frantic and unreasonable" grief may well have been
panic at the thought that he had left it too late.

In public Baldwin spoke fair words about the new King, but in private the
well-informed and astute Prime Minister expressed himself differently. Tom
Jones quotes Baldwin as being "distinctly nervous about him [the new
King]".[7] And Jones himself wondered "whether it is going to be a case of the
Prince in Shakespeare's *Henry IV*, and the King in *Henry V*".[8] On 20th
January the Prince, as he then was, had come to tea with the Baldwins. In a
letter written on 24th January Tom Jones noted:

> When Mrs Baldwin left them to talk, she said, "We have faith in you," which
> touched him, and he held her hand and pressed it for a noticeable moment. He
> told S.B. that he was glad he was P.M., and S.B. remarked to me: "You know
> what a scrimshanker I am; I had rather hoped to escape the responsibility of
> having to take charge of the Prince as King. But perhaps Providence has kept
> me here for that purpose. I am less confident about him than Lucy [Baldwin]
> is."[9]

Baldwin, Jones and other well-informed men were aware of the former Prince's preference for older, married women such as Mrs Ward and Lady Furness, and popular singers such as Florence Mills (who launched the song 'I can't give you anything but love'). Hector Bolitho wrote of him:

> Frequent chastening made the Prince of Wales secretive, stubborn and more self-willed than ever. Still in tune with his generation, he came to look upon his father, the Archbishop and some of the older Ministers as a critical and unsympathetic company, designed to frustrate his natural eagerness. He, therefore, made his own life as he wished. It took him into three worlds. One was in the circle of friends which he gathered about him, often to the distress of his father, who suspected their influence. . . .
>
> For some sad reason their eldest son was not equipped with this power to judge, and early in his life he was inclined to gather about him those people whose familiar manner made it easy to talk with them, rather than those whose loyalty and respect made their manner seem reserved. This incongruity first showed itself during his American and Dominion tours . . . when his official duties were ended he often sought his pleasure in society which was unsuited to the needs of the heir to the throne. It was as if the burden was so heavy for him that when he needed relaxation he ran to the extreme of gay and casual people whose objects in life were different from his own. [10]

Baldwin was aware of the new King's close friendship with Mrs Simpson, a gay, witty and attractive American commoner who had been divorced from one husband and, with her second, Ernest Simpson, had been drawn into the circle of princely friendship during the early 1930s. Some people have suggested that the opposition to the King's friendship with Mrs Simpson sprang from the fact that she was an American. Support for this view is given by Tom Jones's pejorative use of the term "the American woman" in a letter written on 24th January 1936. [11] However, the British aristocracy had long learned to welcome American brides, such as Lady Furness, Lady (Nancy) Astor and Lady (Emerald) Cunard into their families.

It may have been that the fact that Mrs Simpson was divorced made her *persona non grata* in Establishment circles. Born into an old and wealthy American family, she had married a US naval officer in 1916. In 1927 she had obtained a divorce from him because of his desertion. Six months later she was married in London to an Englishman, Mr Ernest Simpson. Viscount Lee wrote: "The 'upper' class deeply resented Mrs Simpson, of whom *The Times* acidly observed that 'she has failed to retain the affection of two previous husbands, both of whom are still living.'"[12] But the upper class had long since learned to come to terms with divorce and had accepted *paramours* without much difficulty. King Edward VII's long list of 'lady friends' was well known to at least an inner circle, which did not try to freeze out Mrs Keppel or the others on whom the King bestowed 'his favours'.

It might well be that the reason for the growth of opposition to the new King's friendship with Mrs Simpson lay in her inability to play her expected part. As Mrs Keppel was heard to remark: "Things were done differently in my day."[13] As we shall see, Mrs Simpson seems to have gone out of her way to offend those members of the royal family whom she met. It could be this, rather than any sense of moral outrage, which lay behind the increasing hostility shown to the King's friendship with "the American woman".

The then Prince of Wales first met Mrs Simpson in 1930. Their friendship had ripened into love, and the Prince's friendship with Mrs Ward came to an end in 1934 as he concentrated his attentions on Mrs Simpson. He managed to get the Simpsons included on the list of guests at a ball held at Buckingham Palace a few nights before the wedding of the Duke of Kent and Princess Marina. Robert Lacey in *Majesty* quotes 'other sources' which "assert that George V actually asked his son whether Mrs Simpson was his mistress, and that it was only on being assured that she was not that an invitation was sent to her husband".[14] In *Edward VIII* Frances Donaldson retells a "strange story told by Sir Maurice Jenks, a former Lord Mayor of London, to Baldwin" in 1936. Jenks had been President of a Masonic Lodge to which Mr Simpson applied for membership, his candidature supported by the then Prince of Wales. The Lodge turned down the application, and the Prince demanded an explanation. Jenks told him that Masonic Laws forbade the entry of the husband of another member's mistress. The Prince "gave his word that this was not the situation", and Simpson's application was then accepted.[15]

We do not know whether the Prince of Wales was lying or not. Certainly Mr Simpson seems to have been either a *mari complaisant*, aware of his wife's unfaithfulness, or a naïve innocent. The couple appeared in public along with the infatuated Prince. In his own *King's Story* the former King Edward admits that by the end of 1935 he had come to the conclusion that he had to marry Mrs Simpson, that the country would never accept a divorced woman as queen, so that he would have to give up his claim to the throne in favour of his brother Bertie. He claims that he would have spoken to his father about this if it had not been for the peculiar circumstances of the year of Jubilee – with the Gloucesters' wedding, the death of Princess Victoria and his father's ill-health all combining to make a serious discussion almost impossible. We may doubt whether such a son could have spoken to such a father on such a subject, no matter how favourable the circumstances. We may, however, wonder why this father, with his rigid ideas on duty, did not speak to his wayward son. We know that he was aware of this "latest friendship" and that he tended to disbelieve the Prince's assurance of its platonic nature. Lady Airlie tells us that he discussed this problem with the Archbishop of Canterbury, Cosmo Lang,[16] and that he also asked the Duke of Connaught to interfere in the affair. He had discussed the problem with Baldwin, hoping that "my eldest son will never marry ...".[17] But if we have some cause to blame the father for not having tried to talk to his son, we also have a good reason to believe that concern over his eldest son's behaviour was at least a contributory factor to the King's ill-health at the end of 1935.

So it was that on his accession the new King was, in Harold Nicolson's words, "in a mess". Nicolson was a member of a party on 13th January 1936 with Lady Sibyl Colefax. He wrote:

> Changed for dinner. ... Then on to the Phoenix Theatre for the first night of Noël Coward's play. Sibyl breaks to me the fact that the other two members of our party are the Prince of Wales and Mrs Simpson.
>
> Mrs Simpson is bejewelled, eyebrow-plucked, virtuous and wise. I was impressed by the fact that she forbade the Prince to smoke during the entr'acte in the theatre itself. She is clearly out to help him. ... Nobody pays any attention to him, and what is odd is that the waiters do not fuss unduly. The Prince is extremely talkative and charming. I have a sense that he prefers our sort of society either to the aristocrats or to the professed highbrows or politicians. Sibyl imagines that she is getting him into touch with Young England. I have an uneasy feeling that Mrs Simpson, in spite of her good intentions, is getting him out of touch with the type of person with whom he ought to associate.
>
> Go home pondering on all these things and a trifle sad. Why am I sad? Because I think Sibyl is a clever old bean who ought to concentrate upon intellectual and not social guests. Because I think Mrs Simpson is a nice woman who has flaunted suddenly into this absurd position. Because I think the P. of W. is in a mess. And because I do not feel at ease in such company.[18]

It is one of the facets of this tragedy that it might have been averted if there had been someone who could have spoken to the wayward and headstrong Prince. Instead, he came to the throne in a peculiar situation. Stanley Baldwin told Tom Jones: "When I was a little boy in Worcestershire reading history books, I never thought I should have to interfere between a King and his mistress."[19] There had been all the signs throughout 1934 and 1935 that the relationship between Edward and Mrs Simpson would create both personal and constitutional problems. But no one had tried to deal with this problem until now, in January 1936, it was too late.

We have seen that on 23rd January the new King and the other members of the royal family accompanied the dead King's body through the streets of London on its way to the Lying-in-State. The Imperial Crown had been brought from the Tower and secured to the lid of the coffin. This crown is surmounted by a Maltese cross, a jewel set with a great sapphire, eight medium-sized diamonds and 192 lesser diamonds. Edward VIII (as Duke of Windsor) described the almost prophetic incident which occurred during this procession: "... The jolting of the heavy vehicle must have caused the Maltese cross to fall. ... I caught a flash of light dancing along the pavement. ... I wondered whether it was a bad omen."[20] So did others. Lady Lee wrote of the "wicked rumour . . . in circulation; that it had fallen off into the gutter as the coffin passed 'Simpson's' in the Strand."[21] The cross was retrieved by the Company Sergeant-Major bringing up the rear of the two files of Grenadiers. Two Members of Parliament, Walter Elliott and Robert Boothby, happened to be standing at this point. They heard the new King remark: "Christ! What will happen next?" Elliott remarked to Boothby: "A fitting motto for the coming reign."[22]

13

The brief reign of Edward VIII

WHILE THE NEW KING watched his own Proclamation Ceremony at St James's Palace, peeping from a window with Mrs Simpson by his side, the Duchess of York was still recovering from pneumonia at Royal Lodge. Her immediate concern, apart from getting better, was to consider the new responsibilities which now fell on her and her husband. She would have to share more duties with Queen Mary. Indeed, while Queen Mary remained in mourning, the Duchess would be, in a sense, the first royal lady in the land. Her husband accepted the task imposed on him by the new King of sorting out the family's financial affairs and settling the late King's estate. His first duty was to provide a report to show how to reduce the cost of running the Sandringham estate.

This took the Duke off to Norfolk, but doctors considered that East Anglia would be too cold for the Duchess. She went to stay at Compton Place, Eastbourne, a property owned by the Duke of Devonshire, where she remained until the beginning of April when she and the Duke went to spend Easter at Royal Lodge.

There was public recognition of the new position of the Yorks in the nation's life. By an Order in Council the words "Our Gracious Queen Mary, the Duke of York and the Duchess of York" were inserted into the Anglican prayers, liturgies and collects for the Sovereign and the royal family. Loyal toasts were given a new form: after the first toast to "The King", there was to be a second, to "Queen Mary, the Duke and Duchess of York and other members of the royal family". They were now to be differentiated from "other members of the royal family". Ambassadors came to pay their respects to the Yorks after presenting their credentials to the new King, and their London home at 145 Piccadilly became, as it were, the home of "the monarch who may be".

On his part the new King started his reign with a burst of energy. He was assiduous in reading all the official papers that were sent to him. He scribbled his comments in the margins before returning them in their red boxes. But there was early evidence that this feverish activity could easily be diverted into triviality – as with the case of the clocks at Sandringham. Ever since Edward VII's time, the clocks at Sandringham had been kept exactly half an hour fast – in the hope that this might get guests out of bed early in the morning to join the shooting parties. George V had kept 'Sandringham time' as a symbol of an old order, a link with his father and his own childhood. Even as the King lay dying, the difference between 'real' and 'Sandringham' time led to some small mistakes. "I'll fix those bloody clocks," the Prince is said to have yelled, and, indeed, the Sandringham clockmaker was kept busy working through the night of George V's death putting all the Sandringham clocks back to Greenwich Mean Time.[1]

The new King also made other breaks with tradition. He received all the ambassadors together instead of individually, as had been customary on the accession of a new monarch. He declared that the ribbons of Orders would not be worn in the open air and so would not be worn at the King's Birthday Parade. He decided that King George V's racing yacht, *Bluebottle*, was to be broken up. He made many changes in his household and on the estates at Sandringham and Balmoral. Many people lost their jobs, and the overall impression was of a man interested in minor things with an inability or unwillingness to concern himself with the greater.

There was, on the other hand, a welcome for the 'breath of fresh air' which he promised to bring and for his love for 'the modern', such as the aeroplane. He inaugurated the 'King's Flight' so that aircraft and pilots were kept ready for his travels. Whereas his father had always used the royal 'We', the new King used the first person singular, as in his first broadcast on St David's Day, 1st March 1936:

> I am better known to most of you as the Prince of Wales – as a man who, during the War and since, has had the opportunity of getting to know the people of nearly every country of the world, under all conditions and circumstances. And although I now speak to you as the King, I am still the same man who has had that experience and whose constant effort it will be to continue to promote the well-being of his fellow-men.[2]

But to people 'in the know' all was far from well. Harold Nicolson gives an account of a meeting with J. H. Thomas, the former railwayman who was Secretary of State for the Colonies in the National Government:

> 26th February 1936
> King's Bench Walk, E.C.4
>
> Jim Thomas really minds the death of the King. He says he has lost one of his dearest friends. And what makes it so odd is that this is true. The King adored him and he always spent a fortnight at Balmoral every year. . . . "And now 'ere

we 'ave this little obstinate man with 'is Mrs Simpson. Hit won't do, 'arold. I tell you that straight. I know the people of this country. I know them. They 'ate 'aving no family life at Court."[3]

The new King's private life was in marked contrast to that of his brother 'Bertie'. The latter found his pleasure in the company of his wife and children, whether at 145, at Royal Lodge or in the homes of their friends – such as Compton Place where he stayed with the Duchess during part of her convalescence. As if in tribute to their family life, Queen Mary spent Easter at Royal Lodge with the Yorks, and the Duchess went out of her way to make life as pleasant as could be for the widowed Queen. She accompanied her on motor trips through the countryside, went with her when she visited friends and persuaded her to join in the celebrations for Princess Elizabeth's tenth birthday. What "the smiling Duchess" did not realize was that her domestic happiness was itself a sharp reminder to the bachelor King of his own problem of being in love with a married woman.

And by the beginning of April the King's behaviour was itself the cause of concern. Politicians and civil servants were alarmed when they realized that not only did he not read his 'papers' but he left them lying around at Fort Belvedere. When they came back to the Cabinet Office, some of these confidential papers were stained with the rings of wet glass bottoms. The initial energy had been dissipated and in its place was a lazy sloppiness. In part this was due to the King's character defects, which were confirmed by the boorish behaviour of the close circle of friends he gathered around him. Nicolson gave an account of a party which he attended on 2nd April 1936 when the Ladies Oxford, Cunard and Colefax brawled in public in an attempt to win the attention of the new King – who was more concerned with Mrs Simpson. Nicolson concluded his account with the telling comment: ". . . . the whole setting is slightly second-rate. . . ."[4]

The energetic, popular 'Prince Charming' had become a devotee of the second-rate, while his slower, duller, nervous, stammering brother had grown and developed. Whereas the one tended to ignore his public duties, the other set out to make his work both interesting and challenging. It is not surprising that after his accession the King should have withdrawn from the company of his brother and the rest of the royal family and have sought the company of the 'second-rate'. It seemed as if the new King was determined not to play the part of a reformed 'Prince Hal' as Jones had hoped.[5] He preferred to shine against the backcloth of the 'second-rate' rather than try to match his brother's devotion to duty, determination to succeed and developing sense of responsibility.

But there were even more serious reasons why the politicians and civil servants were uneasy about the King's behaviour. It seemed that he was unaware of the true nature of his position as constitutional monarch. He had given some indication of this ignorance before his accession, when, in June 1935, addressing a British Legion rally in the Albert Hall, he had spoken in favour of a proposal to "stretch forth the hand of friendship to the Germans".[6] German newspapers took this as an indication that the British government was anxious to become more friendly to the Hitler government. It was, in fact, an expression of the then Prince's own personal admiration for the Fascist dictators. What neither the Prince nor the Germans understood was that it was a constitutional impropriety for a member of the royal family to make such a political utterance. Kings and princes are not allowed the freedom of a personal indulgence in political matters; they have to subordinate their own inclinations and tastes – or cease to be royal.

Germany's leaders believed that "here was a future King of England favourable to them. . . ." Addressing a crowd of about twenty thousand, "Goering then turned to the question of Anglo-German relations and expressed Germany's pleasure at the recent declaration of His Royal Highness the Prince of Wales. The German ex-servicemen and the German nation cheerfully grasped the hand which had been stretched out to them. . . ."[7]

King George remonstrated with his son on his injudicious remarks. However, after his accession, there was worse to come. In March 1936 German troops marched into the Rhineland, breaking not only the Versailles Treaty but also the Locarno Pact by which Britain, France and Italy had agreed to guarantee the French, Belgian and German frontiers. There is evidence in the autobiography of Hitler's companion Albert Speer that Hitler always termed the re-militarization of the Rhineland the most daring of all his undertakings. "We had no army worth mentioning; at that time it would not even have had the fighting strength to maintain itself against the Poles. If the French had taken any action, we would have been easily defeated; our resistance would have been over in a few days. . . ."[8]

During this crisis there was a series of meetings between French and English Ministers; there was talk of implementing the terms of the Locarno Pact and of making war against Germany. Frances Donaldson's *Edward VIII* provides the documentary evidence for the role of the King throughout this period. He spoke to the Italian Ambassador and the London representatives of German newspapers and made it clear that he was opposed to any firm action being taken against Germany. Indeed, he was anxious to promote an alliance between Germany and Britain – contrary to the wishes of his government and, as far as could be judged, the majority of his people.[9]

It is not surprising that the German Foreign Minister, Ribbentrop, decided that he could do more good as Ambassador in London than in the Foreign Ministry in Berlin. The Abdication later in 1936 was a disappointment to Ribbentrop and the other Nazi leaders, who had sensed "the likelihood of success . . . because of Edward VIII. . . ." Indeed the Germans thought that,

"Edward VIII had to abdicate since it was not certain whether, because of his views, he would co-operate in an anti-German policy."[10]

Baldwin's initial reaction to the King's failure to appreciate his true constitutional position – of reigning but not ruling – was to instruct civil servants to make a careful selection of the papers that were sent to the King. Some required a royal signature; these had to be sent. But sensitive, confidential papers were withheld. The King did not seem to notice that, in return for his own unconstitutional behaviour, his Ministers were depriving him of his constitutional rights of access to all official papers. Baldwin was saved, in this instance, by the King's own laziness.[11]

By the time of the crisis over the Rhineland, the Duchess of York had almost recovered. On 9th March she wrote to the royal physician, Lord Dawson of Penn: "I am really very well now and I think am now suffering from the effects of the family break-up – which always happens when the head of a family goes. Though outwardly one's life goes on the same, yet everything is different – especially spiritually and mentally. I don't know if it is the result of being ill, but I mind things that I don't like more than ever before. . . ."[12]

Among the "things" which she minded in March 1936 may have been reports about the King's evident infatuation with Mrs Simpson. Her sense of what was 'royal' must have been outraged at reports that he ran at her beck and call – sometimes to fetch her nail-file if she had left it upstairs, sometimes to get cushions to make her more comfortable. Her sense of the respect due to the dead King and to the widowed Queen must have been shocked by reports of the successful party held at Fort Belvedere, the King playing his own bagpipes around the dining-table.[13]

On her return to London the Duchess helped the widowed Queen Mary plan the arrangements for her move out of Buckingham Palace and into nearby Marlborough House. We know from Lady Airlie that the mother often spoke in sorrow about the behaviour of her son, now also her King. It has to be assumed that she also spoke to the Duchess about her concern over his private life, including, for example, his refusal to attend church each Sunday. She was also reminded of the possible effects of his behaviour on herself and her family by the growing interest shown by the Press and the public at large in her elder, but still very young, daughter. This interest in the 'future Queen' grew to the point where it was felt necessary to invite journalists into 145 Piccadilly. The resulting publicity was well down to Annan's "inconceivable banality". There was wide publicity given to the Post Office engineer sent to repair the telephone at 145 who smacked the little Princess's bottom when she rummaged in his tool bag. "She ran away, and her mother seemed rather pleased," he told a reporter.[14]

The royal family preferred this sort of favourable, if banal, publicity to that which they were getting in newspapers in the USA and Europe. Foreign newspaper-owners and editors were not parties to the self-denying ordinance which the British Press lords imposed on themselves and their editors. There was widespread publicity given in foreign newspapers to the growing intimacy between the King and Mrs Simpson. The British public was kept in blissful ignorance of all this.

Lulled by the pictures of "the smiling Duchess", "the future Queen Elizabeth" and "inside 145", the British public was led to believe that all was well in the royal *ménage*.

Indeed it was the King himself and not the newspaper proprietors who seemed determined to bring Mrs Simpson's name before the public. In the summer of 1936 he insisted that her name should appear in the Court Circulars which listed the names of guests at his evening dinner-parties. At the first of these, the guest of honour was the Prime Minister. Others present included the Duke and Duchess of York and Mr and Mrs Ernest Simpson.[15]

In July the King gave another party, and again the Court Circular gave the list of guests – the Duke and Duchess of York, the retiring Viceroy of India, the Marquess of Willingdon and his wife, Winston Churchill, some politicians – and Mrs Simpson. Mr Simpson was not present, as was made clear to that portion of the reading public which was interested enough to read the Circular in the leading newspapers. On 13th July Harold Nicolson met Ramsay MacDonald: "He talks about the problems of the King's appalling obstinacy and the unfortunate Court Circulars in which Mrs Simpson's name appears as a guest. He says it is making a bad effect on the country."[16] MacDonald exaggerated, as London-based politicians tend to do. 'The country' was not yet aware of the significance of an announcement which few read and even fewer understood. But it is certain that Mrs Simpson's presence at these parties annoyed the Duchess of York. She felt that she and the Duke were being 'used' by the King to give an air of respectability to his 'friendship' with Mrs Simpson. At the July party, Winston Churchill brought up the subject of King George IV and Mrs Fitzherbert, the great marriage scandal of the late eighteenth century. Lady Hardinge tells us how the Duchess "very firmly said '*That* was a long time ago.'"[17] The Duchess was unwilling to give even the hint of a suggestion that she might be willing to countenance any development of the King's relationship with "the American woman".

Mrs Simpson realized the importance of trying to win over this influential member of the royal family. If the Duchess became favourably inclined towards her, then probably Queen Mary and certainly the Duke of York would also become less antagonistic. But the harder Mrs Simpson tried to win the sympathy and support of the Duchess, the more she seemed doomed to fail. In her book *The Heart has its Reasons*, she recalled the reception she received in the spring of 1936:

That spring David bought a new American station-wagon. . . . It was amusing to observe the contrast between the two brothers – David all enthusiasm and volubility as he explained the fine points of the machine, the Duke of York quiet, shy, obviously dubious of this new-fangled American contrivance. . . . We all walked through the garden. Our conversation, I remember, was largely a discussion on the merits of the garden at the Fort and that at Royal Lodge. . . . David and his sister-in-law carried on the conversation, with his brother throwing in only an occasional word. It was a pleasant hour; but I left with a distinct impression that while the Duke of York was sold on the American station-wagon, the Duchess was not sold on David's other American interest.[18]

"Crawfie" was present on this visit, and in her book she commented on the distinctly proprietary manner in which Mrs Simpson treated not only the infatuated King but also Royal Lodge, which was the Yorks' home and very much their personal creation. Miss Crawford wrote of how this "smart, attractive woman drew the King to the window and suggested how certain trees might be moved, and a part of a hill taken away to improve the view". It is hardly surprising that the atmosphere was "ice-cold" – so noticeably cold in fact that Princess Elizabeth asked "Who is *she?*" as soon as the King and Mrs Simpson had left the room.[19]

In the summer of 1936 the King decided to go on a cruise on the yacht *Nahlin*, chartered from Lady Yule. During late August and early September he visited the Dalmatian coast in a way which attracted world-wide attention. In Dubrovnik he was greeted by twenty thousand peasants in national costume who shouted the Yugoslav equivalent of "*Vive l'amour*". When the yacht sailed through the Corinth Canal, the King was filmed wearing only a pair of shorts, to the delight of the crowds who gathered to yell their obscenities. On the return trip he appeared stark naked in a Viennese bath-house – and provided good copy for newspapers, newsreels and photographers from all over the world, except Great Britain. A contemporary and a close friend of the King's, 'Chips' Channon, noted in his diary; "The Mediterranean cruise was a Press disaster."[20] Robert Lacey in *Majesty*, written in 1977, says: "The unreality of the *Nahlin* cruise beggars description." Certainly it gave strength to the argument that the King seemed to have taken leave of his senses – a point which was to be repeatedly made by members of his immediate family during the coming winter.

As if to add point to the contrast in life-styles, the Yorks spent part of their summer holiday at the Bowes-Lyon family estate in Durham, visiting pits and the homes of miners. They also stayed with the Duke of Northumberland at Alnwick Castle before the Duke of York returned south to "one of the most important engagements of the year" – his Boys' Camp. At the end of August the Yorks were united again at Birkhall, on the estate of Balmoral, to which the King brought Mrs Simpson to stay in early September. The Duchess had invited the Archbishop of Canterbury to spend part of his holiday with them in Birkhall; he wrote: "A delightful visit. They were kindness itself. The old house is full of charm, and the Duchess has done much with the garden. Strange to think of the destiny which may be awaiting the little Elizabeth, at present second from the throne."[21] The King did not invite his Archbishop to stay at Balmoral, nor, at this time, did the Archbishop comment on the different patterns of behaviour of the two elder sons of King George V.

The King invited the Yorks to play a prominent part in the entertainment he hoped to provide for Mrs Simpson and her friends during their stay at Balmoral. The Duchess, duty-bound, did go over, but she made little attempt to disguise the anger she felt at being 'received' at the royal home where Queen Mary had been so gracious a hostess. Nor did she hide her anger when informed that Mrs Simpson was sleeping in what had been Queen Mary's room. It was obvious that the King meant her to be treated as if she were already his queen, although she was not yet divorced from Ernest Simpson.

All this offended the Duchess's concept of what was fitting, what was 'royal' in terms of behaviour. But perhaps the thing that offended her most was that the King was so infatuated that he was prepared to ignore his public work – and to make use of her husband in an effort to cloak his own laziness. Months before, he had been invited to open some new hospital buildings at Aberdeen when he came to Scotland for his summer holiday. He had refused on the grounds that he would still be in mourning for his father who had died eight months earlier. Those nearest him knew that this mourning had not put a brake on his attending Ascot in June; nor had it dampened his enthusiasm for club life – or the legendary cruise. Nor, when making his excuses, had the reverence for mourning prevented his nominating the Duke of York to take his place. All this might have been distasteful to the Duchess, who shared with Queen Mary a very real pride in carrying out her public duty. To add to the insult – to the concept of royal duty, to her husband and to her own sense of propriety – as her husband drove off to the Aberdeen Infirmary, the King was arriving at Ballater Station to meet Mrs Simpson, whom he put in the front of the car beside him.[22] Henry Channon noted: ". . . The visit to Balmoral was a calamity, after the King chucked opening the Aberdeen Infirmary, and then openly appeared at Ballater Station on the same day, to welcome Wallis [Mrs Simpson] to the Highlands. Aberdeen will never forgive him."[23] Nor would the Duchess, Queen Mary and other members of the family.

Lady Airlie was Queen Mary's almost constant companion during this painful period. She wrote: ". . . Press cuttings began to be showered on Queen Mary from British residents all over the world accompanied by letters urging her to stop the gossip. . . . One morning in November she showed me a cutting from the Baltimore *News-Post* saying that, after her divorce had been made final, Mrs Simpson would marry the King of England. I exclaimed that I did not believe it. . . ."[24]

Lady Airlie may not have wanted to "believe it", but what was to be the end of the affair if not marriage? The Duke of York, in the words of his biographer, "would not bring himself to believe that if faced with the choice of the crown or his marriage, the King of England would opt unhesitatingly for Mrs Simpson".[25] But, as we shall see, the Duke's optimism proved to be unfounded. The brief reign was drawing rapidly to its almost inevitable close.

14

The Abdication

IN OCTOBER 1936 THE BRITISH people knew nothing of the King's relationship with Mrs Simpson. They had been kept in the dark by a deliberate policy of the Press barons. In *The Abdication of King Edward VIII*, Lord Beaverbrook explained why he had agreed with the King's suggestion that he use his influence to keep Mrs Simpson's name, and in particular her application for a divorce, out of the British papers, though people in the USA and on the Continent were regaled with what an Englishman living in the USA referred to as "the poisonous publicity attending the King's friendship with Mrs Simpson".

The Prime Minister went to see the King on 20th October. His son told Harold Nicolson that they: "walked around and around the garden at Fort Belvedere discussing the business [of the divorce and the King's friendship] and then returned to the library".[1]

The King's private secretary was Major Alexander Hardinge, a brother of Diamond Hardinge with whom the then Lady Elizabeth Bowes-Lyon had stayed in Paris in 1923. After Baldwin had left the King, Hardinge called at 145 Piccadilly to tell the Duke that Edward VIII's abdication was, at least, a possibility. The Duke and Duchess had for some time been aware that their daughter might one day become queen; now, for the first time, it was, semi-officially, explained that the burden of sovereignty might well fall on them. The Duke hoped that would not happen; during the next two weeks he tried to persuade his King-brother to follow the path of duty and not of self-indulgence – but in vain. The Duchess, conscious of the role she would have to play as supporter of her shy husband, did her best to continue to lead a normal life.

In her memoirs, Lady Hardinge, wife of the King's secretary, wrote: "Go out to see the Duchess of York, who is an angel as usual. Much cheered by those delicious children who came in from the swimming-bath with terrific accounts of their exploits."[2]

On 27th October Mrs Simpson was granted a decree nisi; she would be free to re-marry within six months – just in time for the Coronation, which had been fixed for May 1937. It is not surprising then that, when news of the divorce came through, there was speculation in London 'society' and among politicians as to whether, in Harold Nicolson's words, ". . . the King will make her Duchess of Edinburgh and marry [her]. The point is whether he is so infatuated as to insist on her becoming queen. . . ."[3]

The next stage in the developing crisis was reached on 13th November. The King had enjoyed favourable publicity on the opening of Parliament on 3rd November and during a three-day visit to the fleet which ended on 13th November. It seemed to his secretary, Hardinge, that he was tending to overlook the grave situation in which he was bound to find himself. Hardinge, as a good secretary, thought it his duty to write a letter, which was waiting for the King when he arrived at Fort Belvedere on 13th November. In this Hardinge warned the King that the British Press could not maintain their silence forever and that, when the "outburst begins . . . , the effect will be calamitous . . .". Hardinge warned him that, if he insisted on ignoring the government's advice, there would be a General Election ". . . in which Your Majesty's personal affairs would be the chief issue, and . . . even those who would sympathize with Your Majesty . . . would deeply resent the damage which would inevitably be done to the Crown. . . ." Hardinge begged the King to ask Mrs Simpson to "go abroad *without further delay*".[4]

The angry King did not reply to this letter from a friendly secretary, whom he now distrusted. This was a pity, because Hardinge was aware that, on that same day, Baldwin had met not only members of the Cabinet but Attlee, the Leader of the Opposition Labour Party, and Walter Citrine, the General Secretary of the TUC, who had just come back from a tour of the USA. Attlee offered Labour's support, while Citrine's reports of the way in which the US newspapers were dealing with "the King's affair" only made Baldwin more resolved to bring it to as speedy an end as possible.

On 16th November the King saw Baldwin again and confirmed that he intended to marry Mrs Simpson – as king, if this was possible, but as an ex-king if necessary. That same evening Edward VIII dined with his mother and told her of his "irrevocable determination to marry Mrs Simpson". Of this sad meeting he later wrote: "The word 'duty' fell between us."[5]

As for duty, he told his new secretary, Walter Monckton, that: "If they were wanting someone exactly reproducing his father, there was the Duke of York."[6]

On the following morning, 17th November, the King told his brothers that he was prepared to abdicate if this were necessary. The youngest brother, the Duke of Kent, described him as "besotted".[7]

In July 1938 his mother wrote him a letter in which she referred to these family discussions: "You will remember how miserable I was . . . you did not seem able to take in any point of view but your own. It seemed inconceivable to those who had made such sacrifice during the war that you, as their King, refused a lesser sacrifice. After all, all my life I have put my country before everything else, and I simply cannot change now."[8]

When the Duchess heard that the self-indulgent King was 'volunteering' the Duke of York for the throne, she was very angry. She condemned the King's presumption, selfishness and lack of consideration for his mother, the Duke, herself and the children. She and the Duke went, as usual, to Royal Lodge for the weekend, the Duke constantly telephoning his brother at Fort Belvedere ". . . to try and help him in his hour of need".[9]

In his own, later, account of the crisis the ex-King wrote: "Bertie was so taken aback . . . that in his shy way he could not bring himself to express his innermost feelings. . . . This . . . was not surprising, for . . . it was he who would have to wear the crown if I left, and his genuine concern for me was mixed up with the dread of having to assume the responsibilities of kingship."[10]

After that sad weekend the Duke and Duchess returned to 145 Piccadilly, where the Duchess went down with an attack of influenza – brought on more by strain and shock than by the bad weather of that winter. During the rest of the 'abdication week' she was confined to bed. Her maid found her one day reading Chapter 14 of the Gospel of St John, which starts "Let not your heart be troubled. . . ." The same chapter ends: "Arise, let us go hence."[11] When next the Duchess left 145 for Royal Lodge, she went as Queen.

On the following day, 18th November, the King visited Dowlais in South Wales, once the 'iron capital of the world'; now sixty per cent of the men were unemployed. As he walked around the slag heaps, the small cottages and the silent steelworks, the King was heard to say: "Something must be done . . . you may be sure that all I can do for you I will. . . ."[12] The Welsh cheered; they sang their hymns and waved their miners' lamps in the darkness. Their former Prince, now their King, would provide the help they needed. That, at least, was the popular belief among people who did not know about the family meeting of the day before. In fact, there was little he could have done, even if he had stayed on the throne; it is, after all, Ministers who rule while kings merely reign. But he had no real intention even of remaining, let alone of helping. While he was in Dowlais Mrs Simpson was telling Lady Colefax that: "All sorts of people had come to her . . . begging her to leave the country. 'They do not understand that if I did so the King would come after me regardless of anything. They would then get their scandal in a far worse form than they are getting it now.'"[13] She appreciated that nothing would be allowed to stand in his "besotted" way.

There was, perhaps, one way in which the King might have kept his throne and still have married Mrs Simpson. Esmond Harmsworth, son of Lord Rothermere, owner of the *Daily Mail*, worked out the plans for a morganatic marriage.

Such marriages were common among the royal Houses of Europe, but apart from George IV's marriage to Mrs Fitzherbert, and the two marriages contracted by that monarch's brother the Duke of Sussex, no member of the British royal family had ever made such a marriage, by which the wife renounces her claims to her husband's title.

In his diary, Tom Jones noted: "Harmsworth told Lothian that . . . Mrs S. had told him . . . she would accept an inferior position as the King's wife, e.g. Duchess of Cornwall. . . . H. then went to see the King and put the same proposal to him. He too was prepared to fall in with this. Lothian offered to find out through me how this plan would be regarded by S.B. I 'phoned No. 10 and fixed breakfast for tomorrow morning."[14] This plan was put to Baldwin, who was angered at the signs that the Press barons were trying to get the King to renege on the agreements that they had reached for his abdication. Baldwin also believed that Mrs Simpson had "got at" the King and that she was trying to outwit the government and get the King to act against the advice offered by his Ministers. It is not surprising that he rejected this scheme, which would have required a special Act of Parliament as well as the agreement of the governments of the Dominions. Frances Donaldson's *Edward VIII* documents the discussions about this scheme and the opinion of the Attorney-General on the proposed Act of Parliament: "If it had been an honest recital, it would start 'Whereas the wife of the King is Queen, and whereas the King desires to marry a woman unfit to be Queen, be it hereby enacted, etc. . . .'"[15]

On 26th November Harold Nicolson noted: ". . . if the King insisted on marrying, the Privy Council would assemble in force and insist that he either abdicate or they resign . . ."[16] as Hardinge had foreseen. And it was also being borne in on people that the King was Head of the Church of England, which in 1936 held Christian marriage indissoluble until death. It was inconceivable that he would be able to carry off the consecration of the Coronation with a wife who had figured in the divorce court. The Archbishop of Canterbury (whose successor was to play a part in Princess Margaret's decision not to marry the divorced Peter Townsend) let it be known that he would feel unable to officiate at the King's proposed wedding. In his memoirs Lord Home has shown that public opinion in Scotland, "with its strong church-going public", was very much opposed to the proposed marriage and was not at all influenced by the clamour of the Press barons in London.

Malcolm MacDonald, Colonial Secretary, was responsible for sounding out opinion in the Dominions. In *Men and Places*, he showed that the Dominion governments and peoples were overwhelmingly against the proposed marriage of the once-popular King. Nearer home, the opposition of the Labour Party had already been made clear by Attlee. As Tom Jones noted: "He thought his popularity was such that he could 'get away' with her."[17] What he had ignored was the simple people's appreciation of real worth. The Australian who had spoken of the Duke of York's having to "work at his job",[18] had a counterpart in the former Anzac soldier who, according to Tom Jones, asked his Prime Minister, Bruce, "Why did he take her to Gallipoli [on the *Nahlin*]?"[19]

Meanwhile the Duke and Duchess of York travelled to Edinburgh on the night of 29th November for his installation as Grand Master Mason of Scotland. He wrote: "I hate going to Scotland to do what I have to do as I am so worried.... I feel like the proverbial 'sheep being led to the slaughter' which is not a comfortable feeling."[20] In Edinburgh their reception was tumultuous, as if the people wanted to offer their special sympathy and support. Then, as throughout the whole period of the crisis, the Duchess faced the future with courage. She was calm and showed great self-control, acting as a support for her husband and Queen Mary, who was the rock around which the family gathered.

In an editorial *The Times* spoke of the reception: "... the special affection for the Prince in whose posterity another race of Scottish descent may someday be called to the imperial throne".[21]

While the Yorks were in Edinburgh, the crisis entered a new phase. The Bishop of Bradford, Dr Alfred Blunt, addressing his Diocesan Conference on 1st December and speaking of the King's forthcoming Coronation, remarked that the benefit of the consecration he would receive depended, in part, on "the faith, prayers and self-dedication of the King himself". He asked people to pray for the King – "a man like ourselves" – that he might receive the grace "which he will so abundantly need ... if he is to do his duty properly". The Bishop then added: "We hope that he is aware of his need. Some of us wish that he gave more positive signs of his awareness."[22] The Bishop later claimed that he was referring to the King's frequent absence from Sunday services. Others, however, believed that he was attacking Edward VIII's friendship with Mrs Simpson. On 2nd August the *Yorkshire Post* published an account of the Bishop's speech and ran its own editorial, in which it referred to Mrs Simpson. A copy of this was sent to the London papers – too late, however, for them to do much about it. However, on Thursday 3rd December the London papers decided to end their long silence on "the King's affair".

As the Duke and Duchess of York left Euston Station after an overnight journey from Edinburgh, they were met by glaring headlines on "The King's Marriage". Along with the headlines were articles, photographs and reports which gave the British people their first taste of the revelations to which foreigners had been treated for months past. The provincial Press was more hostile to the proposed marriage than the London Press which, *The Times* apart, was under the control or influence of the Beaverbrook-Rothermere axis. The King was badly shaken when he read this section of the Press. "They don't want me," he remarked sadly.[23] In the House of Commons, MPs, while still influenced by the London Press, had begun to take account of the opinions expressed in articles in the local constituency papers. "Baldwin rises to answer some unimportant questions and is received with cheers from every part of the House . . . he says that no constitutional crisis 'has yet' arisen," wrote Nicolson, who went off to a meeting where "I find a deep and enraged fury against the King himself. In eight months he has destroyed the great structure of popularity which he had raised."[24]

The Duke of York went to see Queen Mary, and he also met the King with Walter Monckton, "who said he would leave the country as King after making a broadcast to his subjects and leave it to them to decide what should be done". But the King was not to be allowed to dictate how things would be done. As Nicolson noted on 3rd December: "The Cabinet met all day. I gather that Attlee and Sinclair [Leader of the Liberal MPs] both refused to form alternative governments and that the King will be forced to abdicate. The Duke of York will call himself 'King George VI' which indeed he is. We are all staggered. . . ."[25]

That night the King went to Marlborough House to see his mother and the Duke and Duchess of York. After again failing to get her to see why 'duty' would not impel him along its path, he asked the Duke of York to see him the next day at Fort Belvedere. The Yorks left to return to 145 Piccadilly. Here, on the following days, came the officials – to discuss things with the man who, it seemed, was to be the new king.

But there was no visit from the Prime Minister or any Cabinet Minister. They had decided to give the King "a few more days" before announcing his abdication – not, it seemed, that they hoped he would change his mind. Rather they spent their time discussing whether the Duke of York was, in fact, fit to take the throne.[26] (This, as we shall see in the next chapter, was a major cause of the Duchess's continuing dislike for her brother-in-law.) The public knew nothing of these ministerial doubts. They were sure that the Duke would be the next King. They gathered outside the house in Piccadilly to cheer people going in and out and to shout "Long live King Albert", the name they assumed he would take.

Over that weekend there were frantic attempts by an unholy alliance of what Tom Jones called "a few fools" to rally support for the King. In 1966 Randolph Churchill wrote: "I asked Beaverbrook why, if he was so far from being a monarchist and one who scarcely knew the King, he had himself gone to so much trouble on his behalf. He replied laconically: 'To bugger Baldwin'. . . ."[27] The Press lords had never forgiven the Prime Minister for having described them as: ". . . aiming at power, and power without responsibility – prerogative of the harlot throughout the ages." It was Beaverbrook and Rothermere whose papers came out in support of the King. It was Beaverbrook who put up Churchill as a stalking horse in the Commons to plead on 9th December for delay. And also siding with the King were such unlikely opposites as Oswald Mosley, leader of the British Fascists, and Harry Pollitt, leader of Britain's Communist Party.

But, over that weekend, MPs had been back to their constituencies and had discovered the deep revulsion felt by the mass of the people. As Nicolson said in a note for 9th December: ". . . The people . . . *want* the King to abdicate. I mean opinion in the House is now almost wholly anti-King. If he can first betray his duty and then betray the woman he loves, there is no good in the man. Thus, although he may keep his throne, if he renounces Mrs Simpson he will have lost the respect of his subjects."[28]

By 8th December the government seemed to have made up its mind that plans for either the Duke of Gloucester or the Duke of Kent to succeed to the throne could not be implemented. On that evening the Duke of York met his brother and the Prime Minister at Fort Belvedere.

On Wednesday 9th December he went to see Queen Mary "and when I told her what had happened I broke down and sobbed like a child".[29] In fact the Duke had with him "the paper drawn up for David's abdication of the throne of this Empire because he wants to marry Mrs Simpson!!!!!", as Queen Mary noted in her diary. The King signed this instrument of his abdication on Thursday 10th December, and the Abdication Bill was rushed through the Houses of Parliament on the following day.

The Duchess of York was still suffering from influenza. On Thursday 10th December at 1.52 pm she became Queen Elizabeth. Her first visitor was Queen Mary, who curtsied to her as she lay back in her sick-bed. We know from "Crawfie" that both women wept at this meeting.

By the next day the new Queen had recovered sufficiently to write to the Archbishop of Canterbury:

I can hardly now believe that we have been called to this tremendous task and (I am writing to you quite intimately) the curious thing is that we are not afraid. I feel that God has enabled us to face the situation calmly. . . [signed] for the first time and with great affection,

Elizabeth R.[30]

15

Queen Elizabeth and the Windsors, 1936–72

ONE OF THE MOST FREQUENT comments on the Queen Mother is that she has "great charm". Even the Duchess of Windsor recalling their meeting at Royal Lodge in 1936, noted: "*Her justly famous charm* was highly evident . . . [and] the beauty of her complexion and the almost startling blueness of her eyes."[1] [My italics.] But beneath that charm and accompanying her kindness there is also a streak of determination. Nowhere has this been more evident than in her attitude towards the Duke and Duchess of Windsor (the erstwhile King Edward VIII and Mrs Simpson). There is no record of her having said or written any critical comment of either of them, but all the external evidence proves that she had little regard for the Duke and a long-lasting dislike of the Duchess.

Her antipathy was made evident at the meeting to which the Duchess of Windsor referred. The Duchess's opinion of her brother-in-law and Mrs Simpson could hardly have been improved by their conduct during the ill-advised cruise on the *Nahlin* and by his behaviour at Balmoral in August and September 1936. The Queen Mother shared the belief common in the royal family that worry over Mrs Simpson had helped shorten the life of George V. That the duty-conscious monarch should have been hurt by the inconsiderate behaviour of his heir was bound to have been resented by the Duchess, who, as we have seen, had a great admiration and affection for her father-in-law.

But the major reasons for her unbending attitude are to be found in the events of the period immediately surrounding the Abdication and George VI's accession. On Saturday 5th December, when Edward VIII had decided to abdicate, Baldwin asked him not to discuss this matter with his family immediately but to allow the government a few days to discuss whether the Duke of York, and after him Princess Elizabeth, would be sufficiently capable of restoring the tattered image of the monarchy.[2] We have it on the authority of Dermot Morrah that: "It was certainly considered at this time whether, by agreement among the royal family, the crown might not be settled on the

Duke of Kent, the only one of the abdicating King's brothers who at that time had a son to become Prince of Wales, and so avoid laying so heavy a burden upon the shoulders of any woman."[3]

We can only imagine the feelings of the Duchess of York in her home at 145 Piccadilly as she heard of the comings and goings over that weekend among the officers of the royal household and government Ministers. Although, as we shall see, she did not welcome the possibility of becoming Queen, and although she knew that her husband was positively appalled at the prospect of becoming King, it cannot have been other than a weekend of humiliation for her. She resented that people should consider "unfit to be King" the man she both respected and loved, whom she had helped to mature and whom she had seen behave as royal ambassador in Australia with such success. It is not surprising that she resented the behaviour of the couple who had exposed her husband to this public humiliation.

And when, finally, the government decided to allow her husband to become King, she had to cope with the fears of the man who believed that he was "unprepared and untrained" for that position. There is, as yet, no record of what the then Duchess of York felt at the report of her husband "sobbing" at the meeting with Queen Mary on 9th December. Even though she was confined to bed with influenza, she had to bolster his courage and help him overcome his natural reluctance to take on this new position. We have some evidence of his need for such support from Tom Jones's account of a meeting with Mr and Mrs Baldwin on 11th January 1937 – almost a month after his accession: "To No. 10. Tea in the drawing-room with Mrs Baldwin just back from a weekend at Sandringham. . . . The King craved time to adjust himself to his new station and its duties. All his life he had been outshone by his brilliant brother and there had been times when, as a boy, he had felt envious that eighteen months should make so much difference."[4]

To Tom Jones and the Baldwins the King's fears may have been of little more than academic or perhaps constitutional significance. To the new Queen they were of very real and personal concern. It was she, and not the members of the government, who had to live with the man who had been exposed to his own inferiority complex by the behaviour of his more selfish and self-confident brother.

One of the reasons for the original ministerial hesitation at approving the accession of Prince Albert, Duke of York, was the fear that he would be unable to overcome his natural shyness and that he might relapse into the stammering, uncertain manner which had formerly been such a burden to him and to his wife. But he had so well overcome his handicap that there was very little evidence of shyness or of stammer during the long and arduous tour of New Zealand and Australia. But then, as if to compound the new Queen's problems and harden her attitude towards the Windsors, there was the

In the garden of Royal Lodge, Windsor, 1940. The Queen has her "charming smile" in spite of the strains of the War, while the Princesses were "knitting for Victory".

The King and Queen visiting one of the districts destroyed by bombing, 1940. Their courage at this time, and the Queen's consistent and sincere interest in the welfare of the people won them a special respect and affection.

July 1941: the Queen supervising the Princesses at their lessons in the open air at Windsor Castle.

1941 and a visit to the East End after it had suffered from heavy bombing by the German Luftwaffe. As one of the women said, the Queen was "bloody marvellous".

Inspecting the harvest at Sandringham in 1943 – and saving petrol as part of the war effort.

A family photograph taken after a party to celebrate Princess Elizabeth's eighteenth birthday in 1944. *Standing, left to right*: the Duke of Gloucester and his wife, Princess Margaret, the Princess Royal, Princess Marina, the Duchess of Kent and Lord Lascelles, husband of the Princess Royal. *Seated*: Queen Mary, the King, Princess Elizabeth and the Queen.

On the balcony of Buckingham Palace on VE Day, May 8th 1945. With the Prime Minister, Winston Churchill, the Royal Family responds to the cheers of the crowds.

The King and Queen with Prime Minister Smuts on top of Table Mountain, Cape Town, during their South African Tour, 1947.

Christmas 1947 and the
King and Queen
enjoying a village
concert.

The King and Queen
on their way down Fleet
Street to St Paul's for
the service of
thanksgiving on their
Silver Wedding day,
1948. The enthusiasm of
the crowds on this
unprecedented occasion
was a sign of the respect
in which the royal
couple were held.

15th December 1948 and the christening day of Prince Charles.

2nd October 1950 and Prince Charles demands his share of attention after the christening of Princess Anne. The grandmother and great-grandmother hope they can cope – and Prince Philip seems to be siding with his son.

The world-famous photograph of three sorrowing Queens at the lying-in-state of King George VI, 11th February 1952.

The royal cortège passing through the streets of Windsor en route for St George's Chapel for the burial of King George VI, 15th February 1952.

The Queen Mother – and grandmother – helping Prince Charles to follow the ceremony of his mother's Coronation, 2nd June 1953.

The newly-crowned Queen Elizabeth II, Prince Charles, Princess Anne, the Duke of Edinburgh and the Queen Mother on the balcony of Buckingham Palace after the Coronation.

unfortunate broadcast made by the Archbishop of Canterbury on 13th December 1936. Dr Lang used this opportunity to attack the former King; then he said of the new King: "In manner and speech he is more quiet and reserved than his brother (and here I may add a parenthesis which may not be unhelpful). When his people listen to him, they will note an occasional and momentary hesitation in his speech. But he has brought it into full control, and to those who hear him it need cause no sort of embarrassment, for it causes none to him who speaks."[5] Logue was, not surprisingly, furious at this stupid, if well-intentioned, reference to the King's speech defect[6] and could vent his anger in both spoken and written word. We have no record of the reaction of the new Queen to this publicity; nor do we know what effect it had on George VI. We can only hazard that their reaction against Lang must also have spilled over into anger at those who had put the King into the position of being publicly reminded of his speech defect.

The new Queen's anger with the Windsors was reinforced by her awareness of the way in which Queen Mary treated them. That she never forgave the former Mrs Simpson is borne out by this passage from the memoirs of the then Duchess of Windsor: "His mother continued to write to him . . . but . . . even Queen Mary, for all her love of her eldest son, could not make room in her heart for something that had altered the natural order of monarchy. . . . In his mother's eyes he had become something different and apart . . . his place at the hearth had gone, along with his place on the throne. As for me, *I simply did not exist.* . . ."[7] [My italics.]

In 1944, when the Duke was Governor of the Bahamas, the Duchess of Windsor wrote a letter to his mother and gave it to a retiring Bishop of Nassau who was returning to Britain and was to have an audience with Queen Mary. She received a letter from the Bishop, who told her that the Dowager Queen had asked about her son and his work. "But when the Bishop mentioned what I was doing . . . there was no response. He met a stone wall of disinterest."[8]

The Duchess discovered that Queen Mary's anger and resentment was continuing and deep. And we can surmise that this anger would have fuelled that of Queen Elizabeth, for whom the older Queen had a great sympathy and with whom she shared many confidences.

As Britain and the world passed through the 1940s and 1950s, the anger did not weaken. Indeed there were new developments which served to reinforce and deepen it. In 1952 George VI died at the relatively early age of fifty-nine but Edward, the former King, died when he was aged seventy-eight, the Duke of Gloucester at seventy-four: the Windsor men tended to live beyond their "three score years and ten". It is generally agreed that a major cause of George VI's early death was the burden he had carried of trying to restore the image of the monarchy. Those who wished were entitled to say that his brother's Abdication was a major cause of his early death and were then justified, in their own eyes at least, in being angry at the selfish behaviour of the man who gave up the throne.

The Queen had no constitutional power and so was unable, directly, to affect the way in which the Windsors were treated. But as Queen Consort she had a great deal of influence over her King-husband.

We have already seen that Queen Mary, as late as 1944, refused even to talk about the Duchess of Windsor. If she had any influence over her son, it would have been thrown into the scales against the Windsors. And it was Queen Mary who said: "The Yorks will do it very well" when she had been made to accept the inevitability of the Abdication of her favourite son.[9] She appreciated that it would be "the Yorks" and not "my second son" (that is, the Duke alone) who would do it very well. She, more than most, appreciated the influence and importance of the role that her son's wife would play in the new monarchy. And, in our consideration of the way in which the Windsors were treated after 1936, we should see the hidden hand and influence of Queen Elizabeth.

At first George VI seemed to make life as easy as he could for his brother. It was he who arranged that the Windsors would receive an annual income of about £25,000. As with all questions of money values, it is difficult to say what such a sum, paid in 1937, would be worth in today's currency. We might take as a yardstick the contemporary price of suburban housing (about £400), the price of a family car (£100–£150) or the wage of coal miners (£1·50 per week).

The government had agreed to allow the departing King to make a final broadcast to the British people. There was some dispute over the way in which he should be introduced. There were those who wanted him to be called simply 'Mr Edward Windsor'; it was George VI who pointed out that, if he was 'made' a commoner, he would have the right to return to the country and stand in a Parliamentary election. As the King said, neither Baldwin nor the leaders of the other political parties could have wanted that. Others suggested that he should be introduced as 'Lord Edward Windsor' – until George VI pointed out that a simple peerage would entitle him to take a seat in the House of Lords where, again, he might become the focus for political activity unwelcome to the Conservatives, Liberals and Labour alike. Indeed, George VI pointed out, since he had been born to a royal duke, he was entitled to be called 'His Royal Highness', and it would be advisable – in the light of the danger of his becoming politically active – to make him a royal duke in his own right. So it was that the former King was introduced on the night of the broadcast as "His Royal Highness Prince Edward".[10]

During the first hectic days after the Abdication, George VI kept in close touch with his brother by telephone. Indeed, there is evidence that the former

King maintained his long-standing domination over the new King, as can be seen from this letter written by 'Fruity' Metcalfe who was the ex-King's companion in his temporary home near Vienna:

> Tonight he [Edward] was told that HM wanted to talk on the 'phone to him. He said that he couldn't take the call but asked that it be put through to him at 10 pm. The answer to this was that *HM said he would talk at 6.45 pm tomorrow* as he was too busy to talk at any other time. It was pathetic to see HRH's face. *He couldn't believe it.* He's been so used to having everything done as he wished. I'm afraid he's going to have many more shocks like this.[11] [My italics]

Further evidence about these telephone calls is provided in the papers of Walter Monckton quoted by Frances Donaldson. Here we can also see the first signs of a hardening of attitude against the Duke of Windsor.

> It was he [Walter Monckton] who had the appallingly difficult task of persuading HRH to abandon the habit of telephoning regularly to his brother. Ever since the abdication, the Duke had taken it upon himself to advise the King on the questions of the day. "This advice" Monckton writes, "often ran counter to the advice which the King was getting from his responsible Ministers in the government. This caused him trouble which no one could understand who did not know the extent to which, before the abdication, the Duke of Windsor's brothers admired and looked up to him."[12]

In 1966 the Duke of Windsor wrote a series of articles for the American Press in which he recalled that: ". . . The King told him that these telephone calls must cease. The Duke asked him if he was serious, and the King replied that he was, adding that the reason for this must be clear to his brother."[13] Here, the Duke believed, was evidence that Queen Mary, Queen Elizabeth and the rest of the Court were influencing his brother against him.

By March 1937 there were signs that the King's attitude had hardened, as can be seen from this account of a meeting between Lloyd George and the new monarch:

> 17th March 1937
> D. [David Lloyd George] dined at Buckingham Palace last night, his first encounter with the King and Queen as such. He was rather nervous about his reception after what had happened and his championship of Edward, but they were most gracious to him. . . . H.M. is *most anxious* that the Duke should not return to this country, but D. told him that he did not take that view and thought that H.M. would be wiser not to oppose it. "*She would never dare to come back here,*" said H.M. "There you are wrong," replied D. "She would have no friends here," said H.M. D. did not agree. "*But not you or me?*" said the King anxiously.[14] [My italics.]

But the rift between the two brothers did not become final until May 1937. On 3rd May Mrs Simpson's divorce became absolute. If all had gone as

Edward had once hoped, this would have been followed by a wedding and, on 12th May, the Coronation of himself and his Queen. Instead he and Mrs Simpson listened on French radio to the commentary on the Coronation of his brother and Queen Elizabeth, and the Duke of Windsor's wedding did not take place until 3rd June.

By then the former King had received a letter from George VI telling him of the statement which appeared in the *London Gazette* on 28th May: "The King has been pleased by Letters Patent under the Great Seal of the Realm bearing date the 27th day of May 1937 to declare that the Duke of Windsor shall . . . be entitled to hold . . . the title . . . of Royal Highness so however that *his wife and descendants if any shall not hold the said title.* . . ."[15] [My italics.] It was, once again, Walter Monckton who brought the letter in which George VI explained to his brother the significance of the Letters Patent – for him and his wife-to-be. George VI hoped that Edward would not consider it "an insult". But, as the Duchess of Windsor recalled, "He exclaimed 'I know Bertie – *he couldn't have written this letter on his own.* Why in God's name would *they* do this to me at this time?'"[16] [My italics.] We do not know who "*they*" were, but it is not hard to imagine that the two Queens – Mary and Elizabeth – at least supported this decision not to accord the title 'Her Royal Highness' to the Duke's wife. As far as the former King was concerned, this was the "insult" which more than any other set him apart from his family. Unless people were prepared to accept his wife as 'HRH', he would not return to England. And there was little chance that the royal family would change their attitude.

Frances Donaldson gives an account of a discussion between George VI and Prime Minister Neville Chamberlain in 1938:

> The Prime Minister thought that the right course was for the Duke of Windsor to be treated as soon as possible as a younger brother of the King who could take some of the royal functions off his brother's hands. The King himself, though he was not anxious for the Duke to return as early as November 1938 (which is what the Duke wanted), was not fundamentally against the Prime Minister's view. *But I think the Queen felt plainly that it was undesirable to give the Duke any effective sphere of work.* I felt then, as always, that she naturally thought that *she must be on her guard* because the Duke of Windsor, to whom the other brothers had always looked up, was an attractive, vital creature who might be the rallying-point for any who might be critical of the new King who was less superficially endowed with the arts and graces that please.[17] [My italics]

For his part, Edward insisted that his wife be accorded the title of HRH. Harold Nicolson met the Windsors at Somerset Maugham's house at Cap Ferrat on 5th August 1938 and wrote:

> When they arrived, Willy [Maugham] and his daughter went into the hall. We stood sheepishly in the drawing-room. In they came. "I am sorry we were a little late," said the Duke, "but Her Royal Highness couldn't drag herself

away." He had said it. The three words fell into the circle like three stones into a pool. "Her" (gasp) "Royal" (shudder) "Highness" (and not an eye dared to meet another).[18]

Here, then, the two irreconcilables: Edward insisting that his wife be granted the title accorded to the wife of every other royal duke, and the monarchy refusing to do so; Edward refusing to return to England unless he could bring his wife and be ensured that she be received as HRH, facing a Court and government not anxious that he should return and determined that, if he did so, it would be on their terms and not his.

This helps to explain why he did not attend the wedding of his niece Princess Elizabeth in November 1947, or her Coronation in June 1953. He did come to George VI's funeral in 1952, and he was at his mother's deathbed in 1953 – but on both occasions he came alone.

It has been one of the many pleasant features of our present Queen's reign that she went out of her way to try to ease relationships between the Windsors and the rest of the royal family. In 1966 she invited both the Duke and the Duchess to attend the ceremony of the unveiling of the plaque at Marlborough House in memory of Queen Mary, and the Duchess of Windsor met the Queen Mother and Elizabeth II – the first public recognition of the Duchess by a British monarch. In May 1972 the Queen visited her uncle as he lay dying of cancer of the throat in a Paris nursing-home. Eight days later he died. His body was flown to England in an aeroplane of the Queen's Flight – one of his own modernizing innovations. His body lay in state in St George's Chapel, Windsor. When the Duchess flew into England, she was taken to Buckingham Palace, where she stayed throughout the rest of that week. On Saturday 3rd June 1972 (the thirty-fifth anniversary of the Windsors' wedding) she watched the Queen ride out from the Palace to the Trooping of the Colour, which included a special tribute to the dead Duke. That evening Prince Charles accompanied the Duchess of Windsor to see her husband's body as it lay in the Chapel. On Monday 5th June the former King was buried in the grounds of Frogmore and on the following day the Duchess flew out of England. No one from the royal family went to see her off at the airport. It could be that the Queen's attempt at easing relationships was limited to bringing her uncle, rather than his wife, back into the family circle.

To some people close to the Queen Mother it seems strange that, "The Abdication is the *one* subject that is never mentioned in this [Clarence] House." After all, if it were not for the Windsors, the Queen Mother would, today, merely be the ageing relict of a Duke of York, as unknown to the public as is the Dowager Duchess of Gloucester. It might be that the Queen Mother would have preferred to have had a simpler, more private life with her husband and her children. If so, her fulfilment of her role of Queen and now Queen Mother, is all the more remarkable.

PART IV: 1936–1939

16

The role of the new monarch

THE EVENTS OF THE short reign of Edward VIII culminating in his abdication meant that, as George VI said at his Accession Council: "I meet you today in circumstances which are without parallel in the history of our country."[1] We have seen that there were serious doubts as to the fitness of this shy, nervous younger brother to cope with the problems created by his elder brother. In examining the role of the new monarch we will have an opportunity to see how and why the fears of the doubters, such as Prime Minister Baldwin, were laid to rest, and to look at the special qualities which George VI brought to his arduous task of repairing the damage done by the behaviour of Edward VIII.

At 11 am on 20th December 1936 the new King attended his Accession Council at St James's Palace, eleven months from the date of the accession of the former King (who had sailed at 2 am that morning from Portsmouth). At his accession the ex-King had been confident and full of life; George VI was obviously under great stress, his face showing signs of the ordeals of the last few weeks. When he spoke, it was in a low voice and with many hesitations: "Your Royal Highnesses, My Lords and Gentlemen. . . . Now that *the duties of sovereignty have fallen upon me I declare to you my adherence to the strict principles of constitutional government* and my resolve to work before all else for *the welfare of the British Commonwealth of Nations*."[2] [My italics.] His choice of words seemed to be deliberate. He was aware of the criticism of his brother's unconstitutional behaviour, and he was aware of the significance of the role played by the Crown as the most important link in the chains which bound the Commonwealth together. We have reason to be grateful for the way in which he carried out his duties throughout his reign.

On the following day prayers were said for the new royal family in churches throughout the Empire.

For the couple who took their religious beliefs seriously, these prayers were of great significance. It was their task, as they saw it, to use the grace with which they hoped to be endowed and by which they would be strengthened to repair the damage that had been done to the institution of the monarchy, the fabric of national life and the peculiar relationship which exists between the Mother Country and the nations of the Commonwealth.

The new Queen appreciated the finer qualities of the new King and was resolved to do all she could to help these to bloom in the new circumstances in which, reluctantly, they found themselves. (This will form the subject matter of Chapter 17.) But the new King was less confident in his own abilities. By nature shy, he had lived in the shadow of a more glamorous brother. Now he seemed in danger of being overwhelmed by the tasks facing him. In *George VI*, Wheeler-Bennett gave an account of a meeting between the new King and his cousin Lord Louis Mountbatten on 11th December, the first night of the reign. They were at Fort Belvedere, watching the former King complete his preparations for his departure.

"Dickie, this is absolutely terrible," the new King said in great distress. "I never wanted this to happen; I'm quite unprepared for it. David has been trained for this all his life. I've never even seen a State Paper. I'm only a naval officer. It's the only thing I know about." And Lord Louis was able to give him consolation. "This is a very curious coincidence," he replied, "my father once told me that, when the Duke of Clarence died [in 1892], your father came to him and said almost the same things that you have said to me now, and my father answered 'George, you're wrong. There is no more fitting preparation for a King than to have been trained in the Navy.'"[3]

But (as we have seen) there was more to his career and character than that. In 1954 Clement Attlee wrote of the King whom he had served as Prime Minister:

He took great interest in social questions, especially in the welfare of industrial workers. He grew to have a wide knowledge of social and industrial problems. He was never happier than when in the camps for boys of all classes which he organized. . . . Happy in his marriage and in his family life, it might well have seemed that his lot was cast in easy and pleasant places. But in circumstances of great difficulty he was called upon to take up the burden of kingship. He responded to that call with that *high sense of duty* which was, I think, his outstanding characteristic. . . .[4] [My italics.]

What was the nature of the role which the new King was expected to fill? Enoch Powell has said that: "The monarchy is emotional, symbolical, totemistic and mystical." Others have suggested that the British people see the monarchy as a symbol of what they feel to be the essence of English life. They hope to see represented in the monarchy not merely themselves but that best self which they would like to develop and sustain in their own persons – but often fail to do because of the difficulties and self-sacrifice involved. The new King was well fitted to play this role. But what of more practical roles?

In *English Constitution* the Victorian writer Walter Bagehot defined the constitutional role of the monarch who had the right to be consulted by his Ministers and the duties of encouraging and, if needs be, warning them. We have seen that King Edward VIII tended to neglect the papers which had to be read as part of the consultative process. Attlee shows King George VI as a "hard worker" at his papers, so that he had a "close familiarity" with the problems that faced his Ministers. We have also seen that the former King had tended to act outside the defined parameters which evolved over the years. George VI's promise to adhere to "the strict principles of constitutional government" was intended to reassure those, such as Herbert Morrison, who were concerned at the behaviour of the former King whose "visits to the distressed areas and . . . impatience with the situation [and] government . . . were constitutionally dangerous and not inconsistent with those Fascist tendencies with which (quite possibly unjustly) he is credited".[5]

One major issue in the Abdication Crisis was the King's refusal to accept the advice of his Ministers over the matter of his proposed marriage. Some people supported the Beaverbrook line that "he had the right to marry the woman he loved", but Harold Laski, a left-wing political philosopher writing in the *Daily Herald* on 6th December 1936 and taking his cue from Bagehot, declared: "He [the King] may advise. He may encourage. He may warn. But if the Cabinet stands firm in its advice, the King must in our constitutional system necessarily give way".[6]

The new King started off, as Baldwin told Lady Airlie, with ". . . a lot of prejudice against him. He's had no chance to capture the popular imagination as his brother did. I'm afraid he won't find it easy going for the first year or two".[7] And there was more than prejudice. During the period between his accession and his Coronation in May 1937 there was a deliberate campaign aimed at creating the impression that he was unfit to reign in his brother's stead. There was, said the rumour-mongers, his stammer, his relatively poor presence and his lack of intellectual ability as shown by his relative failure as a student before and after his entry into the Royal Navy. The Beaverbrook Press gave credence to these rumours with slanted reports which suggested, among other things, that the Coronation service was going to be shortened for fear that the new King would be unable to cope. There was no truth in such reports. Nor was there, or is there, any correlation between academic success and the development of those qualities required by a public figure. In *My Early Life* Winston Churchill wrote of his own failure when with his tutors: ". . . We descended into a dismal bog called 'sums' [and] the inhospitable regions of examinations . . . a great trial to me. . . . I did not do well in examinations."[8] His words could have been echoed by the new King. Attlee described George VI as a "hard worker" possessed of "a good judgement" – neither of which attributes was examinable and both of which were qualities which his wife had always seen in her husband.

The new King was in no doubts as to the problems that lay ahead. In *Monarchy in the Twentieth Century* Sir Charles Petrie quotes a "staunch Conservative MP" as saying that if in December 1936 a straight vote of the House of Commons had been taken, not less than one hundred votes would have been cast in favour of the establishment of a republic. This is only a matter of opinion. However, the Independent Labour Party did move a 'republican' amendment to the Abdication Bill on 10th December. Although this was defeated by 403 votes to five, the significant fact was that such an extreme amendment was proposed and debated.[9]

There is little doubt that the stability of the monarchy had been threatened by the events surrounding the abdication. The new King was fully aware of this. In November, while still Duke of York, he had written to one of the King's assistant private secretaries: "If the worst happens and I have to take over, you can be assured that I will do my best to clear up the inevitable mess, *if the whole fabric does not crumble* under the shock and strain of it all."[10] [My italics.] And on 31st December, still trying to come to terms with what had happened, he wrote to the Prime Minister: "I am new to the job but I hope that time will be allowed to me to make amends for what has happened."[11] In hindsight we can appreciate how well he made "amends".

George VI was not on his own in trying to refurbish the tattered image of the monarchy. Queen Mary, deservedly popular in her own right, used her influence to help the transition from one monarch to another. As one of the royal family (probably the new Queen) wrote to her: "Thank God we have all got you as a central point because without it, [the family] might easily disintegrate."[12] Then the King had the support of his wife, as we shall see in the next chapter. Together they proved the truth of Queen Mary's verdict, "The Yorks will do it very well."[13]

George VI had spoken of the welfare of the Commonwealth. He appreciated that one of the major functions of the monarchy in the twentieth century has been to act as a focal point for the loyalty and the affections of the peoples of the Commonwealth. There was a danger that in the aftermath of the Abdication Crisis there might be calls, particularly from Australia and Canada, for a final break from the informal links with Britain. However, each of the independent Dominions agreed to what had happened in London and passed Bills or Orders in Council to give constitutional assent to the abdication of one king and the accession of another.

When examining the role of the new King, we have to take into account the way in which, deliberately or subconsciously, he modelled himself on his father. George V had won a special place in the minds of his peoples, as his son appreciated:

... The King himself in the role of the bearded paterfamilias, his devoted and queenly wife, their four grown sons and a daughter, not to mention the rising generation of grandchildren – he transformed the Crown as personified by the royal family, into a model of the traditional family virtues. . . . The King . . . became the living symbol not only of the nation but also of the Empire, the last link holding together these diversified and scattered communities.[14]

One of the first decisions made by the new King, known in the family as 'Bertie', was to take the name 'George VI' – a deliberate, public and conscious effort to indicate a return to the traditions of his father's reign. He brought back his father's private secretary, Lord Wigram, to be a lord-in-waiting and to act as his personal adviser. Within a few days of his accession, Baldwin, who had been pessimistic so soon before, was confidently predicting: "What will endear him to his people is that more than any of his brothers he resembles in character and mind his father. . . ."[15]

On 10th December Baldwin had spoken in the House of Commons, explaining for the first time what had happened during the past few weeks. In the course of this speech he declared:

The Crown in this country through the centuries has been deprived of many of its prerogatives, but today, while that is true, it stands for more than it ever has done in our history. The importance of *its integrity* is, beyond all question, far greater than it has ever been . . . the guarantee in this country, so long as it exists in that integrity, against many evils.[16] [My italics]

This sense of "integrity" was to mark the reign of George VI. His elder brother had tried to live a double life – a public one divorced from his private one. For the new King there was no such dichotomy: the dutiful husband and father brought to his public life the same care and attention that he had devoted to the development of his private life. And he brought from his private life a sense of security and a concept of morality that enabled him to carry out the difficult tasks of his public life.

In his private life the King, like his wife, found great comfort in religion. It is, then, not surprising that he should have seen his Coronation as an opportunity to show the people that the ceremony had a spiritual significance. Bagehot had written of the sovereign as the "head of our morality". The King hoped that his Coronation would bring out "magnificently" the true meaning of a Christian State.

The Archbishop of Canterbury spent part of the Easter holiday at Windsor going over the Coronation service with the two monarchs. He found them "most appreciative and fully conscious of its solemnity". On the Sunday before the Coronation they went from Royal Lodge to Buckingham Palace to receive the Archbishop for a private service of spiritual preparation. The Archbishop wrote: "I met them in their room. After some talk on the spiritual significance of the Coronation, they knelt with me; I prayed for them and for their realm and empire, and I gave them my personal blessing. I was much moved, and so were they. Indeed, there were tears in their eyes when we rose from our knees."[17]

On 12th May 1937 they drove in the Gold State Coach from the Palace to Westminster Abbey. As if to ensure that people should appreciate the link between George V and the new monarchy, Queen Mary broke with tradition and drove in the procession to the Abbey – the first Dowager Queen ever to do so. She watched her son and his Queen "as if in a trance of consecration", move through the solemn ritual of consecration and coronation.

Lady Rhondda was in the Abbey and, in *Notes on the Way*, she gave an account of the service, during which a minister read the Gospel story in which Christ advised His followers to "Render . . . unto Caesar the things which are Caesar's, and unto God the things that are God's." Writing of the colourful pageantry in the Abbey which reflected the might and riches of a great empire, she noted that Caesar had received his tribute. Then she went on:

> One had forgotten that another kingdom than Caesar's existed. But, as the Service began, the values of that other kingdom imposed themselves. . . . It was partly no doubt, the effect of the very beautiful old words. But I believe it was partly, too, the effect of the personality of the two chief actors in the drama. . . . More and more one found oneself considering those two people who had almost certainly been reluctant to take on a duty which to them at least would seem to hold in all probability neither profit nor pleasure. For here . . . were a man and a woman who were deeply concerned with those other values, to which they themselves had paid and were paying the tribute of sacrifice.[18]

Harold Nicolson gave an account of an interview which Ramsay MacDonald had with the King and Queen on 27th May 1937: "Poor old boy, he was pleased by the kindness they had shown to him. He told the Queen that the King had 'come on magnificently since his accession'. She had been pleased. 'And am I doing all right?' she asked. 'Oh you . . . ,' Ramsay had answered with a sweep taking all that for granted."[19]

And the two continued to grow. On 10th December 1937 Archbishop Lang wrote to them:

> It falls to me as much, I suppose, as to any public man to meet all sorts and conditions of people, and to learn what is in their minds. I find everywhere the same testimony to the impression which Your Majesty and the Queen have made upon your people during the first year of your reign.
>
> At first the feeling was one of sympathy and hope. It has now become a feeling of admiration and confidence.

I have noticed, all who have in any way come into contact with Your Majesty have noticed, how remarkably and steadily, if I may presume to say so, you have grown into your high office. Thus the courage with which a year ago you accepted the burden of a great responsibility suddenly thrust upon you, has been amply vindicated.[20]

In less than a year the King had shaken off the doubts which had assailed him in December 1936 and was well on his way to shaping a new monarchy.

17

The role of the Queen Consort

THE ACCESSION OF HER husband meant that Elizabeth Bowes-Lyon became Queen Consort, the first British-born Queen Consort since Tudor times. As such she stepped into a position which is at once legally defined and yet remains amorphous. Its legal standing – her place in the Constitution – is defined in Anson's *Law and Custom of the Constitution*: "The Queen Consort is a subject, though privileged in certain ways. Her life and chastity is protected by the law of treason. She has always been regarded as free from the disabilities of married women in matters of property, contract, and procedure. ... She has her separate officers and legal advisers. But in all other respects she is a subject, and amenable to the law of the land."[1]

As Queen Consort she was accorded the title of 'Her Majesty', her own coat-of-arms and a Standard which flew over Buckingham Palace whenever she was in residence without the King. Her income, granted by Parliament, was fixed at £40,000 a year, although in the event of her becoming a widow she would receive £70,000 a year, as did Queen Mary. In her new position she had a greatly enlarged personal staff – from pages to private secretaries, all of whom owed their first allegiance to her and whose salaries were paid out of her £40,000.

These and similar changes may be called 'official'. Other changes flowed from her new constitutional position. Lady Cynthia Asquith, who had been invited to 145 Piccadilly on the morning of 11th December 1936 when the instrument of Abdication was ratified by Parliament and George VI became King, tells of Princess Elizabeth looking at a letter on the hall table addressed to 'Her Majesty, the Queen'. "That's *Mummy* now, isn't it?" she asked Lady Cynthia. The younger Princess, Margaret Rose, complained: "I had only just learned how to spell York – YORK – and now I am not to use it any more. I am to sign myself Margaret all alone."[2]

As 'Her Majesty', Elizabeth Bowes-Lyon became the first lady in the land, a position previously held by the very popular Queen Mary. The new Queen

1954 and the gardener-Queen
Mother introduces her
grandchildren to the tasks
involved in her favourite
hobby. The close relationship
between her and Prince
Charles is evident in this
photograph.

24th November 1954 and a
family reunion on her return
from the triumphal tour of
Canada and the United
States. Prince Charles has a
big hug for his grandmother at
Waterloo Station while
Princess Anne waits to give
her own greeting. The Duke
of Edinburgh is on the left as
the Queen, with her back to
the camera, greets a member of
her mother's entourage. Prime
Minister Churchill stands in
the centre waiting to offer a
welcome on behalf of the
government.

The Queen Mother gives her horse, Devon Loch, a good luck pat in the paddock at Sandown on 21st January 1956, where the horse ran in the Mildmay Memorial Chase.

Talking to children who had come to watch her launch the tanker *British Queen* at John Brown's shipyard, Clydebank.

20th April 1966 and a relaxing period after many public ceremonies during the first days of the Royal Tour of New Zealand. Here she is trying her luck at trout-fishing on Lake Wanaka, where her unqueenly garb might have shocked the locals but would have been familiar to the fishermen on many rivers in Scotland.

"One of the most amazing Queens since Cleopatra . . ." Harold Nicolson.

Trooping the Colour, 14th June 1970, and an enthusiastic welcome for the popular
Queen Mother as she drove with Prince Charles, Princess Anne and Princess
Margaret's daughter, Lady Sarah Armstrong-Jones.

1st August 1975 and only three days to go for the birthday of the hard-working and popular Queen Mother. The *Daily Mirror* caption under this photograph read: "We ain't 'arf proud of our old Mum."

4th August 1976 and the Queen Mother's seventy-sixth birthday. As she left Clarence House she was greeted by a crowd singing *Happy Birthday* – and to their delight she stopped and conducted them through their piece. Here she was photographed with the Queen, Prince Philip, Prince Edward (*left*) and Prince Andrew in the garden of Clarence House.

13th June 1977 and the Queen Mother walks with Prince Charles in the procession of Knights of the Garter on their way to St George's Chapel, Windsor, where the Queen was to install two new Knights.

June 1978 and the Queen Mother leaves Buckingham Palace with Princess Margaret on their way to the Trooping the Colour. This was Princess Margaret's first public appearance after her divorce from Lord Snowdon – and the Queen Mother showed her motherly concern by choosing to drive with her daughter through the crowded streets and to an enthusiastic welcome.

tried to ensure that the older Queen was not 'pushed out' further than was constitutionally necessary. She could not, for example, do other than sit with her husband at the State Opening of Parliament – a role which Queen Mary had filled in George V's days, but in less formal matters, such as public patronages and presidencies, the new Queen used a great deal of tact. In theory, on her husband's accession, the former Duchess of York had to give up all her former patronages while she became, as it were, the heir to those traditionally linked with the wife of the monarch. But Queen Mary had held many of these posts for over twenty-five years and was anxious not to break all these links both with her own past and with the present public. As far as was possible, the new Queen allowed her to retain these patronages, although she was compelled to take on some which were of a more official nature. So it was that the net rapidly widened, for not only did she quickly resume her former patronages but she took on new ones. She became patron of the Silver Rose Ball to raise hospital funds; on 20th December it was announced that she was to be Patroness of the Governess's Benevolent Institution, and within days came announcements linking her with the preservation of old houses, the Red Cross, the Westminster Abbey Organ Fund, the Friends of York Minster, the Royal Horticultural Society, the National Council of Girls' Clubs, the Victoria League, the Royal National Lifeboat Institution, Queens' College, Cambridge . . . and the list grew of societies, institutions and organizations which she was to sponsor, visit, inspect and help with her close interest.

But, arduous and time-consuming though this aspect of her work was to be, it nonetheless may be described as the external side of her role. Along with her staff she planned her visits, prepared her speeches, carried out – with a real and lively interest – the work that was expected of her. But this was the 'working' side of her life and was only a part of that role which she might be expected to play as Queen Consort.

There were, as we will see, other and, perhaps, more important facets of that role. To these as well as to her 'working' life she brought a great deal. As the latest in a long line of the Glamis nobility she had, as it were, in 'the bone and the blood', a sense of history and an appreciation of the values of tradition. As part of her Glamis inheritance she had a concept of duty and service, based in a measure on her sound religious faith. And part of her character was that charm and vivacity which had made her a popular figure when she was merely Lady Elizabeth, had won her the soubriquet of "the smiling Duchess" and would make her a very popular and much-loved Queen and later Queen Mother.

There was one other feature which she brought to her new role. We have seen that she admired both King George V and Queen Mary and that, in return, she had won their very deep affection; thus it is not surprising that when she stepped into her new role she was very conscious of the fact that it had lately been filled by Queen Mary. One of her main aims was to model herself, in part, on the older Queen. Not that she would be as formal, as rigid or as aloof as King George V's wife had always been. But the new Queen, like the old, was conscious of the value of tradition, aware of her public duty and service so that in the new reign there was an element of continuity. If the new King appealed to his people because he was so much like his father, the new Queen would strengthen that popularity by ensuring that her family life and her own public life would be modelled, in many important respects, on that of Queen Mary.

One of her first aims, as she saw it, was to ensure that her husband-King was provided with a home to which he could return after his day's work, and that this home should give him that warmth and love which he was going to need if he were to overcome the 'prejudice' which Baldwin sensed in December 1936. She had, as we have seen, provided such a base at 145 Piccadilly. For the first few weeks after his accession the King had to use Buckingham Palace as his place of work – leaving 145 after breakfast and not returning until late in the evening. Meanwhile, the Queen had to supervise the breaking-up of that home and plan the move across to the Palace, into which the family moved on 15th February 1937. It had been relatively simple to make 145 Piccadilly into a comfortable home. The Palace, on the other hand, was a massive building which was part office, part museum, part State Rooms and only part home. But within a very short time the new Queen had come to grips with the problem of home-making in this difficult milieu, as Lady Airlie pointed out:

> I pitied most of all the new Queen. In the fourteen years of her marriage she had remained completely unspoiled, still at heart the simple unaffected girl I had known at Glamis, carrying out her public duties with an efficiency that won Queen Mary's admiration, but finding her true happiness in her home and her own family circle.
>
> When I first had tea with her in her sitting-room at Buckingham Palace, a few weeks after King George's accession, I saw that the room was already beginning to show the traces of her own personality – the little feminine touches which I had always associated with her. "It looks homelike already," I said spontaneously. The King, who had come in for a few minutes, smiled proudly . . . "Elizabeth could make a home anywhere."[3]

And in that new home she re-created as far as was possible the family atmosphere which had been a feature of their lives at 145 Piccadilly. She could not, of course, enjoy the same freedom as she had once done; never again would she simply drive out to call on friends, go shopping or dance in a night club. There were to be no more private visits to the cinema such as she and her husband had once enjoyed. Now all was official; she was guarded by detectives and surrounded by protocol.

There was, however, a chance to escape from this during the weekends at Royal Lodge which they continued to use as their country home, and where the King, Queen and Princesses continued to hack, saw, make bonfires and enlarge the garden.

One of the Queen's constant aims was to shield her children from the glare of publicity and to ensure, as far as was possible, that they had a pleasant upbringing. Miss Crawford was with the two Princesses on the day their father left 145 as Duke of York and returned as King. She wrote:

> Lilibet and Margaret had run as usual to give their father a final hug as he went off, looking very grave, dressed as an Admiral of the Fleet. . . . When the King returned, both little girls swept him a beautiful curtsey. I think perhaps nothing that had occurred had brought the change in his condition to him as clearly as this did. He stood for a moment touched and taken aback. Then he stooped and kissed them both warmly.[4]

The King and his brothers and sister had always to curtsey to their mother and bow to their father when entering or leaving a room. The new Queen did away with this practice, although she insisted that the children continue to pay this respect to their grandmother, Queen Mary. She wanted no such formality in her relationship with her children nor between them and their father-King. She was, after all, the daughter of Lady Strathmore, of whom *The Times* wrote in an obituary:

> She possessed a genius for family life – a most rare and priceless gift.
>
> It was once said of her by an older woman that she was perfect in all her relationships of life, and when one thinks of her as daughter, wife and mother, one realizes that it was true and she had friends in every walk of life.
>
> The Archbishop of Canterbury, the Most Reverend Cosmo Gordon Lang, speaking at Lady Strathmore's memorial service, said: "She raised a queen in her own home, simply, by trust and love, and as a return the Queen has won widespread love."[5]

It is not surprising that the daughter of such a mother should have created a happy family atmosphere even in such unfavourable surroundings as Buckingham Palace. In doing so she gave her own daughter a set of pleasant memories that were to help to ensure a pleasant childhood for the present royal children.

And the new Queen used her position as 'the first lady' to cement relationships in the wider royal family which had come under strain during the Abdication Crisis. She was wise enough to see that Queen Mary had been "the central strong point" around which the family had rallied during those harrowing days. She also had enough self-confidence to be willing to allow the older Queen to remain a potent figure. Lady Airlie, constant companion to Queen Mary, noted: "The King showed great kindness to his mother, and the Queen with loving intuition constantly asked her advice, which pleased her very much."[6] When, as was inevitable, changes had to be made at Buckingham Palace, Sandringham and Balmoral, the wishes of Queen Mary were consulted and respected. So much was this the case that on 22 December 1936 the older Queen noted in her diary: "Left London with Bertie, E. and their children for dear Sandringham to spend Christmas there, my staff running it this year. . . . Happy to be back in the old Home."[7]

This ability to consider the wishes of the older Queen and to co-operate with her, ensured that the transition into the new reign was smoother than might have been the case and helped to remind the public that the new reign was going back to a popular, traditional pattern. All this would have been so very different if Edward had continued to reign. People were reminded of his insensitivity by his marriage to Mrs Simpson on 3rd June 1937 – the date of his father's birthday and his final slight to the memory of that popular monarch.

The new King was fully aware of the important part which the Queen would play in his reign. During his speech to his Accession Council he said: "With my wife and helpmeet by my side I take up the heavy task which lies before me. . . ."[8] He concluded his first message to Parliament with the words: "It will be my constant endeavour, with God's help and supported as I shall be by my dear wife, to uphold the Honour of the Realm and promote the happiness of my peoples."[9]

Almost twenty years later Clement Attlee wrote his appreciation of the work of George VI. In the course of this he referred to him as: "happy in his marriage and in his family life . . . in all his work he had the help and support of the gracious lady who was an ideal Consort. As Queen and wife and mother she won a firm place in the hearts of the people."[10]

We have seen how she had helped him develop in the years between their marriage and their accession. She was to continue this work to such an effect that one biographer has claimed that: "It was widely felt that it would have been quite impossible for the Duke of York to have taken on the kingship without his wife." She and the King were, inevitably, more apart than they had been before December 1936. He had his papers to read, statesmen and politicians to meet, and public duties to perform. She also had a busy public life. But they still managed to take lunch and dine together almost daily and, when apart, to have long conversations over the telephone. He would consult her about his official papers – something that his father and grandfather never did with their wives. When he was discussing affairs with his private secretaries, she would often go into the room, and, although she did not take part in the discussions, she knew what was going on and was the better able to help him reach decisions. As one official noted, it was common for him to say: "I have talked to the Queen about that, and I shall do such and such."[11]

Between this King and his Consort there was a relationship different from that between King Edward VII and Queen Alexandra, and King George V and Queen Mary. In a sense this happier official relationship was merely a reflection of their happy marriage. The Queen's eldest sister, Lady Elphinstone, said of them: "They were so particularly together; they both leaned so much on the other. It was Queen Elizabeth's gift to be able to encourage and reward the King with a look or a smile."[12]

She had sustained him during the harrowing days after 4th December, when the politicians discussed his suitability as successor to his brother. She had helped him earlier with his speech therapy. But perhaps the best public evidence of his dependence on her and her ability to "reward with a look or a smile" was provided by their behaviour when he had to make a public speech. The *Northern Whig and Belfast Post* carried a report of a speech which the King made during a coronation tour of Ulster: "His speech finished, the King turned to the Queen with a slight smile, to receive in turn a quick smile of encouragement that captured the sympathy of everyone who noticed it." And when this tour was over, the same newspaper declared: "At his side was the smiling and radiant Queen, whose grace and charm, added to the splendid qualities of mind and heart, have enthroned her in the affections of the whole Empire . . . they have not merely heightened their personal popularity but have made the throne even more securely founded upon the solid base of constitutional usage and popular assent."[13]

As if to mark his debt of gratitude to his wife-Queen, on 14th December 1936 the new King conferred on her the title of 'Lady of the Most Noble Order of the Garter'. This was only two days after his accession and was also his own birthday. As the new Queen wrote to Queen Mary: "He had discovered that Papa gave it to you on his, Papa's, birthday, 3rd June, and the coincidence was so charming that he has now followed suit and given it to me on his birthday."[14]

There was a Royal Tour of Scotland between 5th and 11th July 1937 as part of the Coronation celebrations. The people of Scotland had always welcomed "the girl from Glamis", and now that she was their Queen her reception was doubly warm. As if in celebration of her position *vis-à-vis* the Scottish people, the King invested his wife with the Order of the Thistle in St Giles's Cathedral.

But there was much more to being Queen than was evident to the wider public. In his memoirs the former King Edward wrote: ". . . The ceremonial façade actually disguises an occupation of considerable drudgery . . . and" he continued, "this represented for me the relentless daily round."[15] (We have seen that he found this too much.) For the Queen Consort, as for the King, there was "an occupation of considerable drudgery". Like her husband the new Queen was assiduous in carrying out this facet of her new role. In part this was due to her sense of having been consecrated during the Coronation service in May 1937. The Bishop of St Albans wrote to her:

> I am quite sure that those whose privilege it was to be near Your Majesties must have felt – as I did – that this sense of reality was mainly due to the lovely way – in spite of the elaborate ritual and ceremonial – in which Your Majesties, together, made us all realize that your coronation meant for you both, first and foremost, the offering of yourselves and all you had to give in life-long service to God and your fellow men, in simple faith that He would give you the power equal to the task.[16]

During his Coronation broadcast the King had said: "To the Ministry of Kingship I have in your hearing dedicated myself, with the Queen at my side, in words of deepest solemnity...."[17] And we can be sure that she shared with her husband this sense of "Ministry". She was not merely doing a job as well as she could, she was, in a religious sense, setting out to serve – her husband, her family and the people. And one facet of that serving role was to offer to the people an example of family life and private conduct which were to show the people, in Bagehot's words, to "believe that it is natural to have a virtuous sovereign". After the scandals of the short reign of the last King, such an example was badly needed, and it was to be one of their proudest boasts that they had fulfilled another of Bagehot's requisites – to fulfil the people's expectation that "domestic virtues are as likely to be found on the throne as they are eminent when there".

Looking back on his experience, Dr Fisher, the former Archbishop of Canterbury noted:

> One of the things that stand out ... is the astonishing sequence that has been given to this nation. After the worldly setting of King Edward VII's reign came King George V and Queen Mary, remarkable examples of plain and humble Christian duty. Then there was the interlude of Edward VIII, so full of promise and yet so full of frustration. After that came King George VI and Queen Elizabeth; again extraordinary examples of plain Christian grace and duty with, in the case of the King, a triumph over the natural disabilities of shyness and stammering. They were just the people to restore again the quietness and happy confidence of the people in their royal family.
>
> If there are to be monarchs at all, there could not conceivably be any more fitted than our royal family to represent their people, and to represent to their people a sane, progressive, keen, creative and godly outlook on life.[18]

We have seen that one of the new King's major tasks was to repair the tattered image of the monarchy in the eyes of the people. In this, as in all else, his 'helpmeet' played a vital role. MacDonald, with his "'Oh you...' and a sweep taking that all for granted", had played an ageing politician's tribute to the early success of her fulfilment of that role. Reports of the success of their Coronation tours spoke, as did the Belfast newspaper, of the appeal which she made to the British people. At the end of the first month of their reign the Queen was asked if she was not tired after all the ceremonies and tours. "Not a bit! We are trying so hard to do it well." This is an echoing of the sentiments of the Australian who had seen the Yorks during their Australian tour in 1927.

The 'Yorks' had lived up to Queen Mary's expectations that they "will do it very well". They had, indeed, and, as the next few chapters will show, they were to repeat their success in both France and the USA, where they won massive support, not only for the British monarchy but for the British people, at a time when such support was to prove vital.

18

The visit to France, 1938

IN 1970 ANDREW DUNCAN WROTE *The Reality of Monarchy*, a full account of a year in the life of Queen Elizabeth II. It is a lively and vivid recital of the "occupation of considerable drudgery". During that year there were thousands of hands to be shaken, hundreds of gifts to be officially received and others to be handed over; there were dozens of lunches and official dinners; there were speeches of welcome and of thanksgiving on departure – and always, it seems, hundreds of miles to be travelled.

For the Queen's mother, life had been somewhat less hectic, if only because air travel was still in its infancy. But, that apart, King George VI's Queen led the sort of life that Duncan described. There was no Andrew Duncan to provide a year-long diary of her work in the 1930s, but, fortunately, many people have left accounts of meetings with the King and Queen and from these we can get an idea of the variety and extent of the work in which she was involved.

In *Times to Remember*, Mrs Rose Kennedy, the wife of the US Ambassador in London, gives an account of her first official visit in 1938 to Buckingham Palace:

> The first protocol visit, which was quite exciting, came only two days after my arrival. Ambassadorial wives – accompanied by their husbands – were always received by the Queen, a gracious form of welcoming them to the country. So, on 18th March, Joe and I arrived at Buckingham Palace and precisely to the minute of our appointed time were ushered into a beautiful sitting-room where Queen Elizabeth came forward to meet us.
>
> She had such a happy, natural smile and friendly manner that I felt at ease with her at once. . . . She and Joe chatted a bit about Anglo-American relations, but soon she wanted to hear all about our children, their ages and school plans, their feelings about coming to England and so forth.[1]

For Mrs Kennedy it may have been "quite exciting"; for the Queen this was a visit by only one of the large number of ambassadors and their wives. Today the Kennedys; tomorrow the French; then the Germans, and so on almost endlessly. And that she had "such a happy natural smile and friendly manner" for all these diverse people, with all of whom she "chatted a bit", is the unsought tribute to her ability to accommodate herself to her new role.

Elsewhere in her memoirs Mrs Kennedy tells of a visit to Windsor Castle for a weekend in the company of the King and Queen, the Prime Minister and Mrs Chamberlain, Lord Halifax, the Foreign Minister, and Lady Halifax, and some lesser ministers.[2] Mrs Kennedy was impressed by the ceremonial, the dinner, the conversation as they walked in the garden, and by a band concert. But for the Queen this was yet one more weekend of public duty which had her 'on call' the year round. And it was not only Prime Ministers who were called to the castle: "The new Sovereigns made a habit of inviting their Ministers for a night to Windsor," wrote Lady Diana Cooper, wife of the then Secretary of State for War, Duff Cooper. In *The Light of Common Day*, Lady Diana quotes from a letter she wrote at the time of their visit:

Windsor Castle   16th April 1937
We were warned to present ourselves at the Castle at 6 pm or thereabouts. . . .
Alec Hardinge appeared and warned me that dinner was at 8.30 pm; leave dining-room with gentlemen at 9.30 pm, but gentlemen don't stop, they walk straight through us to the lu [sic] and talk and drinks. Girls gossip until 10.15 pm, when the men reappear . . . and at 10.30 pm it's "Goodnight".

11.15 pm . . . The King and Queen said goodnight to the cringing company and the party broke up. I waited for my husband . . . tearing round to one and all saying "Where's Duff?" At last I'm down to a butler, who replies with an inscrutable face: "He is with the Queen."

He came back at 12.30 am, one hour so-called drinking tea with the Queen. She put her feet up on a sofa and talked of kingship and "the intolerable honour" but not of the [Abdication] crisis. Duff so happy. . . .[3]

From conversations with ambassadors and their wives, ministers and their wives, as well as from listening to her husband, the Queen was well aware of the dark clouds which were looming ever larger on the international scene in 1937 and 1938. On 14th March 1938 Hitler's army invaded Austria; the German dictator announced that the union of the two countries, the *Anschluss*, was merely "a German family affair". His plans for the annexation of at least part of Czechoslovakia were proclaimed to the world on 24th April by Konrad Henlein, the leader of the Nazi party in Czechoslovakia. The government of that unfortunate country turned to their ally, France, to ask whether France would honour her agreement to defend Czechoslovakia in the event of a German invasion. The French did not send a reply but instead asked the British government for a promise of its support in the event of a Franco-German war over Czechoslovakia. It was against this background that the government hastily arranged a State Visit by the King and Queen to the President of the French Republic. The original date for the departure had been 28th June, but all their plans were thrown into confusion by the death of Lady Strathmore on 23rd June. The King and Queen were at the funeral at Glamis, after which they stayed for a few days at Birkhall while the Press wondered whether the State Visit would be cancelled. However, the Queen's idea of duty and her wish to provide continuing support for her rapidly developing husband, overcame her natural inclination to spend more time in mourning for her mother. It was agreed that the Visit would start on 19th July.

At first sight it may appear somewhat "bizarre and banal" to note that all the clothes which Norman Hartnell had designed for the Queen to wear in France were now declared unsuitable – as the Queen was still in mourning. It was Hartnell who pointed out to the Queen that white was a colour which royalty traditionally wore during a period of mourning – and, by the time the Queen set out, all her silks, satins, velvets and lace were ready. The stunning effect of "the little Queen" dressed in white crinolines was to play an important part in the success of the visit. This visit recalled memories of that made by King Edward VII in 1903 when Franco-British relations were anything but cordial. He had "captured Paris by storm". As Sir Frederick Ponsonby remembers:

> . . . Wherever we went . . . loud and repeated cheering. It was the most wonderful transformation, and all in three days. It was all very well for Lord Lansdowne [the Foreign Secretary] to claim afterwards the credit for the *Entente Cordiale*. . . . As the French Ambassador in London remarked, any clerk . . . could draw up a treaty, but there was no one else who could have succeeded in producing the right atmosphere for a *rapprochement* with France.[4]

It was hoped that the visit in July 1938 would have an equally beneficial effect on Anglo-French relations and that the Ministers accompanying the King and Queen would find, in the hoped-for cordial atmosphere, common ground in their determination to stand up to Hitler.

But there were commentators who pointed out that the last State Visit to France had been made by King George V and Queen Mary. They had gone there in April 1914 – to cement the *rapprochement* of which Ponsonby had written. And within four months of their return home, war had broken out. Was it possible that the same pattern would follow this visit?

The answer to that question lay in the future. What was certain in July 1938 was that the Queen, like Edward VII, "captured Paris by storm". Hartnell had provided her with a series of dresses based on the crinoline, a deliberate attempt to revive memories of the costumes worn by Empress Eugénie, well calculated to win French approval. Lady Diana Cooper travelled with the royal pair, and her husband, now First Lord of the

Admiralty, was to use the visit as a chance to discuss naval matters with his French counterpart. Lady Diana wrote from Paris: "We saw the King and Queen from a window, coming down the Champs Elysées, with roofs, windows and pavements roaring exultantly, the Queen a radiant Winterhalter...." Later she wrote: "Each night's flourish outdid the last. At the opera ... shining with stars. [At] Malmaison ... I talked to two crying old ladies who begged for my place on the royal path. *'Vous la voyez toujours. Si seulement nous avions un roi.'*" And of the crowds which gathered to cheer the two monarchs, Lady Diana noted: "I can never forget it."[5]

This may be dismissed as the over-enthusiastic writing of a member of the royal circle. A more telling comment on the effect of the Queen's visit may be that of Paul Reynaud, Prime Minister of France during the traumatic days of the collapse of that nation in 1940. Reynaud went to see President Lebrun at this hour of defeat and in *In the Thick of the Fight* he recalled: "On seeing me off, [Lebrun] said sadly, in allusion to the visit of the British sovereigns to Paris: 'Do you remember that charming little Queen a year ago?'"[6] That this visit should be remembered by these men at that moment in their country's history is a dramatic indication of the impact it must have made on hard-bitten politicians.

On the morning of the last day of the French visit, 21st July, the King presided at a review of fifty thousand French troops at Versailles. The proposed fly-past by the French air force was cancelled because of low cloud, but in the afternoon, when the King and Queen attended a concert in the chapel of the Château at Versailles, the peace was shattered as the air force undertook its belated fly-past. Wave after wave of aircraft passed over the chapel, their shadows fleeting across the sunlit walls, their engines drowning the music. Both the King and Queen remembered this as a "macabre experience", an ominous harbinger of what was to come.

On 22nd July the King undertook his last ceremony, when he unveiled a memorial to the eleven thousand members of the Australian Imperial Forces who fell in France during the First World War and who had no known grave. After he had laid his official wreath, the Queen went forward and laid down an armful of red poppies picked in the nearby fields that morning which had been given her by a schoolboy. Both of them had in mind not only the eleven thousand remembered at this memorial but the two hundred thousand Australians who had been killed or wounded during the great holocaust which had been "the war to end war". Their State Visit had been a great success for them and for the King's Ministers, who had been given an opportunity of long and serious discussions with their French counterparts. Some commentators wondered whether this visit would have the same consequences as had followed the last State Visit. Within four months of George V's visit to France, the First World War had started. Britain declaring war on Germany on 3rd August 1914. The consequence of the visit of George VI and Queen Elizabeth was less forceful.

On 3rd August 1938 Lord Runciman arrived in Prague. The British and the French had agreed to send a mission to persuade the Czechs to accept some form of compromise with the Sudeten Germans. In the confident expectation that reasonable men would be able to find a rational solution to the Czech-Sudeten problem, the British went on their holidays as usual. The Queen's standard flew above the royal yacht *Victoria and Albert* on 26th July when she and the Princesses embarked at Portsmouth. Two days later the King joined them, and they attended Cowes Regatta before sailing into the North Sea. On 2nd August the King attended his Boys' Camp at Southwold in Suffolk, while the Queen stayed on board the anchored yacht. Later the family went on to Balmoral and, they hoped, a pleasant summer holiday. It was not to be.

On 4th September the Czech government, as anxious as the British and French to avoid war, produced its proposals for the solution of the Sudeten problem. The Sudeten Germans were to be allowed to have their own form of totalitarian government in an autonomous region inside the borders of the Democratic Czechoslovakian Republic. This too easy victory did not fit in with Hitler's plans; he ordered all Germans inside Czechoslovakia to rise in revolt on 7th September and used this as an excuse for the leaders of the Sudeten Germans to break off their negotiations with the Czech government.

On 12th September Hitler addressed a mass rally at Nuremberg. While he did not declare war, he "spat on Czechoslovakia" and ordered a stepping-up of the rebellion by the Germans inside that country. There was an increase in the hand-to-hand fighting between Germans and Czech forces, and the world waited for Hitler to declare that he had to intervene to protect his fellow-countrymen.

The King travelled to London on the night train on 14th September, arriving almost at the same time as the Prime Minister, Neville Chamberlain, was leaving Heston Airport to fly to see Hitler at Berchtesgaden. On the following day the Prime Minister was back, reporting to the King at the Palace that he had persuaded Hitler to hold up his planned invasion for a week. French Ministers were summoned to London for discussions during which, as Tom Jones revealed, they "besought our [Ministers] to avoid it [war] at all costs. They could only put seven hundred planes in the air! [while] our Ministers [Hoare and Kingsley Wood] responsible for air defence knew that London was at Germany's mercy."[7]

On 21st September the Queen travelled to London to be with the King during this crisis. On 22nd September Neville Chamberlain flew once more to see Hitler at Godesberg to put before him a plan for the solution of the Czech problem. When he returned on 25th September, he told the King that war was imminent. Germany was determined to use force to solve the Czech problem if the Czechs had not handed over the Sudeten areas by 1st October. The British government started its own preparations for war: children were evacuated from London and other crowded areas; gas-masks were issued to the civilian population; trenches were dug in London parks to provide some sort of cover for people undergoing aerial bombardment; lonely Spitfires patrolled the skies above London, while on Horse Guards Parade and Westminster Bridge aircraft guns were mounted.

During that weekend the King and Queen did not go to Royal Lodge as was their normal custom. They were supposed to have gone to Glasgow for the launching of the world's largest liner, the *Queen Elizabeth* on 27th September, but the King decided that he could not be away from London while there was a real danger that war might break out. So it was that the Queen travelled on her own on the train, which left London on the evening of 26th September. Princess Elizabeth and Princess Margaret met her at Ibrox Station in Glasgow and together they visited the Empire Exhibition, the Queen having her usual unperturbable manner, which impressed people who were well aware of the crisis. As *The Times* reported: "A great multitude of people gave them a welcome which the tension of the moment seemed to charge with a deeper and more personal feeling than would have coloured enthusiasm at a less critical time."[8]

On 28th September the King held a Privy Council to confirm by a Royal Proclamation the preparations that had already begun – the mobilization of the fleet and the calling-up of the Auxiliary Air Force, and to declare a State of Emergency giving the government "appropriate powers". That afternoon the Prime Minister addressed the House of Commons. He outlined the developments which had taken place since the Runciman Mission had first gone to Czechoslovakia, gave an account of his own efforts to maintain peace and arrange a compromise with the Germans, and showed why war now seemed to be inevitable. Then, as Harold Nicolson wrote:

He said that his conversation with Herr Hitler had convinced him that the Führer was prepared, on behalf of the Sudeten Germans, "to risk a world war". As he said these words, a shudder of horror passed through the House of Commons.

"I came back," he added, "to London the next day." The House was tense with excitement. He then told us how the Anglo-French plan was described by Hitler at Godesberg as "too dilatory". "Imagine," he said, "the perplexity in which I found myself." This remark aroused a murmur of sympathetic appreciation from all benches.

"Yesterday morning," began the Prime Minister, and we were all conscious that some revelation was approaching. He began to tell us of his final appeal to Herr Hitler and Signor Mussolini. I glanced at the clock. It was twelve minutes after four. The Prime Minister had been speaking for exactly an hour. I noticed that a sheet of Foreign Office paper was being rapidly passed along the Government bench. Sir John Simon interrupted the Prime Minister, and there was a momentary hush. He adjusted his pince-nez and read the document that had been handed to him. . . . All the lines of anxiety and weariness seemed suddenly to have been smoothed out; he appeared ten years younger and triumphant. "Herr Hitler," he said, "has just agreed to postpone his mobilization for twenty-four hours and to meet me in conference with Signor Mussolini and Signor [sic] Daladier at Munich." . . . That was the end of the Prime Minister's speech and when he sat down the whole House rose as a man to pay a tribute to his achievement. I remained seated. Liddall [the Conservative Member for Lincoln] behind me, hissed out, "Stand up, you brute."9

Chamberlain flew to see Hitler at Munich. On 30th September he returned in triumph. At Heston Airport he waved the text of the Agreement for Anglo-German Friendship which he had signed with Hitler. At Downing Street he went onto the balcony to tell the cheering crowds that he had achieved "Peace in our Time". Later that evening he appeared with the King and Queen on the balcony of Buckingham Palace to receive the applause of the crowds which had gathered to greet the man who had achieved "Peace with Honour".

Few people in Britain agreed with the forthright Churchill who addressed the Commons during the debate on the Munich Agreement:

We really must not waste time after all this long debate upon the differences between the positions reached at Berchtesgaden, at Godesberg and at Munich. They can be simply epitomized, if the House will permit me to vary the metaphor. £1 was demanded at the pistol's point. When it was given, £2 was demanded at the pistol's point.

Finally the Dictator consented to take £1 17s 6d and the rest in promises of good will for the future. The German dictator, instead of snatching the victuals from the table, has been content to have them served to him course by course . . . a disaster of the first magnitude has befallen Britain and France. . . .10

Churchill had been wrong about India, Ireland, the Abdication. Many thought that here he was wrong again. The British people preferred to think that there was going to be no war.

19

The visit to the USA, 1939

WITHIN WEEKS, THE EUPHORIA which had accompanied the Munich settlement had faded. The King's private secretary noted:

> 19th October [1938]
>
> The PM agreed with the King that the future policy must be the cultivation of friendly relations combined with intensified rearmament. It was essential that the Cabinet should be united and back him up in this new foreign policy. He was determined to get more aeroplanes, better ARP and some kind of National Register.[1]

The failure of the policy of trying to negotiate with Hitler was made clear in March 1939. In the first week of March the leaders of the Ruthenian and Slovak minorities went to Germany to ask Hitler to help them gain their independence from the Czechs. On 14th March Hitler announced the independence of both territories; on 15th March the President of Czechoslovakia was summoned to Berlin and was bullied into agreeing to place the rest of his country under German protection. That evening Hitler was in Prague, issuing a proclamation that "Czechoslovakia has ceased to exist".

For Chamberlain, all this came as a shock. On 10th March he had declared publicly that "the outlook in international affairs is tranquil".[2] On 17th March he denounced Hitler as "a perjurer", went on to declare that, while he was willing to surrender much for the sake of maintaining peace, "there is one thing I must expect, and that is the liberty we have enjoyed for hundred of years, and which we would never surrender".[3]

On 21st March Hitler made his first demands on Poland. Coincidentally, the French President, Loubet, was in London on a return State Visit. This gave the British and French Ministers an opportunity to formulate a common policy in the light of Hitler's attitude to Poland. This, which amounted to a revolution in British foreign policy, was announced to the House of Commons by a belligerent Chamberlain on 31st March:

In the event of any action which already threatened Polish independence, and which the Polish government accordingly considered vital to resist with national forces, His Majesty's Government would feel themselves bound at once to lend the Polish Government all support in their power. I may add that the French Government have authorized me to make it plain that they stand in the same position as does His Majesty's Government.[4]

On 27th April came the announcement of a second revolutionary decision. For the first time in the history of the country the government proposed to introduce compulsory national service in peacetime. Many historians have blamed Chamberlain for not having adopted a more warlike policy at an earlier stage. This is to ignore the fact that the country as a whole was in favour of a policy of appeasement and pacifism throughout the whole of the 1930s. This is clear from the success of the Peace Pledge Union and the welcome given Chamberlain on his return from Munich. British attitudes were typified by the notorious debate in the Oxford Union in February 1933 when, by 275 votes to 153, the undergraduates voted in favour of the motion: "That this House will in no circumstances fight for King and Country." Hitler's brutal repudiation of his Munich Agreement united the country as no Prime Minister could have hoped to do. In April 1939, following the announcement of peacetime conscription, there was another, less well-remembered debate at the Oxford Union when, by 423 votes to 326, the undergraduates voted in favour of the motion that "In view of this country's commitments and the gravity of the general situation in Europe, this House welcomes conscription."

It was against this background that the government decided that the King and Queen should undertake a State Visit to North America.

In France the King and Queen had walked in the steps of previous monarchs. Their State Visit to Canada and the USA was the first ever made to North America by a reigning sovereign.

During the coronation in 1937, Mackenzie King, the Prime Minister of Canada, had suggested that the King and Queen should visit his country. By August 1938 it had been agreed that the visit would take place in 1939. Franklin Delano Roosevelt, the President of the USA, was quick to seize the opportunity to send an invitation to King George VI: "I need not assure you that it would give my wife and me the greatest pleasure to see you, and frankly I think it would be an excellent thing for Anglo-American relations if you could visit the United States. . . ."[5]

It is difficult to remember that at that time there was no 'special relationship' between the USA and Great Britain. This was to be the product of close wartime collaboration. In the 1930s many Americans, including important politicians, thought of Britain as the world's leading colonial power. Since they traced the origins of their country back to the war against this colonial power, they tended to take a critical and hostile view of Britain's role in India and other parts of Asia, in Africa and the West Indies. For many Americans living in the Middle or Far West, Europe, including Britain, was very far away. (For Britain's similar attitude to distant parts of Europe, it is worth recalling that in September 1938, during the Czech crisis, *The Times* had a leader which said: "How horrible, fantastic, incredible it is that we should be digging trenches and trying on gas-masks here because of a quarrel *in a far-away country between people of whom we know nothing. . . .*"[My italics.][6]) American newspapers now reminded their readers that they had sent their sons to help in the First World War and that the Europeans had given them no thanks for their trouble. It was better, these isolationists argued, not to get involved in the affairs of these old countries, some of which, in any case, were smaller than many States in the USA. Even as late as December 1938, Ambassador Kennedy told the American Press that he wanted the USA to "keep out of it. . . . I feel more strongly than ever that this nation should stay out – absolutely out – of whatever happens in Europe."[7] It was fortunate that the subsequent visit by the King and Queen more than offset this unfavourable attitude by a leading American.

One of the purposes behind the State Visit to the USA was to break down the isolationist hostility of the majority and to remind the Americans of their own European roots. However, Roosevelt was conscious of the fact that his political opponents in the USA would be critical if the King and Queen were accompanied by the normal retinue of diplomats, politicians and advisers. So it was that, when the King went to the USA, he did so with only a small personal staff. This, as we shall see, was to be of some importance for him and the Queen.

They arrived in Canada on 17th May to undertake an arduous tour during which they crossed the vast country by train. In towns and cities there were crowds, official ceremonies and public appearances. (Some indication of the nature of the journey may be seen from the fact that the Queen required on average six changes of costume each day.) And there were small gatherings at each station, each small wayside halt, along the route. For their benefit the two visitors would step out onto the observation platform to wave. For the eager crowd which had patiently waited – sometimes into the small hours of the morning – the visit was to be a memorable event in the life of their parish or town. For the visitors there was the "drudgery" of being woken at 4 am to be told that they were due in at some station where they had to appear cheerful and bright to see and be seen.

Once again it was the Queen who captured the headlines through this two-week tour. "A Queen who smiled like an angel", "We will remember her smile", were two typical headlines. As she was laying a foundation stone in Ottawa, she heard one of the stone-masons speak and realized that he was a

Scot. She took the King across to where he and other fellow-Scots were standing and in the sight of the crowd of seventy thousand the two visitors laughed and joked and won roars of approval from the watching Canadians who had been afraid that the tour might be a frigid, formal affair. Here was the first of the 'walkabouts' for which the present Queen was to become famous.[8]

Within a week of their arrival they had won such a degree of popularity that one Provincial Premier declared: "Any talk that they may hear (in the UK) about Canada being isolationist after today is just nonsense." And the Governor-General, Lord Tweedsmuir, wrote to a friend in London:

> The visit is going to have an enormous effect in Canada and in the United States . . . as a demonstration of our unity of spirit. Our monarchs are most remarkable young people . . . as for the Queen, she has a perfect genius for the right kind of publicity . . . at the unveiling of the War Memorial, where we had some ten thousand veterans, she asked me if it was not possible to get a little closer to them . . . it was an amazing sight, for we were simply swallowed up . . . the American correspondents were simply staggered. They said that no American President would ever have dared to do that. It was a wonderful example of what true democracy means and a people's King.[9]

And their impact on people in the USA was just as immediate and as great. They crossed over from Canada just after ten o'clock on the night of 7th June 1939 and arrived in Washington on the following day. Mrs Roosevelt noted in her diary: "In the course of a long life I have seen many important events in Washington, but never have I seen a crowd such as lined the whole route between the Union Station and the White House . . . they have a way of making friends these young people."[10] And the headline, "The British re-take Washington", was supported by an editorial in the isolationist *Washington Post* noting that the welcome was "not the result of calculated government dragooning to create the effect of popular enthusiasm but wholly voluntary and sincere".

A change in US attitudes towards Britain and Europe required a change of mind on the part of politicians. It was significant, therefore, that the King and Queen met many of them and their wives. One senator was so impressed that, as he shook the King's hand, he remarked, "My, you're a great Queen-picker."[11] It was even more important to win the support of the men closest to the President. One of the more influential of these was Harry Hopkins, Special Adviser and Personal Assistant to the President. His eight-year-old daughter had been disappointed when the King and Queen wore 'ordinary clothes' during their journey through Washington, and it was the Queen who suggested that the little girl should be in the hall of the White House on the evening when they would be leaving for a dinner-party at the British Embassy. Then the child saw the Queen in her sweeping crinoline, her jewels and her diadem. Mrs Roosevelt was present and noted:

"The illusion was so perfect that she curtsied to the Queen and ignored the King." They stopped to speak to her and, as they moved on, she turned to her father to say: "Oh, Daddy, Daddy! I have seen the Fairy Queen."[12]

And they made their impact on a wider public. For example, there were four million people lining the route of their journey to the World's Fair; on their later progress through the streets of New York there were "enormous crowds", and as they made their way back to the President's home at Hyde Park the "parkways . . . lined with close-packed masses of people and cars". One observer noted: "No American ever received such an ovation from his countrymen."[13]

But behind all this well-deserved public enthusiasm were the harsher realities. Since the King had no Ministers or advisers with him, it was he and not his Ministers who had to hold private conversations with the President. They spoke of 'when', not 'if', war would come. The President explained that he hoped he would be able to persuade his countrymen to come to Britain's aid 'when' it was needed. It was at these talks that Roosevelt explained that he hoped the British would allow the US Fleet to use British Naval Bases in the West Indies from which it could more easily patrol the Atlantic. The visit of the King and Queen was an important step in the breaking-down of American isolationism and in drawing the USA more firmly into the anti-Axis camp.[14]

As for the King and Queen, still fresh to their unexpected roles, their State Visit to Canada and the USA was most important. They had been seen by millions, had won the affection and respect of Canadians and Americans. They had carried out, with style and simple dignity, a multitude of duties. In the process they had become increasingly confident in their abilities. It is little wonder that the Queen was to remark: "It made us, the King and I. It came at just the right time, particularly for us."[15]

They arrived back in England on 22nd June and were given a tumultuous welcome home on a drive through London. Harold Nicolson wrote to his wife:

Such fun yesterday. The House adjourned at 5.15 and we all went out into Parliament Square where the pavements had been kept clear for us. There we stood and chatted for ten minutes, and then the bells of St Margaret's began to swing into welcome and the procession started creeping round the corner. They went very slowly, and there were the King and Queen and the two Princesses. We lost all our dignity and yelled and yelled. The King wore a happy schoolboy grin. The Queen was superb. She really does manage to convey to each individual in the crowd that he or she have had a personal greeting. It is due, I think, to the brilliance of her eyes. But she is in truth one of the most amazing queens since Cleopatra. We returned to the House with lumps in our throats.[16]

They had, indeed, been "made", and this new-found confidence and popularity was to be of great importance to them and the country in the years that lay ahead.

The King and Queen were quickly reminded that the European situation was still in a ferment. On 2nd July they reviewed at Hyde Park twenty thousand representatives of the nation's Civil Defence Forces. The King broadcast a message which told of the deep impression made upon him and the Queen by: ". . . This demonstration of the spirit of service which is everywhere present in the nation today, and which shows itself in the determination to make the country ready to meet any emergency whatever the sacrifices or inconveniences entailed. You know that all our preparations are designed not to provoke war but to preserve peace."[17]

On 22nd July of that last summer of peace, the Queen went with the King and the two Princesses on a visit to the Royal Naval College at Dartmouth. For the King this was a return to old haunts, for the Queen a chance to live vicariously through that enjoyable part of her husband's naval career. It was not evident then that the most significant event of the visit was the meeting between Princess Elizabeth and her cousin, cadet Captain Prince Philip of Greece, nephew of Lord Louis Mountbatten, to whom the King had turned for advice at the time of his accession in 1936. She had never seen him before, and this first meeting was to be of great importance for the future of the monarchy.

On 5th August the King held the last of his Camps. This year there were to be only two hundred boys, and the Camp was to be held at Abergeldie Castle, the King himself being Camp Chief. The Queen and the Princesses entertained the boys to tea at Balmoral Castle and went across to take supper with them. On the last night of the Camp the great bonfire was lit by the King himself. Balmoral pipers played stirring airs, and finally 'Auld Lang Syne' and the National Anthem were sung with unaccustomed fervour. The King and Queen then said goodbye to the boys as they made their way to the waiting coaches. During the next six years the King and Queen met many of these boys — in one or other of the services, in factories or Civil Defence stations, in hospital or at investiture ceremonies. Some they would never see again.[18]

PART V: 1939–1952

20

The Queen and the War, 1939–45

THE ROYAL FAMILY RESUMED their holiday when the last Boys' Camp had finished, but on 22nd August came the news of the German-Soviet Non-Aggression Pact, and the danger of war loomed even larger. The next day the King travelled to London. Queen Mary wrote to the Queen: "I feel deeply for you too, I having gone through all this in August 1914 when I was the wife of the sovereign."[1]

The Queen stayed at Birkhall until 29th August when she travelled to London. As she said: "If things turn out badly, I must be with the King."[2] On 1st September German troops invaded Poland and on the 3rd, having failed to get the Germans to withdraw, Britain declared war. On that Sunday evening the King broadcast. He spoke of the attempts that had been made to maintain peace in the face of great provocation. "We have been forced into conflict . . . to meet the challenge of a principle that Might is Right. And if this principle were established . . . the peoples of the world would be kept in bondage of fear and all hopes of peace and justice would be ended . . . it is unthinkable that we should refuse to meet the challenge." The King ended his broadcast with a declaration of simple faith and a call to the people:

> It is to this high purpose that I now call my people at home and my peoples across the seas, who will make our cause their own. I ask them to stand firm and calm and united in this time of trial. The task will be hard. There may be dark days ahead, and war can no longer be confined to the battlefield. But we can only do the right as we see the right, and reverently commit our cause to God. If one and all we keep resolutely faithful to it, ready for whatever sacrifice it may demand, then, with God's help, we shall prevail. May He bless and keep us all.[3]

During these anxious days when the King was in endless consultation with Ministers, ambassadors and leading members of the Armed Forces, the Queen was, as ever, his greatest support. One friend said: "I have never seen the Queen more closely resemble her mother, Lady Strathmore, than she did

167

in those first days of the war. She was a tower of strength."[4] In November 1939 she communicated some of her own sense of faith, determination and strength in a broadcast to the women of the Commonwealth and Empire, and of Allied Europe: "The greater your devotion and courage, the sooner we shall see again in our midst the happy ordered life for which we long . . . we put our trust in God, who is our refuge and our strength."[5] This was a paraphrasing of the Glamis family motto: "In thou my God, I place my trust without change to the end." This inner faith, strong and sure, had been one of the major facets of the Queen's life up to 1939. It was to be the main reason for the serenity, dignity, assurance and courage which she was to display so amply in the days that lay ahead, during which, as one of her staff remembered: "The Queen never showed that she was worried."[6]

The role played by the Queen during the War falls, almost naturally, into three sections, as, indeed, did the War itself. There was what became known as the 'phony' period when little seemed to be happening. This came to an end with the German attack on the West, in spring 1940, which launched a second period during which it seemed at least possible that Britain, too, would be conquered. This dark time came to an end in 1943 when the tide turned in favour of the Allies.

In the first period the Queen undertook, from the start, a series of tours of the country. She visited Civil Defence points and air-raid shelters, Red Cross centres and ambulance trains, clothing factories and munitions works, dockland areas and troops in training. A million children had been rushed out of London and other large cities, and the Queen visited some of the evacuees in their new homes in Sussex. She was very conscious of the sacrifices made by the people who took these children into their homes and, as a gesture of appreciation, sent each of them a personal message: "I wish to mark, by this personal message, my appreciation of the service you have rendered to your country in 1939 . . . you have earned the gratitude of those to whom you have shown hospitality, and by your readiness to serve you have helped the State in a work of great value."[7] She visited men and women who served on lonely searchlight bases, the men unloading food ships in London Docks and the hospitals which were preparing to receive the expected casualties from enemy action. In the royal train she and the King travelled thousands of miles showing themselves to the people, using their train as a mobile home. At the start of 1940 they went to Clydeside to launch the battleship *Duke of York* at John Brown's shipyard, to visit armaments factories and ARP organizations. A lady-in-waiting remembered only the "bitter winter . . . almost collapsing with cold", during a long inspection of troops ready for embarkation for France.[8] The Queen spoke to almost every man on the parade, remembering, perhaps, the sadness of saying goodbye to her brothers in 1914 and to the men who had stayed in the hospital at Glamis.

But she realized from the start that the War was not only about industrial or military efficiency. Like many of the British people, she put a high value on things of the spirit, so that it is not surprising that she continued to attend concerts and art exhibitions. Pictures from Royal Lodge were exhibited at the National Gallery, where, even during the later air-raids, lunchtime concerts were given and Beethoven and Mozart were played before crowded audiences delighting in this breath of greatness being made available at a time of national stress.

In complete contrast to the Queen's patronage of and attendance at these concerts, was her support for a scheme for providing hot meals for people in blitzed areas. Lord Woolton, the Food Minister, worked out plans for a fleet of travelling vehicles to take meals where they were needed. He knew that he would need "fearless and devoted workers" to drive the vehicles into dangerous areas, and he told the King that he wanted to "call them 'Queen's Messengers' because the women who will take charge of these convoys will indeed be messengers of mercy". The Queen did not see why her title should be used in this way. "What will I have done?" In his *Memoirs* Woolton wrote:

> Then, greatly daring, I said, "But, Your Majesty, don't you know what you mean to all of us in this country? It isn't only your high position that matters; it is the fact that the vast majority of people think of you as a person who would speak the kindly word, and, if it fell within your power, would take the cup of hot soup to the needy person." Whereupon Her Majesty put up her hands and said to me, "Oh, my lord, do you think I mean that? It is what I have tried so hard to be." Indeed it was a very moving insight into the mind of a great lady.[9]

On 9th April 1940 Hitler invaded Denmark and Norway, and the Second period of the War had opened. On 2nd May the Germans attacked the Low Countries. Very quickly they smashed their way through Holland, Belgium, Luxemburg and France. On 24th May they entered Boulogne, and only the Channel stood between the conquerors and Britain. On that day, Empire Day, the King broadcast to his people, calling for a Day of National Prayer on the following Sunday. And throughout this period, "the Queen was perfectly wonderful ... tremendously reserved, she carried on steadfastly with the daily things that had to be done. ..."[10]

There was an unseemly scramble by many important people to get their children out of the country to the safety of Canada or the USA. The left-wing poets W. H. Auden and Christopher Isherwood, who had once called so loudly for a war against Fascism, had led the rush to America when war seemed likely in 1938. Many people thought that the two Princesses should be sent overseas to avoid the danger of their being captured in the event of a German invasion. The Queen's answer to these suggestions was: "The children won't go without me. I won't leave the King. And the King will never leave."[11]

Visitors to the royal home always came away the better for their contact with the Queen. Nicolson wrote: "I cannot tell you how superb she is. I anticipated her charm. What astonished me is how the King is changed. He is now like his brother. He was so gay and she so calm. They did me all the good in the world. We shall win. I know that. I have no doubt at all."[12]

On 10th May Neville Chamberlain had been forced to resign, and Winston Churchill became Prime Minister of a Coalition Government. On the 13th he spoke of "having nothing to offer but blood, toil, tears and sweat". On that same day Queen Wilhelmina arrived from Holland, the first of the royal émigrés forced to flee before the German advance. On 3rd June the "miracle of Dunkirk" saw the embarkation of three hundred thousand troops from France, whose government sought an armistice with the Germans. Britain was now alone.

For the royal family this meant an immediate tightening of security because of fears that the Germans might launch an attack of paratroopers to try to capture the monarchs. They travelled in a bullet-proof car; the Queen carried a steel helmet and practised with a revolver. Lord Halifax, the Foreign Secretary, who had the privilege of walking through the Palace grounds as a short cut to Whitehall, was very surprised one morning to hear the rattle of fire in the Palace grounds: it was the Queen and her ladies-in-waiting on the rifle and revolver ranges. Halifax ceased to use his short cut. The Queen continued with her practices, being determined, as she said: "They won't take me easily."[13]

In September 1940 the Blitz on London began. During one of the first raids the King and Queen happened to be on a tour of Civil Defence centres, and when the sirens went they made their way to a public shelter where they sat with other Londoners, drinking tea. When they were in the Palace and the sirens sounded, they went, with their guests and staff, to a housemaids' sitting-room in the basement which had been reinforced by heavy timbers. Until 1941 this was their only shelter.

During the heavy bombing, their old home at 145 Piccadilly was destroyed along with thousands of other people's homes in all parts of London. Throughout the September days when Londoners were staggering beneath the shocks of the bombardment, the King and Queen would appear, sometimes together, sometimes separately, among the rubble and the ruins. They spoke to their people, offering a word of sympathy and encouragement, listening to sad stories of bereaved parents or old people bombed out of their lifetime's home. Their conduct during these trying times won their people's admiration. As one man said: "For him we had admiration, for her adoration." A Cockney woman put it in her own words as she watched the dainty Queen holding a baby of a mother whose arm had been disabled in the bombing: "Oh, ain't she lovely; ain't she just *bloody* lovely." Churchill put it more sonorously when he wrote to the King: "This war has drawn the throne and the people more closely together than ever before, and Your Majesties are more beloved by all classes and conditions than any of the princes of the past."[14]

On 13th September the Palace was again bombed, this time during the day while their majesties were working at their desks in a room overlooking the quadrangle. Though they were badly shaken and the King wondered "why we aren't dead", they promptly went to talk to the staff busily engaged in clearing up the mess. The Queen said: "I'm glad we've been bombed. It makes me feel I can look the East End in the face."[15] An American woman penned the lines which expressed, albeit in doggerel, the feelings of many Londoners:

> Be it said to your renown,
> That you wore your gayest gown,
> Your bravest smile, and stayed in Town,
> When London Bridge was burning down.
> My Fair Lady.[16]

But the strain of London's bombing and the stress of trying to help provide an air of calm assurance in the Palace and to the world at large was very great. The Queen wrote to Queen Mary: "I feel quite exhausted after seeing and hearing so much sadness, sorrow, heroism and magnificent spirit. The destruction is so awful and the people are so *wonderful* – they *deserve* a better world."[17]

Nor was it only London which suffered from the German bombing. The Queen went to Coventry, Bath, Plymouth and all the other cities and towns which had been attacked. Crowds gathered wherever the royal family went, and always they were given an amazing welcome, even by the homeless and bereaved. I have my own vivid memory of the Queen, dressed in pink, poking her way over the rubble of bombed-out areas of Cardiff, stopping to speak to ambulance men, ARP wardens, knots of housewives and the obviously distressed. When she was given the Freedom of the City of London, tribute was paid that: ". . . During the full weight of the enemy attack on London, the Queen became the shining symbol of her sex. Wherever the bombs fell thickest, there she was to be found bringing comfort and encouragement to the homeless."

And throughout all this she provided an air of serenity, of a calm founded on a deep inner faith. It was she who suggested to the King that he end his second Christmas broadcast of the War with the words: "I said to the man who stood at the Gate of the Year, 'Give me a light that I may tread safely into the unknown.' And he replied, 'Go out into the darkness and put your hand into the hand of God. That shall be to you better than a light, and safer than a known way.'"[18]

One of her ladies-in-waiting said of this period: "Altogether life was rather a strain. Yet, once I had seen the Queen, I felt absolutely all right and able to face anything." And Herbert Morrison, Home Secretary and Minister of Home Security, declared that the example of the King and Queen did more to keep up the spirits of the people than any other single factor.[19]

The onset of the third and final period of the War was signalled by the victory of the British forces at El Alamein in October and November 1942. By May 1943 the Axis troops in North Africa had surrendered and the Allied Forces were poised for the invasion of Sicily. On 11th June 1943 the King left Northolt Airport to travel via Gibraltar to visit the victorious troops. This journey caused the Queen some alarm. She wrote to Queen Mary:

> I have had a few anxious hours because at 8.15 I heard that the plane had been heard near Gibraltar and that it would soon be landing. Then after an hour and a half I heard that there was thick fog at Gib. and that they were going on to Africa. Then complete silence till a few minutes ago, when a message came that they had landed in Africa and taken off again. Of course, I imagined every sort of horror and walked up and down in my room staring at the telephone.[20]

The Queen had seen the Duchess of Kent shattered by the death of the Duke of Kent when his aircraft crashed in August 1942. The death of this younger brother had also had a deep effect on the King and Queen, so that her concern over the King's flight to North Africa was understandable.

Before he left England George VI had appointed the Queen a Counsellor of State, which gave her the privilege of holding an Investiture at the Palace. There had been no public announcement of the King's absence in Africa on a day in June 1943 when 255 officers and men were assembled to receive their decorations: the band played as the doors opened – and in came the Queen. No queen had held an Investiture since Queen Victoria, and the *Glasgow Herald* gave an account of this unusual one:

> On that day a long line of men and women in uniform, headed by the late Wing-Commander Guy Gibson and his dam-busting colleagues, overflowed from the investiture room through a corridor and into a large ante-room.
>
> At that time they did not realize that there was anything unusual in all this, until they noticed one of the palace flunkeys glancing impatiently at his watch. From this they gathered that this particular investiture was taking much longer than usual, "because the Queen is speaking to everyone being decorated".
>
> Although the Investiture began quite early in the morning, it was long past one o'clock when those at the end of the line came to a spot where they could see the Queen, and they were able to note that she was indeed speaking to everyone in turn and showing no signs of tiring from the long session.
>
> When our colleague at last came before her and his answer to her first

question announced his Scottish accent, the Queen seemed pleasured, and she did not let him go until she had extracted from him a potted autobiography.

He left the dais feeling elated, though he confessed that the last few minutes of waiting to ascend the dais were far more nerve-racking than any of his pre-operational 'jitters' on bomber raids over Germany.[21]

She was to hold other Investitures when the King was abroad visiting the troops in Italy in 1944, when she also had the privilege of signing the Royal Assent to several Bills, which, after her signature, became law. But these constitutional niceties were merely highlights in what was the unchanging routine of the wartime Queen. She continued to visit towns and troops, hospitals and airfields, factories and dockyards.

Even though 'the tide had turned', Germany had a number of brutalities to visit on Britain. In June 1944 London was attacked by the first of the 'pilotless planes', the V1 rockets which were filled with explosive. The people of London had hoped that they had finished with aerial attacks. Now, in 1944, they had to withstand bombardment by this new weapon. The Queen wrote to Queen Mary: "There is something very inhuman about death-dealing missiles being launched in such an indiscriminate manner."[22] One flying bomb landed in a corner of the Palace gardens, but, as a lady-in-waiting noted: "There is a tiny passage behind the Belgian suite in Buckingham Palace and when a flying bomb was alerted the Queen would say, 'We'll hide in there.' A very large housemaid was also always sheltering there, taking up the complete width of the passage, and, I must confess, making me feel much safer."[23] But the bombs destroyed parts of London dear to the Queen, including the chapel at Wellington Barracks when many of their friends were at worship. The Queen had already lost a nephew, Captain John Patrick Bowes-Lyon, who was killed in action in 1941. Now, in 1944, she suffered the death of her father, Lord Strathmore. She and the King went to Glamis for the funeral, where the pipers of the Black Watch played the sad 'Flowers of the Forest' on the long walk from the Castle chapel to the family burial ground.

In March 1945 the V1s had been replaced by the more inhuman and more destructive V2s. But there was a general belief that the end of the War was in sight. The Queen began to think of the arrangement that would have to be made for the peacetime visits of important people, including President Roosevelt. On 12th March the King wrote to the President:

I am very glad to hear that it may be possible for you to make your long-promised visit to my country after the conclusion of the Conference at San Francisco.

We shall do our best to make you comfortable here, and it would be a real pleasure to the Queen and myself to have you with us and to continue the friendship which started so happily in Washington and Hyde Park in 1939.[24]

But it was not to be. On 12th April the President was taken ill while at lunch in Warm Springs, California, and within a few hours he was dead. The King ordered a week's mourning for the death of the man who had done so much to ensure an Allied victory. The King and Queen went to the Memorial Service which was held in the President's honour at St Paul's on 17th April. They then went for a short break to Sandringham. It was here that they received the Prime Minister's news that the end of the War was now in sight. The King talked of the broadcast that he would make. He and the Queen emphasized to Sir John Reith, the Director-General of the BBC, that he wished to stress that the post-war society would have to be based on the Christian ethic. "He really does believe it, you know," the Queen told Reith. And there can be little doubt that she shared and perhaps inspired his simple belief.[25]

Although the surrender of the German forces was not signed until the early hours of Monday morning, 7th May 1945, crowds had been gathering at the Palace throughout the Sunday as if in recognition that this was the centre of their hopes and the symbol of their long struggle. Churchill made the official announcement of the end of the War on Tuesday, and by that time there was a 'multitude' outside the Palace repeatedly chanting "We want the King! We want the Queen!" The royal couple and the Princesses made eight appearances on the balcony, waving and smiling to the excited crowd. Their last appearance was just before midnight – by which time the two Princesses had been given permission to slip out through a side door to join the quarter of a million people milling around the Palace.[26]

Some historians have asserted that there is some doubt as to when the King and Queen were fully 'accepted' by the British people. Some believe that the moment of their 'arrival' was the Coronation in 1937; others, quoting the Queen as an authority, claim that it was their visit to the USA which had 'made' them. But there are those who claim that it was the events of the War which more than any other thing gave this King and his Queen a special place in the affections of the British people.

It is doubtful whether George V and Queen Mary were as well known or as popular after their first nine years on the throne as were George VI and Queen Elizabeth in 1945. Their steadfast courage, their continuing presence 'at home' during the worst days of bombing, their hard work and continual encouragement, had won for them the enthusiastic support evident in the first days of peace when they toured London and the rest of the country as if to thank the people for the sacrifices that had been made.

Their conduct during the War was in direct contrast with that of the ex-King, the Duke of Windsor. We know from a number of sources that he was in close touch with the Germans throughout the War. In the summer of 1940 he told a German emissary that his brother was a man "of copious stupidity", while the Queen was "shrewd and intriguing". Before leaving to take up his position of Governor of the Bahamas in August 1940, he let the Germans know that it was "too early for him to come forward. Once times changed he would be ready to return . . . he had already initiated the necessary arrangements." A month later, from the safety of the Bahamas, he sent a telegram to Germany asking for "a communication as soon as action was advisable". As his biographer notes: "In the calmer atmosphere of today [1974] no one would attribute actual guilt in the sense of deliberate treachery to the Duke, but comparative guilt is easier to estimate, and there is no doubt that his actions would have earned fierce reprisals in the atmosphere of, for instance, the French Resistance."[27] It is not surprising that the attitude of the royal family hardened towards the man whose Abdication had been responsible for the "intolerable burden" being imposed on George VI and Queen Elizabeth, and whose conduct during the war was so radically different from theirs.

The country had been well served by its monarchs, who looked forward to some relaxation of pressures now that peace had been restored in Europe.

Mrs Roosevelt with the King and Queen, 1942

WE HAVE SEEN THAT THE King and Queen had been warmly received by the American people and their President during their State Visit in 1939. The fruits of that visit were quickly garnered during the first days of the War when the President was still conscious of the strong isolationist lobby in Congress. When Poland was invaded, he broadcast to the American people promising that he would keep the USA out of the latest European War. He did add, however, that "when peace has been broken anywhere, the peace of all countries is in danger." He was aware that in fighting for the principles enunciated by George VI in his broadcast,[1] Britain was, in reality, fighting on behalf of liberty and justice everywhere.

The President persuaded Congress to alter the 1938 Neutrality Act (which forbade the shipment of arms or munitions to warring countries) so that, under a 'Cash and Carry' scheme, Britain and France were allowed to buy war materials, provided that they paid for them in *cash* and *carried* the goods in their own ships. After the German take-over of western Europe in the spring of 1940, Roosevelt warned the American people that they might become "a people lodged in prison, handcuffed, hungry and fed through bars from day to day by the contemptuous, unpitying masters of other continents".

He persuaded Congress to allow the expansion of the American munitions industry so that, for example, fifty thousand aeroplanes could be produced each year. He sold the British everything that America could spare – rifles, ammunition, heavy guns, even fifty First World War destroyers which could be used to defend the Atlantic convoy routes against submarine attack. In return, Britain gave the USA the right to set up naval bases on British-owned islands off the American coast. In March 1941, in face of stiff opposition, Roosevelt managed to persuade Congress to approve a Lend-Lease system, under which he proposed to allow Britain to have whatever goods she wanted without any talk of the loans which had done much to sour Anglo-American relations in the inter-war years. He proposed to lend the goods to Britain: after the War they could be returned if possible. If, however, they had been used up or destroyed, he argued, they would have been used as much for the benefit of the USA as for Britain, and there would be no charge.

In August 1941 Roosevelt and the British Prime Minister, Winston Churchill, met on the American warship *Augusta* off the coast of Newfoundland. From their discussions emerged the Atlantic Charter in which the United States and Britain promised not to try to increase their own power in the years ahead, either by seizing land belonging to other countries or in any other way. Both countries agreed that peoples all over the world should be given the right to choose the kind of government under which they wished to live and that all countries conquered by force should have their independence given back to them. Both agreed that after "the final destruction of the Nazi tyranny", the nations of the world should join together to try to ensure greater prosperity for all and to protect the future peace of the world.

In July 1941 the decision was made to allow US warships to escort British merchant shipping across the Atlantic so far as Iceland, where they would be picked up by British naval vessels. Britain no longer had to defend the whole of the Atlantic route. This led to German submarine attacks on the US ships in September 1941; American personnel were involved in the War even while their country was still neutral. But in December 1941 Hitler's ally, Japan, launched the attack on Pearl Harbor, and Germany was compelled, reluctantly, to side with her ally and announce that she too was at war with the "military arsenal of the West".

Even as early as September 1941 there had been repeated stories in the US Press that the President's wife, Eleanor Roosevelt, would be visiting England. Certainly there were people in England and in America who were anxious that she should do so, to bring back to the Americans the story of how the British were standing up to the War and to show by her presence that, though officially neutral, the Americans supported the stand being taken by the British.

When the Americans became actively engaged in the War and US troops were stationed in Britain, the demand for a presidential-type visit grew even stronger. In her diary Mrs Roosevelt noted: "There is a very remote chance that sometime FDR may let me go to England this summer [1942] or autumn or winter if by doing so I can serve some good purpose both there and here."[2] She wrote to a friend that the British and American people ought to know "a great deal more about each other" and that "I would like to bring home to the women of the USA what the average household in England is going through."

Plans for the proposed visit were finalized, and letters passed between the Queen and Mrs Roosevelt. Mrs Roosevelt wrote:

Her Majesty, The Queen:
I am deeply appreciative of your very kind invitation to visit you in England. I shall try to come somewhere around the middle of October. I shall be very happy if I might spend two nights with you and His Majesty the King, and after that I think I should devote my entire time to seeing all that I can of the British women's war effort, and our own groups over there. It will be a great pleasure to see you again.[3]

The President wrote to the King:

I wish much that I could accompany her, for there are a thousand things I want to tell you and talk with you about. I want you and the Queen to tell Eleanor everything in regard to the problem of our troops in England which she might not get from the government or military authorities. You and I know that it is the little things which count but which are not always set forth in official reports.[4]

Mrs Roosevelt's arrival was fixed for 21st October. Her plane had landed in Ireland on time, but bad weather there made it impossible for them to go on to England. So she was two days late when the plane landed at Bristol for her to be taken by train to London. She had her first experience of protocol when she asked why they had not flown to London: it was explained to her that the King and Queen never went to airports to meet anyone, whereas it was established tradition for them to meet guests at railway stations.

At Paddington Station "she jumped from the train to grip the Queen's hand" and to be greeted by the Queen with "We welcome you with all our hearts." As she drove in the royal Daimler to Buckingham Palace, she noted the "loud cheers from the waiting crowds" but more significantly "the absence of those security precautions with which the royal family moved among their people" – in strange contrast to the all-enveloping security which hedged American presidents.

When she arrived at Buckingham Palace, she noticed here, as at Paddington Station, the scars of the bombing from which London had suffered in 1940 and 1941. This gave her an immediate impression of what life was like in wartime London. When she entered the Palace, the royal couple showed her to her room – the Queen's own bedroom on the first floor. This, she explained, was an enormous room, which her son Elliott compared with the long corridor at the White House. But if it was a grand, high-ceilinged room, it was also one which was bomb-scarred. None of the windows had any glass, small casements of wood frames and isinglass had been installed. The Queen showed her how the splinters of a bomb had dropped through the ceiling and lodged in the King's wardrobe. Nothing was done to alleviate the discomfort of which she wrote: "Buckingham Palace is an enormous place, and without heat. I do not see how they keep the dampness out. The rooms were cold except for the smaller sitting-room with an open fire. In every room there was a little (one bar) electric fire."[5]

She took tea with the King and Queen around a set table, "as I used to have in my childhood", and met the two Princesses. At 8.30 pm she had dinner – with the King and Queen, Lord and Lady Mountbatten, Mr and Mrs Churchill, Field Marshal Smuts and his son, two ladies-in-waiting, the Master of the Household, the US Ambassador and her son Elliott, whose squadron was based about seventy miles from London. The dinner was a mixture of the great and the simple. "We were served on gold and silver plates, but our bread was the same kind of war bread every other family had to eat. . . . Nothing was ever served that was not served in any war canteen," wrote Mrs Roosevelt.[6] At dinner on the Saturday night, another guest was Lord Woolton, the Minister of Food, who assured Mrs Roosevelt that the meals served at the Palace "might have been served in any home in England, and would have shocked the King's grandfather [Edward VII]".[7]

During the dinner on Friday night Mrs Roosevelt had found the Prime Minister "distrait and withdrawn. I found the PM not easy to talk to. . . ." This was hardly surprising because he was aware, as the others were not, that the Battle of El Alamein had just started. At one point in the dinner he excused himself, went to the telephone and got the latest reports of the progress of the battle. What he heard obviously pleased him because he surprised the other diners by singing 'Roll out the barrel' with great gusto.[8]

On Saturday morning Mrs Roosevelt went to a Press conference at the American Embassy. In the afternoon she went with the King and Queen to look at the destruction that had been wrought by the repeated air attacks. She described the City as "gutted", with St Paul's "gaping to the skies". During this drive through London's East End the Queen remarked that "the only solace in the destruction was that new housing would replace the slums that had been levelled." Mrs Roosevelt saw the ruins of the Guildhall, met numbers of Civil Defence personnel and had it borne in on her "that England's home front was literally part of the battle-front".

On Sunday the King, Queen and Princesses saw her off at the door after breakfast, "more like friends saying goodbye than any formal leave-taking". Mrs Roosevelt then moved into an apartment that the US Ambassador had found for her. The King sent a message to the President on 25th October:

Mrs Roosevelt left us this morning to continue her tour. I would like to tell you what real pleasure it gave us to have her stay at Buckingham Palace. That she should have made the long journey in these dangerous war days has touched and delighted our people and they are very glad to welcome her here. We had some good talks and are looking forward to hearing her impressions of our women's war activities after she has completed the strenuous programme arranged for her.[9]

She stayed in Britain for some three weeks and met the royal family again when she called on them at Windsor Castle on 13th November to pay her farewell visit. The King noted: "She is much impressed with all that she has seen and heard." Mrs Roosevelt recorded her impressions later:

The King and Queen treated me with the greatest kindness. The feeling I had had about them during their visit to the United States – that they were simply a young and charming couple, who would have to undergo some very difficult experiences – began to come back to me, intensified by the realization that they now had been through their experiences and were anxious to tell me about them. In all my contacts with them I have gained the greatest respect for both the King and Queen. I haven't always agreed with the ideas expressed to me by the King on international subjects, but the fact that both of them are doing an extraordinarily outstanding job for their people in the most trying times stands out when you are with them and you admire their character and their devotion to duty.[10]

22

The post-war monarchy, 1945–7

IMMEDIATELY AFTER VE DAY the King and Queen made a victory tour of
South London by car. Huge cheering crowds almost swamped them as they
visited the badly bombed boroughs of Deptford, Lewisham, Streatham and
Greenwich. They also visited other regions of the British Isles, including the
Isle of Man, in July, and the Channel Islands, now freed from German
occupation. They held Victory Parties at Windsor, Buckingham Palace and
Sandringham for the many groups of people who deserved a special
recognition for their work in the War.

Meanwhile, the country had held its first General Election since 1935, in
agreement with a decision explained on 31st October 1944 by Mr Churchill,
who said: "... The termination of the war against Nazism will fix the date of
the General Election . . . it would be wrong to continue this Parliament
beyond the period of the German war."[1]

On 23rd May the Labour Ministers in the wartime government had
resigned, and Mr Churchill continued at the head of a predominantly
Conservative Caretaker Government until the Dissolution of Parliament on
15th June. Election Day was fixed for 5th July. Ballot-papers had to be sent to
the millions of men and women serving overseas, including many still fighting
the war against Japan. It took three weeks for some of these papers to be
returned, and the result of the election was not declared until 26th July. The
result was a massive victory for the Labour Party which won 392 seats to the
189 won by the Churchill-led Conservatives.

So it was that the King and Queen had to deal with a new set of
Ministers who had policies radically different from those which
might have been pursued by a Conservative government.[2] The royal
couple found it strange not to be seeing Mr Churchill. They also missed
the frequent and friendly letters which they had received from the late
President Roosevelt. But, unlike the King, the Queen found it fairly easy
to welcome the development of the Welfare State by the new government;

she had, after all, said of the bombed-out Londoners that they deserved
better.[3]

The Japanese war came to an end on 15th August 1945 which was the day
fixed for the State Opening of the new Parliament. Once again, the people
turned out in their thousands to cheer the royal couple on their way to and
from Parliament, and, later, to call for them to appear on the balcony of
Buckingham Palace. That evening the King broadcast to the people:

> The war is over. You know, I think, that those four words have, for the Queen
> and myself, the same significance, simple yet immense, that they have for you.
> Our hearts are full to overflowing, as are your own. Yet there is not one of us
> who has experienced this terrible war who does not realize that we shall feel its
> inevitable consequences long after we have all forgotten our rejoicings of
> today.[4]

Among the most immediate of the "consequences" was the material
condition of the country. Millions of buildings and homes had been destroyed
or badly damaged; and there was little chance of doing much about them
until the countries of the world had begun once more to produce a flow of
goods and materials. Meanwhile, the people had learned to put up with the
discomforts which had seemed inevitable in wartime but which appeared
more irksome once "peace had broken out". People were tired of rationed
food, shabby clothes and lack of fuel. In the royal homes, as elsewhere,
everything was shabby, walls unpainted, gardens unkempt and bomb
damaged. On one occasion the King asked George Tomlinson, Minister of
Works and responsible for the upkeep of Buckingham Palace: "What about
my windows, George?" "It'll come your turn, Sir," was the reply. When the
men finally arrived to start work on the Palace, the King turned to the Queen,
in the presence of Mr Tomlinson, and said, "It's come our turn."[5]

And because of the War, the King and Queen were very tired. Mackenzie
King found the King "looking older, inclined to be rather excitable". It was
one of the Queen's main functions to disguise her own condition so that she
could give him the comfort that he needed.[6]

The coming of peace brought the royal couple face to face again with the
nature of their role. This had been thrust on them in 1936; they had struggled
to come to terms with their position in the years before 1939 and during the
War had been sustained by their own sense of patriotic duty and the evident
popular support. Now, in 1945, with the enthusiasm of the War behind
them and without the stimulus of having to learn a new role, they had to face
the fact that they would never again know the privacy they had enjoyed before
1936.

During the war years, their two daughters had, almost imperceptibly,
grown up, and in the post-war years the King and Queen had to face the
problems encountered by all parents of growing children. But the nature of

those problems was hidden from them when they went to Balmoral in September 1945 for their first long holiday since before the War. Here, the royal couple hoped they would be able to rebuild that happy family life they had known at 145 Piccadilly and again in the Palace before their lives were disrupted by the War.

For this holiday the King and Queen had invited a large number of their close friends, including the Queen's sisters, Rose and Mary, her brother David, the Eldons, Cranbornes, Salisburys and others. The family and their guests hunted, stalked deer, fished and rode. The King taught Princess Elizabeth the difficult art of stalking; dressed in old clothes and gillies' hats, they spent hours together in the deer forest. The Queen, never addicted to field sports, took charge of the picnics which were centred on her two-roomed cottage, an old school-house on the moor, "one room used as a dining-room with a little table in the centre, and an open fireplace opposite the door; the other, a large room evidently the kitchen with a huge open fireplace with equipment for cooking foods," as Mackenzie King described it.[7]

The evenings at Balmoral, like those far-away evenings at Glamis, were given over to music, cards, games and charades. One evening was made memorable by the ceremony of Beating the Retreat by a Highland regiment in the dusk on the front lawn. Here, like the Glamis family, the Windsors were "more of a clan than a family", surrounded as they were by not only their friends but also by the children of their friends.

But after the pleasure of the autumn holiday there was the return to the world of work and duty.

For the Queen there was a four-fold role to play. In one she had to act as supporter of her husband, the King, although in many ways he had grown so confident and able that she was able to stand to one side and, indeed, to begin to lean upon him for strength and steadfastness. In January 1946 the King wrote to his brother the Duke of Gloucester, then Governor-General of Australia:

> I have been suffering from an awful reaction from the strain of war, I suppose, and have felt very tired, especially down here [Sandringham]. . . . I am perfectly well really but feel that I cannot cope competently with all the varied and many questions which come up. My new government is not too easy and the people are rather difficult to talk to . . . still learning how to run their departments.[8]

Lady Airlie was with the family at Sandringham during that Christmas holiday. She wrote: "I sat next to the King . . . his face tired and strained and he ate practically nothing. When I told him how much I had liked his Christmas broadcast, and how well written I thought the script had been, he looked across at the Queen. 'She helps me,' he said proudly."[9]

The Queen's second role was what we may call her public role. There were many garden-parties which went on through the spring and summer of 1946 and the Victory Parade through London in June 1946, ten months after VJ Day. At this the Queen stood beside the King who took the salute from a dais on the Mall. Eleven million people had jammed into London to see the historic parade, many of whom stayed through the late evening to cheer outside the Palace until, at 12.30, the King and Queen came onto the balcony.

These parties and the Parade were the highlights of her public life. Elsewhere she had to help entertain the Foreign Ministers who were in London in December 1947 for their International Conference, "standing", as Nicolson wrote, "for two long hours . . . Molotov talking to the Queen. . . ."[10]

And there were the societies, institutions and organizations of which she was an active and interested patron; regiments of which she was a lively Colonel-in-Chief; hospitals and schools to be inspected; foundation stones to be laid and factories to be seen.

In what we may call her third role the Queen tried to lead a private life. She took her daughters to Covent Garden Opera House to see performances by the Sadler's Wells Ballet Company and welcomed the revival of racing. In 1946 Ascot was something like its pre-war self, as *The Times* wrote: "Royal Ascot has been restored to the calendar of social events, but, like much in our new peacetime, its grandeur is greatly diminished. . . . The King and the royal guests drove to the course in closed cars, but tomorrow, when the Gold Cup is run for, they will again drive in open carriages drawn by Windsor greys. . . ."[11] And as an extension of that private role the Queen endeavoured to fashion a family life for her husband, her daughters and the wider royal family of which she was very much the first lady. Lady Airlie, who was at Sandringham in January 1946, wrote:

I thought – regretfully at first – how much the atmosphere had changed, but then I realized that this was inevitable for a new generation had grown up since I had last seen it. In the entrance hall there now stood a baize-covered table on which jig-saw puzzles were set out. The younger members of the party – the Princesses, Lady Mary Cambridge . . . and several young Guardsmen – congregated around them from morning till night. The radio, worked by Princess Elizabeth, blared incessantly.

Before the end of the week I revised my impressions. There was no denying that the new atmosphere of Sandringham was very much more friendly than in the old days, more like that of any home. One senses far more the setting of ordinary family life in this generation than in the last. It was the way in which the King said, "You must ask Mummy," when his daughters wanted to do something – just as any father would do.[12]

For the King and Queen one of the sadder effects of the War was that their daughters had grown up without any of the pleasures which they might have known in more normal times. In fact, ever since the accession in 1936, the children's lives had been more circumscribed than they would have been if their Uncle David had remained as king. After the Abdication Princess Elizabeth became Heiress Presumptive to the Throne; her sister Margaret stood second in line, and their upbringing had to reflect these positions.

Princess Elizabeth was, by nature, shy, cautious and serious, a female model of many of her father's characteristics. Lady Airlie was present at her confirmation in 1942:

> I saw a grave little face under a small net veil, and a slender figure in a plain white woollen frock. The carriage of her head was unequalled, and there was about her that indescribable something which Queen Victoria had. Although she was perfectly simple, modest and unselfconscious, she gave the impression of great personality.[13]

Lady Airlie saw more of the Princess during her holiday at Sandringham in January 1946: "In that family setting she seemed to me one of the most unselfish girls I had ever met, always the first to give way in any of the small issues that arise in every home."[14]

There was a very special relationship between the Princess and her father whom she resembled in so many ways. He was aware of how much she missed by being Heir and how much more she lost because of the War. During Christmas 1940 he went to watch her acting out the Nativity story with the children of the Sandringham estate. In his diary he wrote: "I wept through most of it."

But if the daughter had inherited her father's shyness, cautiousness and seriousness, she had also inherited his stubbornness. This was proved by her continued insistence, against his expressed wish, that she should be allowed to 'join up' in one of the services. Like every other sixteen-year-old she had registered at a Labour Exchange in the spring of 1942, but it took her until 1944 before she managed to persuade her father to allow her to join up. She travelled to Aldershot where she registered in the Women's Auxiliary Territorial Service: "No. 230873, Second Subaltern Elizabeth Alexandra Mary Windsor, Age: 18. Eyes: Blue. Hair: Brown. Height: 5 ft. 3 ins."

On VE Day the King wrote in his diary: "Poor darlings, they have never had any fun yet."[15] By this time, as we shall see, the Princess was set on becoming engaged to her cousin, Prince Philip, but the King feared that she had not yet met enough people. He organized parties where his daughter might meet other 'eligible' bachelors, a set of men whom Queen Mary christened "the Body Guard". But, as we shall see, the Princess remained steadfast in her attachment to Prince Philip.

The King was, said Lady Airlie, "a devoted father to both his daughters. He spoiled Princess Margaret and continued to treat her as an *enfant terrible*."

She was very different from her sister, more lively, a lover of music of all sorts and a great mimic. She developed a more extrovert personality than the solemn Elizabeth and was much more outspoken, not to say ill-mannered. She used slang expressions, explaining that she had heard them "at my mother's knee – or some such low joint". Lady Airlie thought "that no two sisters could have been less alike than the Princesses, the elder with her quiet simplicity, the younger with her puckish expression and irrepressible high spirits – often liberated in mimicry. Queen Mary described her as 'espiègle' – which was precisely the right word, although it has no complete equivalent in English, adding, 'At the same time she is so outrageously amusing that one can't help encouraging her.'"[16]

In 1947 the two Princesses went with the King and Queen on a State Visit to South Africa. It was Field-Marshal Jan Smuts who had suggested that the royal family should visit that country, though the King was "uncertain about it" because he was aware of the ill-feeling that many of the Dutch South Africans felt towards Britain. As it turned out, the Dutch, British and the Zulus all combined to make the visit another memorable success.

The King, Queen and the two Princesses left Britain on 1st February 1947. (The country was already in the grip of the most severe winter in living memory. Trains were unable to run so that there was a shortage of fuel at power stations. The electricity supply had to be rationed and this, plus the continued bad weather, made the already grey, drab and austerity-ridden country an even grimmer and unhappier place in which to live.) During the journey on HMS *Vanguard* the Queen was "the brightest light" on board, leading lines of conga dancers and helping to make everyone forget the memory of the gale they had met in the Bay of Biscay. In Capetown they were greeted by a huge cheering crowd, and they had to stand for almost an hour in a blazing sun shaking the hands of the hundreds who had lined up to receive them. As they finished, the Queen spoke to the King and they turned to walk across to where a group of men, wounded in the War, were sitting in their wheel-chairs. The crowd closed in around them and in this, another foretaste of the now traditional 'walkabout' the royal couple were lost to view for fully fifteen minutes. Their visit had got off to a great start. In the evening they had to attend a banquet at the City Hall. Dermot Morrah described the scene:

> It was a long slow process to clear a way for the royal car to the door, and even when they arrived the King and Queen were reluctant to go in to dinner until they had stood for some minutes on the balcony waving smiling acknowledgements of the enthusiasm below. This again was to be a frequent experience all over the country; conscientious officials might work out their programme to the minute, almost to the second, but they reckoned without the King and especially the Queen.[17]

When Princess Elizabeth had seen the plans for the tour she wrote: "My heart rather sinks when I think what is ahead. . . . It is absolutely staggering how much they expect us to do and go on doing for so long at a stretch. I hope we shall survive, that's all. . . ."[18]

Even the experienced Queen had noted that the tour would be "very strenuous". For four weeks the party was constantly on the move through South Africa and Southern Rhodesia. There was an endless procession of official receptions, reviews, speeches and dedications. The party travelled in an ivory and gold 'White Train' which was a third of a mile long and which was meant to be as restful as a travelling home could be. The Queen insisted that they sit by the windows to be ready to wave to some isolated farmer and his family.

The royal family left Capetown on 24th April and arrived back in Britain on 12th May. The long trip had done much for each member of the family. The Queen felt "relaxed". Princess Margaret had formed a close friendship with one of the King's aides, Group Captain Peter Townsend, although neither the King nor the Queen had noticed this as yet. Princess Elizabeth had enjoyed her twenty-first birthday on which she had broadcast from South Africa to the peoples of the Commonwealth, dedicating herself to serve them in what she must have hoped would be a distant future.[19] The King jokingly referred to the fact that they had all appeared to have lost weight because of the arduous nature of their Tour. It was the Queen who first expressed alarm at the fact that he had, in fact, lost nearly a stone in weight. She was also aware that during the Tour he had begun to suffer from severe cramp in the legs and had developed a cough which seemed never to clear up. During the journey home he had not joined in the games – deck-tennis and the like – at which he had once been a good performer. He preferred to rest. But not even the Queen realized how ill he was, and there were major events to distract attention away from consideration of the King's health.

23

A royal marriage, 1947, and a Silver Wedding, 1948

ON 10th JULY 1947 AN ANNOUNCEMENT was made from Buckingham Palace: "It is with the greatest pleasure that the King and Queen announce the betrothal of their dearly beloved daughter The Princess Elizabeth to Lieutenant Philip Mountbatten, R.N., son of the late Prince Andrew of Greece and Princess Andrew (Princess Alice of Battenberg), to which union the King has gladly given his consent."[1]

Behind that announcement lay the stories of a daughter's stubborn tenacity, parents' anxious concern and a very pleasant young man's involved family background.

On 22nd July 1939, as we have seen, Princess Elizabeth and her sister had accompanied their parents to the Royal Naval College, Dartmouth. One set of cadets were down with mumps and another with chicken pox, and the Princesses were left in the care of the Captain's Messenger for the day, eighteen-year-old Prince Philip of Greece. Miss Crawford remembered him as a "fair-haired boy, rather like a Viking, with a sharp face and piercing blue eyes".[2] Although they were distantly related to one another – having the same great-great-grandmother, Queen Victoria, the two young people had never met before. The naïve young Princess was immediately attracted to the athletic, good-looking and extrovert Prince Philip. To the shy thirteen-year-old the eighteen-year-old cadet Prince was, according to "Crawfie", "a strange creature out of another world . . . a hero". As if to emphasize the difference in their ages, the Princess, still following a nursery time-table, was in bed when the Prince came aboard the royal yacht that evening for dinner with a group of other cadets. The next day he entertained the two Princesses again and, when the royal yacht sailed out of the River Dart, he followed in a small rowing boat while the Princess "watched him fondly through an enormous pair of binoculars".[3]

The young Prince's mother was the daughter of Prince Louis of Battenberg (b. 1854) and Princess Victoria, daughter of Louis IV of Hesse and Princess

Alice, daughter of Queen Victoria. Prince Louis had entered the British Navy as a midshipman in 1869 and by 1912 had become so efficient and outstanding an officer that he was made First Sea Lord. When Britain went to war with Germany in 1914, there was an outbreak of hysterical jingoism which led to the demand for his resignation. The people ignored his forty-six years of service, his outstanding ability and the way in which he had prepared the Royal Navy for the War. That he had been born a German damned him in the eyes of the British popular Press. In October 1914 he resigned.[4]

Popular revulsion against all things German caused the monarch and his British cousins to renounce their German names and titles. On 18th July 1917 King George V adopted the name 'Windsor'.[5] Prince Louis took the surname 'Mountbatten' and the title of first Marquess of Milford Haven. His younger son, once Prince Louis Francis of Battenberg, was the Lord Louis Mountbatten who accompanied the King and Queen to Dartmouth in July 1939.

Prince Philip's father was Prince Andrew of Greece, a member of the Danish royal family of Schleswig-Holstein-Sonderburg-Glucksburg, which was Prince Philip's family name, although he preferred to sign himself 'Prince Philip of Greece' even though he did not have a drop of Greek blood in his veins. In 1863 the Greeks had invited a Danish prince to become their first king. In deference to the Greeks' patron saint he took the title of George I. His sister Alexandra married King Edward VII – the Danish royal family being, in Robert Lacey's words, "the most successful exporting dynasty of modern times".[6] The subsequent history of the Greek royal family was confused and bloody. George I had been assassinated in 1913; his son, Constantine, had been deposed in 1917, his successor dying of blood poisoning in 1920. Constantine had been brought back again, only to be driven off the throne for a second time in 1922. His cousin, George II, ascended the throne in 1922, abdicated in 1923, was recalled in 1935 and expelled again in 1941.

Prince Philip had been born on the island of Corfu on 10th June 1921 when his uncle, Constantine, was on the throne for the second time. In 1922 Prince Andrew, Philip's father, was in command of a Greek army corps which was defeated by the Turks under Kemal Ataturk. This defeat led to a revolution in Greece where Prince Andrew came under threat of execution. King George V sent a battle cruiser, the *Calypso*, to bring Prince Andrew and his family to safety. Prince Philip was carried away from Greece "in an improvised cot of orange boxes" on board a British cruiser.[7]

His father became an indolent member of the playboy set. His mother, Princess Alice, turned to her brothers for help. It was George, the second Marquess of Milford Haven, who assumed responsibility for Philip's upbringing, while Lord Louis became his guardian after George's death in 1938. It was the Mountbattens who had sent Philip to Cheam School and then in 1934 to Kurt Hahn's school at Salem. When Hahn was driven from Germany because of his anti-Nazi attitude, Prince Philip was among the pupils who followed him when he opened his school at Gordonstoun in Scotland. As Lady Airlie showed; Prince Philip was known in royal circles:

> Even during the years when he was at his first school in Paris Prince Philip came over to visit his grandmother and his uncles, Lord Milford Haven and Lord Louis Mountbatten. On one of these visits he was taken to tea with Queen Mary at Buckingham Palace, but she told me long afterwards that she only remembered him vaguely as "a nice little boy with very blue eyes". Later, when he was at Gordonstoun and spending part of his holidays with the Duke and Duchess of Kent, he made much more impression on her. "He's very handsome," she told me. "He has inherited the good looks of both sides of the family. He seems intelligent too. I should say he has plenty of common sense."[8]

Lord Louis Mountbatten used his influence to get him into the Royal Naval College, although as a foreigner he could have only a temporary commission. He won the King's Dirk as the best all-rounder cadet of his term. His first Captain's opinion of him was brief: "My best midshipman",[9] while his first Admiral wrote of him as "the best junior commanding officer in the fleet". On 28th March 1941 he took part in the battle against the Italian Fleet at Cape Matapan and he earned his Captain's commendation for "his alertness and appreciation of the situation".[10]

While Prince Philip was winning plaudits from his naval superiors, young Princess Elizabeth was at home with her parents. At Christmas 1940 she persuaded her father to use diplomatic channels to send her Christmas card to Philip in return for the Christmas card he had sent from Athens. She placed a photograph of the Prince on her mantelpiece and, when her parents objected to "her lack of discretion", she replaced it for one of the young naval officer in the bushy naval beard he had sprouted, maintaining, according to "Crawfie", that "that camouflage would fool anyone".[11]

In October 1941 they met again at the Duke of Kent's home, Coppins. For Christmas 1943 he was one of the five guests to dinner at Royal Lodge on Christmas Eve. By this time there were rumours which linked the names of the Princess and Prince Philip. On 21st January 1941 the Conservative MP Henry (Chips) Channon noted in his diary: ". . . an enjoyable Greek cocktail party. Prince Philip of Greece was there. He is extraordinarily handsome. . . . He is to be our Prince Consort, and that is why he is serving in our Navy."[12]

King George of Greece spoke to the King and Queen on behalf of his young kinsman, but the possessive father and anxious mother gave him no encouragement, as can be seen from a letter written by the King to Queen Mary: "We both think she is too young for that now, as she has never met any young men of her own age. . . . I like Philip. He is intelligent, has a good sense of humour and thinks of things in the right way. . . . We are going to tell

George [of Greece] that P. had better not think any more about it for the present."[13]

The Queen, remembering her many suitors, found it hard to believe that her daughter had fallen in love with the first eligible young man she had met. And there was still a series of complications surrounding Prince Philip's nationality. In 1944 the King of Greece agreed that he might give up his membership of the Greek and Danish royal families and apply for naturalization as a British subject. However, the British government advised the King to defer the application because of the confused nature of the Greek political scene in the winter and spring of 1945. The People's Liberation Army, led by Communists and supplied with arms by the Allies, was engaged in a guerrilla war against the German occupying forces. There was no guarantee, in the last days of the war, that this army would agree to the return of King George, who had been driven out by the Germans in 1941. The government thought that the application should wait until the Greek people had made up their minds as to the future of their royal family.

In March 1946, after a period of civil war between those forces supporting the monarchy and others supporting the establishment of a republic, the Greek people voted in a plebiscite for the return of King George. However, he was a very sick man and his heir, Prince Paul, was married to Princess Frederica, the grand-daughter of the Kaiser against whom Britain had fought during the First World War. It was obvious that there would be objections if the heir to the British throne were to announce her engagement to a member of the royal House of Greece with its links with Germany. It was also considered that for a member of the Greek royal family to renounce his nationality would not be very helpful so close to the restoration: some Greeks might consider it a sign that the family was so uncertain of its future that its members were seeking refuge elsewhere. So Prince Philip had to go on waiting, and there could be no talk of an engagement while he was still a member of the Greek royal family. The Queen was glad of this delaying obstacle, as Queen Mary told Lady Airlie in January 1946: "The King and Queen feel that she is too young to be engaged yet. . . . After all, she's only nineteen, and one is very impressionable at that age. . . . Elizabeth seems to me the kind of girl who would always know her own mind . . . like her father. All the same, I think the King and Queen are right to make her wait a while." Then she laughed: "After all, he had to wait long enough for *his* wife and you can see what a success their marriage is."[14]

Although they were forced to wait, they continued to meet. Prince Philip was now stationed at a training establishment, HMS *Royal Arthur*, at Corsham in Wiltshire, and in his black MG sports car he used to drive the ninety-eight miles to London to visit the Princess, sometimes staying overnight at the Mountbatten home in Chester Street.

In 1946 Prince Philip spent his summer leave at Balmoral. During this holiday he formally proposed to the Princess. She, bearing out Queen Mary's opinion that she was "the kind of girl who would always know her own mind . . .", ignored the wishes of her father and mother, the hesitations of governments over the question of his naturalization and the problem of his surname. She accepted his proposal but agreed with her parents' wishes that the engagement should not be made public until the family had returned from South Africa. By then she would be twenty-one years old.

The young Princess's stubborn insistence compelled the government and her father to decide the question of her fiancé's nationality. The King offered him a British title so that he could continue to be known as a Prince. He, however, told the King that he did not want to take advantage of this kind offer but would prefer to be known simply as 'Lieutenant Philip—— RN'. The question of his surname was solved when he accepted the suggestion made by the Home Secretary, Chuter Ede, that he should adopt the name of his maternal grandfather.[15] Accordingly the announcement of 'Lieutenant Philip Mountbatten's' naturalization was made on 18th March 1947 while the royal family were in South Africa.

On 30th January 1947, the day before the family sailed, Lady Airlie had gone to the Palace to give Princess Elizabeth her birthday present. The Princess said wistfully that: "it would be sad to be away from England on her birthday, and then, visibly brightening, added, 'but when I come back we will have a celebration – perhaps *two* celebrations.' This seemed to me to confirm the rumours . . . but only Queen Mary . . . knew."[16]

The announcement of the engagement of the popular Princess gave Londoners the excuse to gather in large crowds around Buckingham Palace. That evening the Queen stood between her daughters on the balcony while the crowds cheered and chanted for the sight of the engaged couple. There was even more public enthusiasm on the day of the wedding, 20th November, 1947. *Country Life* reported: "The crowd was enormous, nothing like it had been seen in London since the coronation ten years ago. And it was a happy, good-tempered crowd obviously determined to enjoy its brief escape from what we have come to call austerity."[17]

The young couple spent the first part of their honeymoon at the Mountbatten home at Broadlands in Kent. The King wrote to his newly married daughter:

> I was so proud of you and thrilled at having you so close to me on our long walk in Westminster Abbey, but when I handed your hand to the Archbishop I felt that I had lost something very precious. I am so glad that you wrote and told Mummy that you think the long wait before your engagement and the long time before the wedding was for the best. I was rather afraid that you had thought I was being hard-hearted about it. I have watched you grow up all

these years with pride under the skilful direction of Mummy who, as you know, is the most marvellous person in the world in my eyes, and I can, I know, always count on you, and now Philip, to help us in our work. Your leaving us has left a great blank in our lives but do remember that your old home is still yours and do come back to it as much and as often as possible. . . . Your ever loving and devoted . . .

Papa[18]

Exactly how "skilful" the "direction" of the Queen had been is the more obvious to us who have seen the daughter grow into a most popular Queen and, it seems, an equally successful mother.

The Queen herself wrote of the wedding day: "What a wonderful day it has been. They grow up and leave us, and we must make the best of it." One of the benefits of having an active son-in-law was that he and the Princess would be able to take on some of the work that had normally fallen to the King and Queen, who were now approaching a comfortable middle age.

As if to remind themselves of their age, the King set aside a day of thanksgiving and re-dedication for their Silver Wedding celebrations on 26th April 1948. At one level this was essentially and primarily a personal event. However, it was made the occasion of another great and spontaneous demonstration of public affection. In brilliant sunshine the King, Queen and Princess Margaret left Buckingham Palace at eleven o'clock. They drove in a state landau drawn by six Windsor greys. Princess Elizabeth and Prince Philip followed in a semi-state landau. Massive crowds lined the route – the Mall, the Strand, Fleet Street and Ludgate Hill. In St Paul's Cathedral was a congregation of four thousand, some old enough to remember the Diamond Jubilee of Queen Victoria, many able to remember their attendance at the Silver Wedding celebrations of King George V and Queen Mary. Although the country was still struggling with post-war austerity, this stately pomp – of the drive and of the service in the Cathedral – provided, in Churchill's phrase, "a flash of colour on the hard road we have to travel".[19]

There was a luncheon in the golden State dining-room at Buckingham Palace where some of the guests were drawn from the royal families of Europe, most of them members of dynasties whose greatness lay in the past. Also present were six of the Queen's eight bridesmaids, all still close friends. As the Queen looked around the room, she saw her brothers and their wives with their children – her nephews and nieces. And when she looked at her married daughter, she knew that in the not-too-distant future she would become a grandmother.

In the evening the King and Queen went on a drive through twenty miles of London's streets. Everywhere their reception was affectionate and enthusiastic. Back at the Palace they were called repeatedly to the balcony to respond to the cheering crowds.

That night both of them broadcast to the nation. The King spoke of the day "of deep significance to ourselves as man and wife" and of the heavy burdens, at times "almost too heavy but for the strength and comfort which I have always found in my home". In reference to the popular enthusiasm which had been so evident, he said, "It has been an unforgettable experience to realize how many thousands of people there are in this world who wish to join in the thankfulness we feel for the twenty-five years of supremely happy married life which has been granted to us." In her turn, the Queen said:

> I, too, am deeply thankful for our twenty-five years of happiness together, for the opportunities we have been given of service to our beloved country and for the blessings of our home and children. The world of our day is longing to find the secret of community, and all married lives are, in a sense, communities in miniature. Looking back over the last twenty-five years and to my own happy childhood I realize more and more the wonderful sense of security and happiness which comes from a loved home.[20]

As that memorable day drew to a close the royal couple could indeed look back over years of "service" and "the blessings of our home". At the age of forty-seven the Queen could reflect that she had learned well the lessons taught by her mother and father. The King, at the age of fifty-two, could reflect that they had taken over the throne at a few days' notice and had been a shining example to the people during the War. They had been the first British monarchs to visit Canada, the USA and South Africa. And the British people were, unwittingly in most cases, bearing witness to Bagehot's comment: "We have come to believe that it is natural to have a virtuous sovereign, and that domestic virtues are as likely to be found on thrones as they are eminent when there."

Later the King wrote to Queen Mary: "We were both dumbfounded over our reception. We have received so many nice letters from all and sundry thanking us for what we have tried to do during these years. It does spur us on to further efforts."[21]

But for the King there were to be few "future efforts".[22]

24

Her last days as Queen Consort, 1949-52

IN THE EARLY SUMMER OF 1948 life seemed set fair for the Queen. Her two daughters were still living 'at home' in the Palace, and she was looking forward to the birth of her first grandchild. The celebrations of the Silver Wedding had shown how popular she and the King were, and they were busily engaged in the plans for their 1949 tour of Australia and New Zealand.

But, "in the midst of life we are in death," said the Psalmist. The Queen had been concerned for some time about the King's health. He had lost weight during the tour of South Africa, when he had also complained of severe cramps in his legs. During the summer holiday in Balmoral, 1948, his condition became worse. He seemed to be easily tired, and his left foot was numb all day, while the pain from this kept him awake most of the night.

On 20th October he was examined in London by his doctor, Sir Morton Stuart. While giving him medicines to relieve the pain, he insisted on calling in specialists who would examine the King on 30th October. Meanwhile, the assiduous George VI kept rigidly to his time-table. He played a full part in the State Visit by the King and Queen of Denmark and presided over the State Opening of Parliament. On 30th October the specialists insisted that yet another of their colleagues, Sir James Learmouth, had to be consulted. He was the country's leading expert on vascular complaints. He could not see the King until 12th November.

Again the King carried on with his public role – taking a march-past of the Territorial Army on 31st October and playing his part in the Remembrance Day Service at the Cenotaph on Sunday 7th November. And throughout this late summer and early autumn he was in constant touch with his Ministers as they battled with the problems of Britain's slow economic recovery and the permanent international crisis associated with the term 'the Cold War'.

On 12th November the doctors told the Queen that the King was suffering from arteriosclerosis, with the danger that gangrene might set in. He might indeed have to have his right leg amputated. In another wing of the Palace the young Princess Elizabeth was being attended by nurses and doctors. The Queen had to go from one bed to another, insisting that the expectant mother must not be worried by news of the gravity of her father's condition. She also undertook not only her own many public engagements but some which the King had been due to carry out. "It was in character that she should carry on. She would never consider a personal anxiety, however acute, a reason for not undertaking any duty," said one of her friends.[1] On the day when the news of the King's condition was made public, she took his place on a private visit to the Royal Naval College at Greenwich.

On 14th November Prince Charles was born, while his grandfather lay seriously ill in another wing of the Palace. But by 15th December the King had recovered sufficiently to take part in the christening of our future monarch, and he was able to go with his family to Sandringham for Christmas. From here he broadcast to the people on Christmas Day:

> The past year has been a memorable one for me. In the course of it I have had three vivid experiences. In April I celebrated my Silver Wedding, then in November I welcomed my first grandchild and finally I have been obliged to submit to a spell of temporary inactivity.... The Queen and I have been deeply touched and much comforted by the expressions of love and loyalty from our people.[2]

The King's condition had responded to the treatment ordered by his doctors and during the holiday he was able to take part in the traditional shooting at Sandringham. When he got back to London he was fit enough to hold audiences and an investiture. Then he was examined again by the doctors on 3rd March. They decided that while his health, in general, was "excellent", he ought to have an operation "of lumbar sympathectomy ... on his right side" to ensure the free flow of blood to his right leg.[3]

The operation was performed on 12th March. Early that morning the Queen, with her daughters, took Holy Communion in the Chapel Royal, St James's Palace. There was great public concern throughout the day, large crowds gathering outside the Palace to wait for the medical bulletins, relieved to see the short but friendly notice on the placards of the newspaper stands: "He's all right." On 21st March Harold Nicolson had an audience with Queen Mary to discuss with her his forthcoming official biography of George V, and during the course of the interview the ageing Queen spoke of the Abdication and the accession of George VI who, she said "... has made good. Even his stammer has been corrected. And now he is so ill, poor boy, so ill." This, adds Nicolson, "in such a sad voice".[4]

While the King convalesced, the Queen carried on with her public duties, telling an audience on one visit "of the person who once prayed to be granted, not a lighter load, but a stronger back". The King recovered sufficiently for him to hold a Privy Council on 29th March and to receive, in April, the Prime Ministers assembled for the Commonwealth Conference. But it was obvious that he would have to curtail his activities. There would be fewer tours and less travelling. This, in turn, would throw a heavier load on the Queen, and the King and Queen were forced, very reluctantly, to call on their elder daughter more frequently.

One sign of Princess Elizabeth's increasing role was given on 9th June 1949 when the King drove in an open carriage to watch the Trooping the Colour. His daughter rode at the head of the Parade. But the King could not, constitutionally, hand over to his heir all the burdens of office, even if he had wanted to. During the summer of 1949 he shared with his Ministers their anxieties over the economy and the international situation. His Prime Minister, Clement Attlee, later recorded: "Few people realize how much time and care he gave to public affairs, but visitors from overseas were often astonished at his close familiarity with all kinds of questions. With this close study went a good judgement and a sure instinct for what was really vital."[5] The Queen shared his anxieties as he discussed with her the problems that were presented to him "in his papers", which he tackled as assiduously as he had in his first years as King.

Throughout the next year there seemed to be a steady improvement in the King's health, so that there were plans drawn up for an Australian tour during 1952. August 1950 was a particularly happy time for the Queen as she watched her husband grow stronger and also celebrated the birthday of her second grandchild, Princess Anne. There had been some hopes that this latest addition to the royal family might be born on the Queen's birthday, but the grandmother-Queen had to wait until 15th August before she could telephone the King at Balmoral that their daughter had had a baby girl.

On her own birthday *The Times* had a leader which said:

> It would be impossible to over-estimate the reinforcement the King has derived from the serene and steady support of the Queen. She has sustained him in sickness and in health, at all times taking her full share in the burdens of royal service and in the time of great anxiety during the King's grave illness, piling new duties upon her already overcrowded programme, in order that no good cause that had been promised the encouragement of royal patronage might be disappointed. She would commend to all what she told the University of Cape Town were the four cardinal virtues of academic life: honesty, courage, justice and resolve, the whole sustained upon the simplicities and the profundities of faith.[6]

On 3rd May the Queen accompanied the King to St Paul's for the declaration of the opening of the Festival of Britain. The next day they toured the South Bank Exhibition on what turned out to be George VI's last important public appearance. On 24th May he was ordered to bed because of an attack of influenza, and the Queen had to carry out, alone, the function of host to the King of Norway who came on a State Visit to London.

He appeared to have recovered by the time the family went to Balmoral in August, where he went shooting and celebrated Princess Margaret's twenty-first birthday on 21st August. However, within a week he had developed yet another chill, and his doctors advised a return to London for a thorough examination and a bronchoscopy to take a sample of tissue from the lung. On 18th September he was told that he would have to have his left lung removed because of a blockage in one of the bronchial tubes. The Queen insisted that she be told the truth about her husband's condition, and it was then that she learned he had cancer.[7] This information was kept from the King, who was aware, however, that, because of his continued loss of weight and the condition of his heart, he might well die under the operation, which was to take place on 23rd September. That morning the Queen left the Palace for the only time during that week. She, her daughters and the Duke of Edinburgh drove to the chapel at Lambeth Palace where they prayed for the King's recovery in a service held by the Archbishop of Canterbury. All over the world prayers were said for him. Harold Nicolson noted:

> "Wilson Harris [editor of the *Spectator*] rings up at 6.15 and asks whether I can do an obituary of the King. This rather startles me. It seemed that Harris had seen Lord Moran [Winston Churchill's doctor] at the London Library yesterday and that Moran had shaken his head gravely. In the evening we listen to the bulletin on the King. He was operated on the lung and his condition will continue to cause anxiety for some days.[8]

On 27th September the King had recovered sufficiently to sign a Warrant authorizing the appointment of Counsellors of State and another which prorogued Parliament so that an election could be held. By 7th October his condition was even better, so that Princess Elizabeth and Prince Philip were able to leave for their State Visit to Canada, which had been postponed because of the operation. During this period the Queen helped make the King's life more comfortable, assisting the nurses and ensuring the smooth running of the household, and played her part as Counsellor of State. She slowly resumed her busy public life, although, as one newspaper put it: "One would wish to express the hope that after her anxious vigil, Her Majesty will not herself undertake too numerous a list of public engagements."[9]

By the end of November the King was well enough to return to Royal Lodge. The Queen had not been there for four months, and it was with a special sense of thanksgiving that, on 9th December, she went to the private chapel to join in the national Thanksgiving for the King's recovery. On 11th December they celebrated the fifteenth anniversary of their accession and on 14th December, the King's fifty-sixth birthday.

Princess Elizabeth and Prince Philip returned from their Canadian visit, and Royal Lodge was the scene of a very happy family reunion. Christmas was spent at Sandringham. The King's recovery seemed to be almost complete; he was even able to go out shooting. At last the Queen felt that she could relax her vigil and begin once again to enjoy a peaceful life. They talked of the training which they hoped to provide for their heir in statecraft and of her forthcoming Australian tour. They planned their own holiday to South Africa due to start on 10th March 1952. But they also discussed the opinions of the doctors, who had warned them that even if he took life much easier, the King might have only a few years left.

On 30th January the whole family went to the Drury Lane Theatre to see *South Pacific*, which was to be a *bon voyage* to Princess Elizabeth and Prince Philip before they left for their Australian tour. On the following day the King went to London Airport to see his daughter off on the first leg of that tour. Oliver Lyttleton, the Colonial Secretary, who was in attendance, later wrote:

> I was shocked by the King's appearance . . . he seemed much altered and strained. I had the feeling of doom, which grew as the minutes before the time of departure ebbed away. The King went on to the roof of the building to wave goodbye. The high wind blew his hair into disorder. I felt with deep foreboding that this would be the last time he was to see his daughter, and that he thought so himself.[10]

Sir Miles Thomas was also present and he remembered "the bitterly cold wind . . . [the King], bracing himself against some inner tension as a man does when he is determined not to let an aching tooth or a sprained muscle interfere with his normal deportment . . . left quickly with the Queen."[11]

The Queen and those who had been fully aware of how gravely ill he had been were not surprised by the King's appearance that day. Rather they were pleased with the rate of his recovery and the fact that he had the strength to be there at all. Back at Sandringham he enjoyed the company of his grandson, Prince Charles, an active three-year-old. On 5th February he felt well enough to go out shooting with friends and farmers. The Queen and Princess Margaret drove across Norfolk to Ludham to see Edward Seago, the artist. In the evening, after tea and a rest, the King went, for the first time ever, to visit the children's nursery. He sat with Prince Charles and Princess Anne while they had supper, helped to tuck them into bed and said a prayer with them before saying goodnight. Then he dined with his wife and Princess Margaret, exchanging stories about the day's events. He went to bed in his ground-floor room which he had used since his illness.

Sometime in that night he died. When his valet failed to wake him for his morning bath at seven-thirty on 6th February, he ran to inform others in the household. The Queen "met the blow with utmost courage. I never knew a woman could be so brave," said one of her staff. She kept the news of the King's death from the grandchildren, ensured that the news was conveyed to Ministers, diplomats and others, including, predominantly, her daughter, now Queen Elizabeth II.

For four days the King's body lay in the chapel at Sandringham from where it was taken for four days of lying-in-state in Westminster Hall before the funeral service on 15th February, thence for burial at Windsor. As the procession passed Marlborough House on that last journey, Lady Airlie was with the eighty-five-year-old Queen Mary: "We sat alone together at the window, looking out into the murk and gloom. As the cortège wound slowly along, the Queen whispered in a broken voice 'Here *he* is,' and I knew that her dry eyes were seeing beyond the coffin a little boy in a sailor suit. . . . We held each other's hands in silence."[12]

Also in the procession was the Duke of Windsor, whose Abdication had thrust the burden of kingship on this younger brother. The silent watchers had a chance to reflect on the different way in which the two brothers had confronted their responsibilities, and the price that the younger had been forced to pay for the strains of sovereignty and the additional stresses imposed by being a wartime monarch.

At her Accession Council his daughter had said, "My heart is too full for me to say more to you today than that I shall always work as my father did."[13] For her, the King's early death meant an abrupt end to the comparative freedom she had known as the wife of a successful naval officer and the mother of two young children. Still only twenty-six, she now had to take on the burdens which the Duke of Windsor had found "intolerable" when he was much older and more experienced.

As for the Queen Mother, as we now have to call her, the death of her husband left a void all the greater because she had done so much, shared so much and loved so deeply. Later she was to write to thank people for the kindness and for their tributes to

> . . . my dear husband, a great and noble King. No man had a deeper sense than he of duty and service, and no man was more full of compassion for his fellow-men. He loved you all [as] he tried to tell you in his yearly message at Christmas; that was the pledge he took at the sacred moment of his coronation fifteen years ago. Now I am left alone, to do what I can to honour that pledge without him.
>
> Throughout our married life we have tried, the King and I, to fulfil with all our hearts and all our strength the great task of service that was laid upon us. My only wish now is that I may be allowed to continue the work that we sought to do together.[14]

Part VI: 1952–1980

25

The working life of the Queen Mother

ALTHOUGH THE QUEEN had been told that the King had cancer, she had hoped that the evident improvement in his health after Christmas 1951 was a sign that he would get better, even if only for a short while. The suddenness of his unexpected death came as a great shock to her. The poet Dylan Thomas had written:

> Do not go gentle into that good night,
> Rage, rage against the dying of the light.[1]

And those nearest to the Queen Mother watched as she emotionally raged, alone and without complaint, at the death of the man with whom she had done so much and with whom she must have hoped to do so much more. Now, for the first time, it became clear that she had come to depend on him. Lady Colville, a friend of Queen Mary's, wrote: "... Everybody realized how much the King had owed to his wonderful consort ... few people realized how much she had relied on *him* – on his capacity for wise and detached judgement for sound advice, and how lost she now felt without him."[2]

As Queen Consort she had been first lady in the land, her position defined by constitutional usage and by law. A widowed queen has no such fixed place. The lives of previous dowager queens offered little encouragement to the active and lively Queen Elizabeth. Queen Adelaide, widow of William IV, had retired at the age of forty-five into the sheltered life of a semi-invalid. Queen Alexandra was sixty-five when Edward VII died: she seemed content to play a very minor role during the early years of the reign of her son George V. His widow, Queen Mary, retained a place in public life while her bachelor son was King. His Abdication brought her into the public eye – as the upholder of tradition and an example of the virtues which the British looked for in their monarchs. But during the War she had gone to live at Badminton, and after 1945 she was a very old lady who returned to lead a quiet life in London.

The lives of these other widowed queens made little appeal to the Queen Mother. Her grief for her husband's death was such that some of her friends feared that she might choose to imitate the example of Queen Victoria. Like Queen Elizabeth, Victoria had relied on her husband, and after the early death of her Prince Consort, Albert, the widowed Queen drifted into a state of near collapse. She withdrew from public life, spoke to her Ministers only through a half-open door and made her sole object the dedication of the dead Prince. Queen Elizabeth was saved from such a fate largely by her own character and by her determination to carry on with the good work which she and her husband had done together.

Others helped her to 'soldier on'. During the War she and the King had learned to value the friendship of Winston Churchill, who in 1952 was Prime Minister: he took it on himself to be not merely a grandfatherly figure to the new, young Queen but also a friendly guide to the widowed Queen, whom he described as "that valiant woman".[3] Her daughter, the new Queen, also helped. She was so obviously in need of help that the selfless Queen Mother felt it essential that she should help get the new reign established. One of the Queen Mother's present staff threw some light on this 'part' when explaining how the ill-fated Peter Townsend had become Comptroller of the Queen Mother's Household at Clarence House. When she moved from Buckingham Palace, "all the people wanted to come with her. It was she who had to tell them that they had a duty to the new Queen, to help her to settle in at the Palace and to ensure that things ran smoothly."[4]

On her part, the new Queen recognized the value of that support – for herself and as a therapy for her mother. Within a week of her accession it was announced that she wished her to be known as Queen Elizabeth, the Queen Mother.[5] As such she would be not merely the grandmother of a new generation of royalty but a symbol for the community – more lovable, less rigid and frigid than Queen Mary. Previous dowager queens have not used the title 'Queen Mother', but the fact that the new Queen had the same name as her mother meant that the new title was essential if public confusion were to be avoided. Nevertheless, in the royal households the title is never used, people referring to 'the Queen' when they mean our present monarch, and 'Queen Elizabeth' when they are referring to the dowager queen. But, however much the family may dislike the title, it has a special appeal for the general public.

There were continued public calls on the Queen Mother – for her patronage of this society and that institution. We have seen that she had been Patron of the North Islington Infant Welfare Centre since 1923 – in its annual report for 1952 she read some words from the poet William Blake: "Labour well the Minute Particulars, attend to the little ones, And those who are in misery cannot remain so long." She had, indeed, gone to play with her two grandchildren even on the day after her husband's death, remarking: "I have got to start some time, and it is better now than later." But in spite of that determination it was some months before she was able to "labour well".

In May 1952 the Queen Mother made her first public appearance since becoming a widow. She had always gone to wish her regiments God-speed before they left for service overseas, and when the First Battalion of the Black Watch was ordered to Korea, she did not fail them. She flew from Windsor Castle to Fife and inspected the Battalion at Crail. Each officer wore a dark mourning band; she was dressed in black, and there was some concern that she might be unable to carry out the inspection. But she spoke to the assembled Battalion, met relatives and Old Comrades, visited the Sergeants' Mess and had her photograph taken with the officers. One soldier wrote: "Her Majesty Queen Elizabeth's visit was a great success, and we appreciated it more than words can say."[6] She had taken her first step into the uncharted world of playing the role of Queen Mother.

Her next public exploit was very different. On 2nd May 1953 the world's first passenger jet airliner, the Comet, flew on its inaugural flight to Johannesburg. While dining with her friends the Salisburys at Hatfield House, she made a comment on this British achievement. The Comet's proving airfield is near Hatfield House. Lord Salisbury had a word with Miles Thomas, the Chairman of BOAC, and a few days later the Queen Mother, Princess Margaret, Group Captain Peter Townsend, the Marquess and Marchioness of Salisbury met Sir Geoffrey and Lady de Havilland on the airfield at Hatfield. They climbed into a new Comet with the chief test-pilot, John Cunningham, at the controls. The plane flew towards Switzerland at about 500 mph. The Queen Mother "replaced her high-heeled shoes with a comfortable pair of casuals" and went forward to the flight deck. John Cunningham allowed her to sit in his seat and to take the controls, explaining to her that if she pushed the central column forward, the plane would get "faster than a meteor". Miles Thomas wrote:

> Her Majesty eased the control forward, the Comet gathered speed. Cunningham gave her a little extra throttle, the mach. needle crept towards the coloured danger sector and suddenly the Comet began to porpoise. Not violently, but just enough to indicate that we had reached the limits of her stability. Quickly, John eased the throttles back, Her Majesty did the same with the controls, and we went back to the same cruising speed as before the royal sprint. That trip was, of course, before the crashes that the Comet suffered through structural weakness, and had that porpoising gone on much longer, the wracking on the structure could well have precipitated a rupture of the skin of the kind that caused the subsequent tragedies. I still shudder every time I think of that flight.[7]

Now that she was no longer 'first lady in the land', the Queen Mother had to move from Buckingham Palace into Clarence House, which had been modernized for her daughter and husband. She also had to move out of Balmoral and back into Birkhall, about eight miles away. She and the then Duke of York had lived here during their early married life, and she welcomed the return to the smaller, more comfortable country house with its happy memories. At weekends she continued to use Royal Lodge which had been the home where she, her husband and their children had enjoyed so much of their lives. The garden which he had planned and on which they had worked together was a constant reminder to her of her great loss but also of many happy days.

In March 1953 Queen Mary died, and the Queen Mother mourned the death of one who had been her great support during the crisis surrounding the abdication. In May came the death of her elder brother Michael, while she was also concerned at the illness of her brother-in-law Lord Granville, Rose's husband, who died in June. In Chapter 26 we will consider the anxieties that bore in on her at this time over Princess Margaret's behaviour and her relationship with Peter Townsend. All in all, Coronation Year was not one of unmixed happiness.

Her daughter's Coronation on 2nd June 1953 was a great State occasion. As in 1937, there were vast crowds on the streets and, a sign of progress, even larger crowds in the television audience that saw the young Queen consecrated to the service of her people as her mother and father had been in 1937. The Queen Mother drove from Clarence House to the Abbey in a glass coach. During the ceremony the young Prince Charles was brought to sit between her and Princess Margaret. When he leaned far out over the Gallery to get a better view, his grandmother pulled him back and he was handed over to his nurse to be returned to the Palace.

Later that evening the newly crowned Queen, her husband and their children came out onto the balcony at the Palace to the cheers of the massive crowds piled around the gates. After a few moments the Queen and Prince Philip moved apart to leave a space. Prince Philip turned, and led out Queen Elizabeth, the Queen Mother, whose appearance was greeted with a special roar of approval for the proud and gracious lady standing with her family and grandchildren around her.

In July 1953 she undertook her first tour as Queen Mother. She and Princess Margaret flew, by Comet, to Southern Rhodesia. The main purpose of their visit was to open the Rhodes Centenary Exhibition in Bulawayo. Their visit was to last sixteen days and when the Queen Mother saw the itinerary that had been planned she complained, "It is not very crowded." She was anxious to be, again, a full-time member of 'the royal firm'. The authorities were only too glad to add other engagements to the schedule. She went to tobacco auctions, laid foundation stones and travelled once again in a royal train through parts of Africa which must have reminded her of her first overseas journey with her husband.

Later that summer she was with the Queen and Prince Philip as they planned their forthcoming visit to New Zealand and Australia for the tour which she and the late King had been anticipating. On 23rd November 1953 she was at London Airport to wave goodbye to her daughter.

While this farewell may have reminded her of previous departures by her daughter, it nevertheless provided her with an opportunity to lead a more active public life at home. The Queen Mother was one of the five State Counsellors appointed to perform royal duties in the absent sovereign's place. In effect she was a deputy Queen, and, for a few brief months, Clarence House became the centre of royal government. Ministers came for discussions, and ambassadors presented their credentials. In the New Year she held six investitures at the Palace to present the awards made in the New Year's Honours List. When she went to receive the Freedom of the Grocers' Company, she was accorded the same privileges as would have been given the Queen. So, on her entry into the City, she was met by the Lord Mayor – as she and her husband had been when they drove to their Silver Wedding celebrations in 1948.

In October 1954 she made a visit to the USA that was to prove to be as important in her life as the 1939 visit had been in that of her husband. In November 1952 a fund had been launched in the USA to commemorate the late King, and the money was to be spent on providing technical training in the USA for young people from the British Commonwealth. When the fund was declared closed, it was natural that the American sponsors should ask the Queen Mother to come across to receive it. She was very doubtful about making this visit. "Who is going to be interested in the middle-aged widow of a King?"[8] She remembered the tumultuous welcome they had received in 1939. That, she believed, was because of the King's presence. To return to the scene of this triumph and to fail would be a bitter blow.

She sailed on the *Queen Elizabeth*, where, in spite of an announcement that people were "not to bother" her, every appearance was greeted by applause – in the dining-room and the cinema or on a walk on deck. This affectionate regard for the widowed Queen was also reflected in the editorial of the *New York Times* on the day of her arrival: "Of all the many reasons for welcoming Queen Elizabeth, the Queen Mother, the pleasantest is that she is so nice. . . ."[9]

The presentation of the cheque was made at a banquet at the Waldorf-Astoria. In full evening dress, the former "fairy Queen" was played in by pipers of the Black Watch. Millions of Americans watched the ceremony on television. *The World Telegram* commented: "The royal lady with the peaches-and-cream complexion and twinkling eyes not only drew a record crowd of

2,800 smart-setters to the Waldorf-Astoria ballroom; she sent them away humming 'God save the Queen' like a first-night audience whistling the top tunes of the hit show."[10]

One of those who applauded was John McGovern, Labour MP for Shettleston Division of Glasgow who had twice been imprisoned during campaigns against unemployment in the 1930s when he had also led hunger marches and a massive sit-down in Princes Street, Edinburgh. Of the Waldorf-Astoria banquet he wrote: "Royal personages were 'untouchables' to me . . . [but] my wife and I had a splendid evening and cheered the Queen Mother heartily. I completely lost my proletarian snobbery. It was amazing that it had to be on American soil that I first recognized royalty."[11]

The conversion of this member of the extreme Left was one small side-effect of the Queen Mother's visit. More significant was her success with the Americans themselves. One afternoon, when she went on an impromptu sightseeing visit to the Empire State Building, the crowds gathered on Fifth Avenue caused a traffic jam, the drivers joining in the cheering. As a British official put it, "The attitude towards our country is warming day by day." Wherever she went the effect was the same: in Harlem she was received by pealing bells and crowds of black Americans; when she visited Saks, the famous department store, the crowds followed her from the streets and into the store. In an attempt to escape, "We shot up and down in the lift, just like a Marx Brothers' film, trying to find a floor where there was not a crowd waiting." Her attempt at privacy was futile. But while this may have proved distasteful to some of her staff and an embarrassment to police and other officials, the enthusiastic reception was welcome on two counts. On a personal level, it proved to her that she was welcome and loved for herself and that she need never have feared coming to the USA in the first place. On a political level, the *Daily Mail* made the point: "She has done more to promote Anglo-American friendship and understanding than all the diplomatic activities of the entire year."[12]

As if encouraged by the success of her American visit, the Queen Mother now entered fully into a public role. At home she not only resumed her old patronages but accepted new positions. And as in the past she was an active and interesting patron. Lord Woolton expressed the feelings of very many when, as Chancellor of Manchester University, welcoming her to one of their celebrations, he spoke of "this gracious lady, who, by her personal and persistent example, has given a fresh and joyous impetus to the meaning of public service".[13]

During the coronation celebrations there was a great public welcome for the new reign. Some people hoped that it would breed 'New Elizabethans'. But the Queen Mother had felt 'left out' of it; the publicity for the 'new' seemed designed to help relegate her to the shadows. However, within a few years it had become clear that, as indeed her daughter had indicated by her new title, she had an important role to play. Elizabeth II came to the throne at a very early age and without that 'training in statecraft' which her parents had planned to give her after her marriage. It is not surprising that she found the "intolerable burden" somewhat heavy. Nor is it difficult to see why so young a Queen decided that she had to be careful to maintain the dignity of the 'majesty' of which she had been warned by her grandmother, Queen Mary.

It may have been in order for Prince Philip to crack jokes with onlookers and to attack politicians, businessmen, trade unionists and the leaders of emergent nations in public speeches and private asides. Lesser members of 'the royal firm' might be genial in company and relaxed in their relations with sightseers, as was the Duchess of Kent. But the young Queen would have agreed with one of her staff: "We don't exist to divert people. We are." Now that she has enjoyed the public acclaim of her own Silver Jubilee and has become much more self-confident, the Queen has shown that she, too, has learned how to relax without losing dignity, and her pleasant smile has become a feature of her public appearances. In the first years of her reign this was not so. It was left to the Queen Mother to provide royalty with its more human and more readily acceptable face. Few people were worthy of a good word in Richard Crossman's *Diaries*, but one honourable exception was the Queen Mother – and this was all the more surprising because the intellectual Crossman prided himself on being an anti-monarchist. But on 1st February 1965 he wrote: "... went to the Festival Hall for the concert celebrating the re-opening. . . . In the second half I sat next to the Queen Mother who was large and cuddly and comfortable and easy. . . ."[14] It was easier for the sixty-five-year-old Queen Mother to allow herself the luxury of appearing to be "cuddly and comfortable" than it was for the Queen to do so. And in playing that "easy" role she was an important member of the royal family, helping to give the family a more pleasant public image.[15]

When talking to her present staff about the Queen Mother's public work, I was told that "without a doubt, her main interest now [1978] is London University". She became Chancellor of the University in 1955, and since then she has played a very active part in its life. "She has visited every constituent College of the University at least once," I was told, and, as Harold Nicolson noticed, such visits were not the empty formal occasions that others often make them. On 30th October 1958 he wrote to his wife:

> I went to Morley College for the opening of the new buildings by the Queen Mother. She was in her best mood and spirits. She has that astonishing gift of being sincerely interested in dull people and dull occasions. . . . You know how much I like people who are good at their jobs . . . and she is superb at *her* job. Somehow she creates such an impression of goodwill and good behaviour. . . .[16]

She presides at the graduation ceremonies which take place three or four times a year at the Albert Hall, where, in her black damask robe with its gold trimmings, she personally hands each graduate the degree certificate. I know from my own students how much the graduates appreciate the fact that they receive their congratulations and certificates not from the Professor or Dean of Faculty but from the Queen Mother. I also know from experience how utterly boring it can be to sit in the Albert Hall while a thousand or more graduates troop one after the other onto and across the platform to meet the Queen Mother. But she does this three or four times a year, and year after year, because she has taken on the job of Chancellor and "she is superb at *her job*".

After the success of her American visit she went on a continuous series of official visits. In 1956 she went to France, then in successive years to Rhodesia and Nyasaland (1957), Canada, Honolulu, Fiji, New Zealand, Australia, Mauritius, Uganda and Malta (1958), Kenya, Uganda, Italy and France (1959), Rhodesia and Nyasaland (1960), Tunisia (1961), Canada (1962), France (1963), the Caribbean (1964), Jamaica, France, Canada and Germany (1965), Canada, Honolulu, Fiji, Australia and New Zealand (1966). On the last of these visits to Australia she visited her grandson, Prince Charles, at school at the Geelong outpost at Timbertop. When we remember that during that visit she had her sixty-sixth birthday, it is easy to understand the admiration that there was for this 'travelling ambassador' and, on the other hand, why she welcomed the coming-of-age of Prince Charles who would be able to take some of the burden from her shoulders. Her staff assure me that there will be no more overseas tours. However, while making this confident assertion, they were also quick to add: "They want her to go to Canada next year..." and who knows what the assiduous traveller may decide to do in her eightieth year? An an indication of her continuing involvement in affairs we need look no further than her acceptance of the office of Lord Warden of the Cinque Ports in September 1978. She will be the first female to occupy this office. One wonders whether she will break her rule and, maybe once, wear the splendid uniform traditionally worn by the Lord Warden.

26

The private life of the Queen Mother

TOURS ABROAD AND VISITS to societies and regiments in this country have to
be planned well in advance. Like all professional people, the Queen Mother
has a well-defined time-table – for each year and each week. Her annual time-
table has an almost unalterable framework. Christmas is always spent with
the family at Windsor – now that Sandringham is not big enough to house all
the nephews, nieces and their children. When the family disperses, the Queen
Mother goes with the Queen for a few days to Sandringham, the home which
her husband had loved so much and where he died.

Easter is "always spent at Windsor. Then in May she goes to her Castle of
Mey . . . back to Windsor for Ascot Week", said one of her staff with a smile.
Summer is spent at Mey although she sometimes goes down to Balmoral for a
few days' fishing. "She always goes to Mey for a week or so in the late
autumn."[1]

In between these holidays at one or other country home, the Queen Mother
lives in Clarence House, which is the London base from which she travels to
her public duties. She leaves on Friday to spend the weekend at Royal
Lodge, the home which she and her husband may be said to have created.
When she goes to Scotland, she normally takes one of her male staff with her
"to help her with the entertaining which she may have to do".[2] When she
goes to Royal Lodge, she goes on her own, perhaps because she does not
intend to do any entertaining, perhaps because she wants to be alone with her
memories of other, happier, fuller days at what is still in fact her English
country home.

If, for the moment, we ignore the public duties which she fulfils, this time-
table is very much like the one followed by her parents and other members of
the landed classes before the First World War.

When a member of the Queen Mother's staff was outlining her annual and
weekly schedules, I noted that "her Castle of Mey" figured at least three times.
I asked why she had felt the need to buy this castle in Caithness when the

royal family had Balmoral and the other home on the estate, Birkhall. The answer was that the Queen Mother wanted a personal home – Clarence House and Royal Lodge being *royal* homes.

She had first seen the Castle of Mey – or Barrogill Castle as it was then called – in June 1952, when she was staying with her friend Lady Doris Vyner in her House of the Northern Gate at Dunnet, only a few miles away from John o' Groats. At this time, when she was just beginning to emerge from the emotional storm which had overtaken her following her husband's death, the calm peace of the flat landscape of Caithness appealed to her. In the 1880s Evelyn Burnaby had written of the district: "We could see no signs of habitation until at last, on suddenly descending by a steep road, we caught a magnificent view, all in a moment, of Stroma Island, with the whole range of the Orkneys perfectly distinct."[3] And that, say her staff, is why she bought the Castle of Mey. Here she can enjoy an almost complete peace.

Lady Vyner took her to see Mey, which was two miles from her own home and six miles west of John o' Groats. As she drove down the mile-long avenue of trees and saw the cannon on the forecourt, the Queen Mother was reminded of Glamis. But Barrogill, or Mey, then up for sale, was a dilapidated shell in 1952. It had been built in 1570 for the fourth Earl of Caithness, whose descendants had lived there for three hundred years. It has a spiral staircase – as has Glamis – leading to a drawing-room from which one looks across the rocky coastline towards the Orkneys. The five-storeyed castle and its wings contain forty bedrooms, eight of which are occupied by a gardener and his family. The twenty-five acres of garden had been badly neglected, but there were still signs of a walled garden, trout ponds and a seawater bathing pool.

The Queen Mother visited Barrogill twice more during June and again when she stayed with the Vyners in August, when the place had still not been sold. She then made a successful bid for it and so became the owner of one of the most northern homes in Britain. Later, when she was given the Freedom of the town of Wick, she explained: "I found the Castle of Mey, with its long history, its serene beauty and its proud setting, faced with the prospect of having no one able to occupy it. I felt a great wish to preserve, if I could, this ancient dwelling. . . ."[4]

And that, say her present staff, was a second major reason for her decision to buy Mey: "It was a lovely little castle which was in danger of becoming derelict."[5] She restored the name, the Castle of Mey, and gave orders for its renovation and modernization. It took three years for this work to be completed, during which time she took a great deal of care about its furnishings. Sotheby's, Christie's and other major salerooms were visited as well as local antique shops in Caithness in an effort to find the pieces which would best fit this ancient home. Here say her staff, was a third reason for her purchase of "my delightful little castle", whose roof almost disappeared in the storms that swept northern Scotland in the winter of 1952–3. She needed, they say, an interest to occupy her time while the wounds healed and she recovered from her husband's death. In 1955 the castle had been restored, and for the first time the Queen Mother's personal Standard flew from its flagstaff.

Since then she has spent a great deal of her time at Mey. She has become an active member of the local community – at flower shows, bazaars, salerooms and agricultural shows. She enjoys fishing for salmon in the Thurso, dressed as one onlooker said "like an old gipsy".[6] But most of all she likes Mey because it is peaceful and is the one home where she has no sad memories.

The Castle of Mey is about one hour by helicopter from Balmoral, and during her summer holiday at Mey the Queen Mother drops in on the royal family at Balmoral where she might well feel, with Tom Moore:

> Fond memory brings the light,
> Of other days around me.

Her younger relations enjoy their visits to "Granny's house" at Mey where they can run free in the estate, along the beach or the empty moorland of the neighbourhood. On her part she enjoys having them with her; like her mother, she too has a "genius for family life".[7]

At her Castle of Mey and Balmoral the Queen Mother enjoys one of her favourite pastimes – fishing. At Mey and Sandringham, as well as at Royal Lodge, she spends a good deal of her time in the garden. These are very private leisure pursuits, and ones which she has enjoyed since she was a girl. Not so with her other, more public, recreation – horse racing. Although, like all girls of her social class, she learned to ride, she was never a 'horsy' woman and had none of the enthusiasm for riding which her elder daughter and Princess Anne have shown since they were young. In this they resembled King George VI, who was an outstanding horseman who enjoyed his membership of a number of hunts.

During her foreign tours the young Duchess of York had gone, as a matter of wifely duty, to race meetings – in New Zealand and Australia. She never rode with her fox-hunting husband but followed the hunt by car so that she could be with him at the end. On his accession to the throne George VI inherited the string of royal racehorses in training at Newmarket, which is not too far from Sandringham so that the King and Queen were able to slip across on private visits when they wished to do so. Just before their coronation, they visited Liverpool and, as part of their visit, went to the Aintree racecourse to see the Grand National. This was the year when the favourite, Golden Miller, refused at a fence, and the race was won by Royal Mail, a horse sired by the aptly named Royal Prince. The superstitious saw in this a 're-run' of the 'crown stakes' when another golden favourite had fallen and another Royal Prince had come to the front.

During the War, horse racing had provided the King and Queen with many hours of relaxation. In 1942 a royal horse, Sun Chariot, was a popular winner of the Oaks at Newmarket, while in 1945 the King's own horse, Rising Light, was placed fifth in the wartime Derby at Epsom. This was the King's first horse, as distinct from those which formed part of the royal stable. On her forty-fifth birthday, 4th August 1945, the Queen went with the King to Ascot and saw Rising Light win an exciting race – which deprived the champion jockey, Gordon Richards, of the privilege of riding all six winners.

The Queen Mother might have remained merely an interested and sometimes excited onlooker if it had not been for the thoughtfulness of Princess Elizabeth, herself an enthusiastic horsewoman. When the King was ill, almost continually, after 1948, the Princess persuaded her mother to become joint owner with her of a horse, Monaveen. This, her daughter thought, would give the Queen Mother some interest outside their home and perhaps provide some relaxation from the tensions imposed on her by her husband's ill-health. The therapy proved more successful than the prescriber dared have hoped.

The horse, running in Princess Elizabeth's name and colours, won his first race for the royal partners and ensured that their enthusiasm was confirmed. Altogether he won four races, finishing fifth in the Grand National in his first season for his new owners. The Queen Mother had become interested in steeplechasing largely because of her friendship with Lord Mildmay, a famous amateur jockey. When he was drowned in 1950, she bought his best horse, Manicou, and raced it under her own name and in her own colours of blue, buff stripes and blue sleeves, with black cap and gold tassel. On 24th November 1950 Manicou won the Wimbledon Steeplechase at Kempton Park, the first time ever that a Queen's horse had won under National Hunt rules and the first time since Queen Anne that a Queen's horse had won in her own colours.

Perhaps the most outstanding horse that she ever owned was Devon Loch. He had been bought in 1955 and won six races for her. But the horse will be best remembered for the race he did not win, the Grand National of 1956. When only thirty yards from the post he was well in the lead, but suddenly, and for no apparent reason, he sprawled almost onto the ground, and the race was lost. Dick Francis, the royal jockey, was in tears;[8] Peter Cazelet, the royal trainer, was upset and in the royal box only the Queen Mother remained calm. Harold Nicolson wrote to his wife:

> At luncheon yesterday I sat between Michael Adeane [Private Secretary to the Queen] and the young Duke of Devonshire. They had both been standing

with the royal party at Aintree when Devon Loch collapsed. They said it was a really horrible sight.

The public and the people in the enclosure took it for granted that the horse had won and turned towards the royal box to make a demonstration, yelling and waving their hats. Then someone shouted out that there had been an accident, and the ovation stopped suddenly as if a light had been switched off. There was a complete hush. The Princess Royal panted: "It can't be true! It can't be true!" The Queen Mother never turned a hair. "I must go down," she said, "and comfort those poor people." So down she went, dried the jockey's tears, patted Peter Cazelet on the shoulder and insisted on seeing the stable-lads, who were also in tears. "It was the most perfect display of dignity that I have ever witnessed," said Devonshire.[9]

She has owned, and still owns, other good horses. In the 1961–2 season she won twenty-three races and for a time was the leading owner of steeplechasers. Her most successful horse in that year was The Rip, which had been bred out of Manicou at North Wootton near Sandringham. In 1964–5 she was among the leading owners, with over twenty winners. On one day at Folkestone in 1964 she had three winners – her four-year-old grandson Prince Andrew enquiring whether "Granny will get a gold medal". In that year, 1965, The Rip was favourite to win the Grand National, but although he jumped the course, he was only able to finish seventh. It would delight her and the race-going public if one day she won the Grand National and/or the Cheltenham Gold Cup.

The enthusiasm of this latecomer to racing has been made evident in many ways. She attends meetings throughout the country and while she is abroad, and she goes to meetings in all sorts of weather. Dick Francis wrote about a day when the heavy rain drove the spectators back to cover so that only six people watched the horses parade. "But H.M. the Queen Mother was waiting under one of the big trees there to see her horse and to give me the usual encouragement before I set off."[10] It is not surprising that a knowledgeable official should say:

Queen Elizabeth is very friendly with other owners, jockeys, everybody – she always goes down among the crowds. She always thanks the head lad and speaks to the stable-lads when she is going round the horses. When jockeys retire or have bad luck, she is the first to be sympathetic in words and in kind. Probably what appeals to her most about racing is its uncertainty, that it cannot be 'laid on'. She is very popular with everyone . . .[11]

And so what started as a therapy has become a favourite occupation. She takes a keen interest in her own horses – visiting the stables, speaking to the lads and the trainer. She has made many new and important friends among the owners and trainers – often slipping out for a quiet evening at one or other of their homes. If she has not been at a meeting, she will try to watch the races on television. Even when she attends a meeting, she normally goes to the camera-room to watch the film of the last three furlongs – trying to recapture perhaps the excitement of the finish. All this makes it easier to understand why one of her staff, when giving me the outline of her time-table, smiled as he said ". . . back to Windsor for Ascot Week".

27

The Queen Mother and Princess Margaret

IT SEEMED UNFORTUNATE that my first visit to Clarence House took place just after the announcement of Princess Margaret's divorce. It was a pleasant surprise to be assured by a member of the Queen Mother's staff that this and the Townsend affair "are all matters of history" and a part of the life of the Queen Mother. To write her story without reference to these sad events would be to produce a travesty of the truth.[1] This reminded me of Cromwell's order that he be portrayed "warts and all". The Queen Mother had taken a similar attitude towards a photographer who had 'touched up' a portrait to remove the wrinkles and lines: "You must show me a little older; one does not stand still."[2]

The Townsend affair may be said to have begun when King George VI decided to appoint Equerries of Honour to his household staff. His aim was to show his admiration for the bravery of so many young men on land and sea and in the air. One of those appointed was Wing Commander Peter Townsend, DSO, DFC and bar, who had won his awards "for outstanding leadership, organization and determination". Within a very short time he had won a special place at the Palace, largely because he could calm the easily angered King, who came to rely on the discreet support which Townsend gave him. The King also admired his ability to organize and, if needs be, re-organize the day's time-table during the last hectic weeks of the War. As one indication of the King's approval, Townsend and his wife were given a grace-and-favour home, Adelaide Cottage, next to Windsor Castle. Here he was always on call when the family were at Windsor. A second mark of approval came when the King agreed to stand godfather to Townsend's second child.

It is not surprising that the fourteen-year-old Princess Margaret should have tended to hero-worship the man whom her father obviously admired and who became, in a sense, one of the family. He stayed on at the Palace after the War, helping to organize the tour of South Africa in 1947 when, once again, his efficiency won the praise of both the King and the Queen, who told him: "I don't know what we'd do without you, Peter."[3] This long and arduous tour lasted nine weeks, during which the party covered six thousand miles. Townsend proved to be an admirable companion for the two Princesses, and especially for Princess Margaret. The elder sister, after all, saw the tour as, in one sense, an enforced separation from her fiancé.

During the King's periods of illness, after 1948, the Queen tended to turn to Townsend for the male support which she needed, confirming his position as an important member of the staff. We have seen that the Queen Mother drew on her own inner resources to overcome the traumatic effects of George VI's death, but Princess Margaret was equally affected by the death of the King, who had spoiled her as a child and with whom she shared a boisterous sense of humour. It is not surprising that she turned to Townsend for that mature male companionship which her father had once provided.

When the Queen Mother and Princess Margaret moved into Clarence House, Townsend, now a Group Captain, moved with them to take charge of the running of what had to be at one and the same time, a home, an office and a State establishment. As one of the Queen Mother's staff explained: "He had seen how the Palace was run, and not many people had that experience."[4]

While he was working for the late King, Townsend was frequently away from home for weeks at a time, and, even when at home, he was often called to Windsor Castle at unexpected hours. After February 1952 the Queen Mother and, more particularly, Princess Margaret made increasing demands on his time. It is hardly surprising that his marriage came under great strain. In December 1952 he obtained a divorce on the grounds of his wife's misconduct.

Up until this time no one seems to have noticed anything special or untoward in the relationship between Townsend and Princess Margaret. Indeed, on reflection, no one seems to have paid much attention to the development of Princess Margaret at all. Her father had spoiled her when she was young; Queen Mary had found her "so outrageously amusing that one can't help encouraging her",[5] and everyone had laughed at her ability as mimic and piano-playing leader of family get-togethers. But no one had thought of the part which she might play in the life of 'the royal firm'. There was a defined role for Princess Elizabeth which tended to isolate the sisters from one another, and her marriage in 1947 left Princess Margaret even lonelier than she had been. It is perhaps not surprising that, given her character and other people's failure to plan a role for her, she should have found her friends among actors, music-hall entertainers and others connected with the theatre. "Chips" Channon met her at Ascot in 1949 and in a moment of perception noted: "Already she is a public character and I wonder what will happen to her? There is already a Marie Antoinette aroma about her."6

What happened was that she fell in love with Peter Townsend, who after his divorce was free to re-marry. In April 1953, a few weeks before the Coronation was due to take place, she told her mother that she intended to marry the Comptroller of her household. Because of the Royal Marriages Act of 1772, she was bound to ask her sister's permission to marry. This Act laid down that no British descendant of King George II could marry under the age of twenty-five without the sovereign's consent. But, it ran on: "In case any descendant of George II, being above twenty-five years old, shall persist to contract a marriage disapproved of by His Majesty, such descendant, after giving twelve months' notice to the Privy Council, may contract such marriage and the same may be duly solemnized without the consent of His Majesty. . . ."7

The new Queen, deeply involved with the plans for her Coronation, was presented with a major problem which had overtones of 1936 about it. We do not know her private attitude towards her sister's plans to marry a divorced and older man. Happy in her own marriage she may have wanted to allow her sister to marry the man of her choice. She and the Queen Mother knew and liked Townsend and may have thought him a suitable partner for the younger Princess, but since the Royal Marriages Act is a statute, the Queen had to ask her Prime Minister to tell her what answer she should make to her sister's request. In 1936 Winston Churchill had wanted the government to allow Edward VIII to marry "the woman he loves". In 1953, as Prime Minister, he told the Queen that a marriage between her sister and a divorced commoner was impossible. The required permission should not be given but the Princess be told to wait for two years when, under the terms of the 1772 Act, she would be free to marry without the Queen's consent. The Queen was constitutionally bound to follow this advice. She was not, however, obliged to accept her Prime Minister's suggestion that Townsend should be dismissed from Clarence House and sent abroad on some government mission or other. This explains why Townsend was with the Princess at her sister's Coronation in June 1953.

After the long ceremony the royal family and their staffs were in the entrance of the Abbey waiting for their carriages to come to take them back to the Palace. Cameramen and reporters were quick to spot Princess Margaret picking stray threads off the breast-pocket of Townsend's uniform and brushing her hand along his row of medals. This almost wifely attention to his dress was enough to encourage foreign reporters to file stories about their love affair. As in 1936, the British Press remained silent. But unlike 1936, this silence was short-lived. Within two weeks *The People* was retailing these stories, arguing in its hypocritical fashion: "The story is, of course, utterly untrue. It is quite unthinkable that a royal princess, third in line of succession to the throne, should even contemplate a marriage with a man who has been through the divorce courts."[8]

The government's reaction was ruthlessly efficient. Townsend had been due to travel with the Queen Mother and Princess Margaret to Southern Rhodesia. The Prime Minister advised the Queen that he should be sent abroad as an air attaché to a British Embassy of his choice and that he and Princess Margaret, while free to write to each other, should promise that they would not meet for a year and that they would meet after that only "in circumstances of absolute discretion". So it was that Princess Margaret travelled to Southern Rhodesia with her mother while Townsend went to the British Embassy in Brussels.

On 21st August 1955 Princess Margaret celebrated her twenty-fifth birthday at Balmoral. Press speculation as to what she would do now had aroused public interest, and over ten thousand people went in coaches and cars to watch her go to church at Crathie. The question had also been discussed inside the royal family and by the Cabinet. The Queen Mother had taken the line that, since her husband would not have approved of a Townsend-Margaret wedding, she could not. The Queen seems to have been uncertain as to what she ought to do. On the one hand she wanted to help the younger sister who had stood by her during the period when their father had seemed opposed to her marriage to Prince Philip. On the other hand she recognized that as official head of the Established Church she had a public duty to oppose the proposed marriage. But, as a complicating factor, she did not want to be the cause of a row which might split the family as it had been split in 1936.

The Prime Minister was then Sir Anthony Eden. It was a sign of the change in social attitudes that even though he had been through the divorce courts he had become Prime Minister in succession to Winston Churchill. Eden's attitude towards the innocent party in a divorce – as Townsend was – had to be coloured by his own experience. But others in the Cabinet took a very hard line, under the leadership of the Marquess of Salisbury. He was a staunch High Anglican and, as a close friend of the Queen Mother, might be thought of almost as her spokesman. He told the Prime Minister that, if the government advised the Queen to give her consent to the proposed marriage, he would resign. Eden's government was already unpopular, and the Prime Minister was not prepared to allow a split over this marriage to weaken further his position in the country. So when he saw the Queen at Balmoral on 1st October he advised her not to give her consent to the marriage. The Queen Mother had left for her Castle of Mey by the time that Eden arrived at Balmoral, seeming to want to wash her hands of the affair now that she had failed over the past two years to show her headstrong daughter where her duty lay.

The affair now took on some of the elements of a tragi-comedy. *Punch* ran a series of cartoons – "tinker, tailor, soldier – group captain . . .".[9] Comedians referred to the proposed marriage, and the popular Press continued to titillate the public appetite with speculative articles. When Townsend returned from Brussels on 12th October 1955, he was followed by dozens of reporters and his visit to Clarence House on the evening of the 13th took place amid the glare of world-wide publicity. On 18th October the Prime Minister saw the Queen and advised her that she should not give her consent to the proposed marriage but that Princess Margaret should be allowed to give notice in a letter to the Privy Council of her intentions to marry Townsend. If Parliament made no objection, the marriage could take place after a year. But, the Prime Minister pointed out, it was highly likely that Parliament would object to Princess Margaret's retaining her royal status after such a marriage. The government would then be obliged to advise the Queen to deprive the Princess of her royal status, her titles and her Civil List allowance which, after marriage, would be £15,000 a year. It was also possible that the government would have to recommend that the Princess and her husband be asked to live abroad permanently.

That same evening Townsend had a private meeting with the Queen Mother, who may by now have come to regret having taken him onto her personal staff in 1952. Members of her present staff do not agree with this: their unspoken attitude seemed to be that Townsend ought never to have allowed the situation to develop as it did. On 21st October the Queen Mother and the rest of the royal family stood in heavy rain as the Queen unveiled the memorial statue to George VI in the Mall. They heard her say: "He shirked no task, however difficult, and to the end he never faltered in his duty. . . ."[10] Some onlookers saw in this an appeal to an errant sister.

On 24th October *The Times* referred to the affair for the first time. In a long editorial the Princess was reminded of her duty and of the choice that lay before her – to remain a member of the privileged family *or* to marry and lose her royal status.

On 26th October the Princess met Townsend at Clarence House. At this long meeting they decided that they could not go ahead with their proposed marriage – and the Princess went to tell her mother and her sister. On 25th October she went to inform the Archbishop of Canterbury of her decision.

On 31st October 1955 the Princess issued a public statement in which she declared that, "mindful of the Church's teaching that Christian marriage is indissoluble, and conscious of my duty to the Commonwealth, I have resolved to put these considerations before any others. . . ." There was a general welcome for what Nicolson called "a great act of self-sacrifice".[11]

Peter Townsend went back to Brussels before taking up a career as a writer. In March 1958, following a world tour, he came to Britain and called at

Clarence House. Once again there was wide-spread speculation; once again dozens of journalists chased after him. This time, however, he merely went back to the Continent. In 1959 he married a twenty-year-old Belgian tobacco heiress. In 1978 he published his own account of the long-drawn-out affair but, conforming to the protocol that governs former royal servants, told us nothing that we did not already know.[12]

By the time Townsend called at Clarence House in March 1958 the Queen Mother had watched her daughter's developing friendship with a young photographer, Antony Armstrong-Jones. She approved of this friendship, arguing that "they are two of a kind". They had similar tastes – in humour, field sports, mimicry – and many common friends among the people of the world of theatre and cinema. The Queen Mother and the Queen were delighted that the Townsend affair seemed to have left no scars.

In 1959 Armstrong-Jones's name appeared frequently on the list of guests at official dinners and luncheons given at Clarence House. He often stayed with the Queen Mother and Princess Margaret at Royal Lodge, Windsor, and spent part of the summer holiday with them at Birkhall. On 26th February 1960, a week after the birth of Prince Andrew, the Princess and Armstrong-Jones announced their engagement. The wedding took place at Westminster Abbey on 6th May 1960, the Queen Mother and the staff at Clarence House being responsible for the despatch of invitations to the two thousand guests.

On 3rd October 1961 Antony Armstrong-Jones was created the Earl of Snowdon and a month later, on 2nd November, he drove his wife from their home at Kensington Palace to Clarence House where, the next day, was born a son, David Albert Charles, Viscount Linley. Almost four years to the day after their wedding was born a daughter, Sarah Frances Elizabeth. On the surface, at least, this marriage seemed to be working.

In fact there was a number of factors which put this marriage under a stress which, as we know, finally proved too much. In part the blame for this lay within the royal family itself. While the Queen and the Queen Mother approved of the marriage and since its break-up have continued to maintain a close friendship with Lord Snowdon, there were others who were less than welcoming. In 1963 J. A. Frere, formerly Chester Herald of Arms and a close observer of the royal scene, wrote: "[Prince] Philip has not actually made things difficult for Tony in any way, but he has done nothing to try to make things any easier."[13] Other members of 'the royal firm' frowned on the Princess's husband because his parents had been divorced – his father in fact married three times, his current wife being a former airline hostess. This was not the stuff of which royalty was made.

In part, the cause of the stress lay within Antony Armstrong-Jones himself. On the one hand he seemed to want to become an accepted part of the royal family: he took a title and sometimes travelled in style with Princess Margaret as a sort of mini-version of the Queen and Prince Philip. On the other hand he wanted to continue to follow his career as a photographer and to maintain his friendships with designers, actors and other people in the 'pop' world. It was difficult, if not impossible, to reconcile the two worlds in which he wished to move, and it might have been better if he had chosen either the royal world – as Prince Philip had done at the cost of his career – or the business world – as Angus Ogilvy did when he married Princess Alexandra of Kent but refused a title and insisted on carrying on a life of an involved businessman. Lord Snowdon, in accepting the title but continuing with his career, tried to get the best of both worlds.

But a good deal of the blame for the break-up of the marriage in 1976 and for the divorce which was announced in 1978 must lie with Princess Margaret. On the one hand she wished to be treated as the Queen's privileged sister, and as such she carried out, faithfully, a number of public engagements. On the other hand she wanted to identify herself with the trendiest fashions of the 'swinging sixties'. While at one time she wanted her husband to behave towards her as Prince Philip did to the Queen – walking deferentially one stride behind her, at other times she wanted him to join her in appearing at the latest club or some jet-set disco. It is not surprising that she had to receive psychiatric help in an effort to find a cure for her neurotic concern for her real identity. Nor is it surprising that in the late 1960s she and her husband had blazing rows in public. Increasingly they tended to lead a separate social life. She found most happiness in her holiday home in the West Indies, a wedding gift from Colin Tennant. It was here in the 1970s that Princess Margaret lived in a well-publicized 'relationship' with Roddy Llewellyn, the son of the Olympic horse-rider Colonel Harry Llewellyn of Foxhunter fame. The young Llewellyn had 'dropped out' of society. In the 1950s Princess Margaret had sought happiness in the shape of a man sixteen years older than her; in the 1970s she looked for happiness in the shape of a man seventeen years younger than her. It came as no surprise when Lord Snowdon announced that he had decided, after consulting the Queen, to seek a divorce.

During their 'unhappy period' the Queen Mother maintained her close relationship with both her daughter and Lord Snowdon. Now she did not allow the divorce to intrude too far into her own private life. On the day on which it was announced, she was due to travel by air to Scotland. When she and her staff boarded the plane early in the morning, she handed round the copies of the papers that had been left on board. Each paper, in its own way, blazoned the news of the divorce. All her loyal but embarrassed staff quickly turned their papers inside out, looking for the sports pages. But the Queen Mother did not give any indication of how she felt about things. During the flight she joked as she would normally have done, in spite of the fact that, as I was told, she felt as any parent must do when the marriage of one of their children had collapsed.

It is a sign of the degree to which attitudes have changed that there was little public outcry when the divorce was announced or when it was finalized. Princess Margaret came in for some public criticism because she seemed to be neglecting her public duties, and there was a small chorus of voices asking that her allowance under the Civil List be cut in 1978. The government paid no heed to this demand, and the public seem reconciled to having a Princess who allows a 'companion' to drive to her palace in a battered blue Ford van.

For the Queen Mother there is still a role to play as supporter of her emotionally disturbed daughter. It was significant that at the Trooping the Colour in June 1978 they drove together in an open landau. It seemed as if the very popular Queen Mother was trying to tell the people that she stood by her daughter, and as if she was trying to draw from the public and towards her daughter some of that sympathy and affection which she had always received.

28

At home in Clarence House

FOR ALMOST TWENTY-SEVEN YEARS the Queen Mother's London house has been the cream-painted Clarence House on the north side of the Mall. This house was designed in 1825 by Nash for the Duke of Clarence who, on the death of his brother George IV, came to the throne as William IV. After he became king he continued to use the house, which is linked with other State departments and with the diplomatic quarters of St James's Palace.

During Queen Victoria's reign the house was occupied first by her second son, the Duke of Edinburgh, and then by her third son, the Duke of Connaught, who died in 1942. By this time it was badly run down and in need of extensive modernization. But it was wartime, and there was neither money nor time to spend on renovating a royal house. The King gave Clarence House to be used as Red Cross offices so that when it was handed back after the War it was a rabbit-warren of makeshift rooms. In 1947 King George VI gave the house to Princess Elizabeth and Prince Philip as their London home, and Parliament voted to spend £50,000 on its modernization, renovation and decoration. It was 1949 before the work was completed and Princess Elizabeth, her husband and her infant Prince Charles moved from Buckingham Palace to their new home.

In 1936 the new Queen Elizabeth had been reluctant to leave her home at 145 Piccadilly to take up residence in Buckingham Palace, but by 1952 she had learned to enjoy life in the rambling palace, with its six hundred rooms, and was equally reluctant to move out of there. By convention, dowager queens, after leaving the Palace, have gone to live at Marlborough House, another of the complex of royal buildings along the Mall, but in 1952 Queen Mary was living there, so another home had to be found for the Queen Mother. It seemed very sensible that she and Princess Margaret should move into Clarence House in what amounted to an exchange of houses between mother and elder daughter. What softened the blow of this move was the knowledge that her immediate neighbour, with whom she shared the garden of St James's Palace, was her life-long friend Princess Mary, the Princess Royal.

My first visit to Clarence House took place on the day after the arrival of the President of Rumania. As I walked down the Mall, I watched a procession in which he drove from the Palace, where he had stayed for the night, to a reception in the City. Then, as if further to confirm the fact that Clarence House is part of a political-cum-diplomatic complex, I had to make my way past a line of official cars waiting to take ambassadors away from a reception which had just been held at St James's Palace. Then on through the aptly named Ambassadors' Court, where even the lamp-posts are crowned with the royal insignia as if to remind passers-by that they are walking on royal ground. The main block of Clarence House, which can be seen from the Mall, is painted a creamy colour. At the back, which is the portion occupied by the Household Offices, one sees that several older houses have been joined together and linked with the main block of the house. These older houses are of that dark purplish-red brick of which St James's Palace itself is built. This serves as a reminder that, at Clarence House, one is in the middle of the area from which monarchs traditionally ruled. Indeed foreign ambassadors are still, in name, sent to 'The Court of St James's'.

The entrance to the Household Offices is via a back door which faces, across the Court, other similar doors of grace-and-favour houses. A uniformed orderly answers the door and at last one is in. My first impression of this portion of the house was of having to go up and down a series of stairs. This, I was told, was because a number of brick-built houses had been joined together, and the stairs served as links between these once-separated portions of the offices.

The Queen Mother moved into Clarence House on 18th May 1953, just two weeks before the Coronation of Queen Elizabeth II. She brought with her a small personal staff which was headed, as we have seen, by Group Captain Peter Townsend. Today she still has a small household staff. Her most intimate 'servant' is her lady-in-waiting, who sees her each morning and who travels with her when she goes out. She has her own quarters in the house and is free to entertain her personal friends who help her to fulfil one of her functions, which is to act as a sort of information service to Her Majesty, who is thus kept informed as to what is going on. Perhaps the most important member of her staff is her private secretary, another of those whom she sees every day and who is responsible for helping her deal with the shoals of letters, for arranging her public duties and overseeing the general running of the household. He is helped by her treasurer, who handles the economy of the house – recruiting domestic staff, paying the bills, wages and salaries, arranging Her Majesty's contributions to various charities and the like. Her Press secretary handles her public relations, meets the journalists, TV reporters and authors looking for interviews.

To handle what was described as "the nuts and bolts", there is an equerry, a young Guards officer, who spends part of his time at the house. His job is to ensure "that the right car arrives at the right time with the right directions to go to the right place", I was told.

One over-riding impression which one gets at Clarence House is that of a quiet cheerfulness. This stemmed, I was told, from the Queen Mother who "has never been angry. Even when one makes a major error, and goes on to say, 'I'm sorry, Ma'am, but...', there is only ever a smile and a, 'Ah, well....'." In this, as in so much else, the Queen Mother is behaving as did her own mother, Lady Strathmore.

When she is in residence at the house, the members of her staff join her for a midday drink before luncheon. Here, as at the times when she is with them individually, she addresses them by their Christian names. They, for their part, address her always as "Ma'am", the men bowing when she comes into the room, the ladies dropping a curtsey.

The critically querulous sometimes ask what the Queen Mother wants with a residence as large as Clarence House. The simple answer is that it is not merely an ageing widow's house, it is also an office and a State apartment. This becomes clearer as one goes through the house with its many rooms. Part of the house is, of course, a home. In this it resembles the homes in which the Queen Mother grew up – at nearby St James's Square, Bruton Street and Chesterfield House. Then she was accustomed to seven- and eight-storeyed homes with many large rooms. At Clarence House she enjoys the same sort of accommodation. She has a morning-room, a long, sun-lit corner room on the ground floor facing the garden and Stable Yard, dominated by two huge display-cabinets housing her collection of china. The furniture is gilt wood made in this country in the eighteenth century. Around the walls are hung a number of paintings, a reminder that the Queen Mother has always been an avid collector and a great patron of young and hitherto little-noticed artists. Here one can see work by moderns such as Sickert, Paul Nash and Augustus John as well as by earlier artists such as Monet.

The morning-room is linked by double doors to the library, a square, high room which was once the hall of the house. It is full of the Queen Mother's own books, a reminder that one of her favourite pastimes is reading. Here she often lunches when alone with her staff or when she has only a few guests, but there is a large dining-room off the library, a long room dominated by a beautiful chimneypiece of white and grey marble and by the long Spanish walnut table which is used when the Queen Mother has a luncheon or a dinner-party. The walls of this room are hung with portraits of the original occupant, King William IV, and of King George III and Queen Charlotte, his father and mother.

The west side of the first floor of the house is occupied by a double drawing-room and the Queen Mother's private sitting-room. Around the walls of the drawing-room are paintings by Augustus John, Wilkie and Landseer, and one by Sir William Richmond of the three Misses Cavendish-Bentinck, the Queen Mother's mother and two aunts. There is a grand piano in this room as well as a television set where the Queen Mother often sits alone to watch her favourite programmes. In her sitting-room there is another beautiful chimneypiece as well as paintings of her husband and our present Queen in her coronation robes. These and other paintings, such as a Fra Angelico, form the background against which the Queen Mother has set out her collection of miniature furniture and enamel.

Until her marriage to Antony Armstrong-Jones, Princess Margaret lived in Clarence House. She had a suite on what was designed as the nursery floor when our present Queen lived there. Here she would entertain her friends, and Clarence House was the centre for parties and dances. The 'home' part of the house is often used by the growing number of younger members of 'the royal firm' for whom a visit to "Granny's house" is a treat.

When the Queen Mother drives to her home, she goes past solid wooden gates off Stable Yard, up to the pillared cream-painted portico of her house. She enters a small hall dominated by the wedding present given to her and her husband by the people of Glasgow – a musical clock topped by the Scottish lion mounted on a crown. She then goes up three steps into a wide corridor which has a number of display-cabinets showing off the splendid service of Worcester china originally presented by George IV to his brother Ernest (later King of Hanover). Here too are several large portraits by Lely, Allan and Ramsay and, in modern contrast, a large picture by Simon Elwes of *The Investiture of Princess Elizabeth with the Order of the Garter by King George VI*. Off this corridor open the various rooms which have been described, including the private sitting-room where in one corner the Queen Mother has her large mahogany desk, its back to the west window. Here is the 'office' part of the house, with its paper-openers, pens, baskets labelled 'Private Secretary' and 'Lady-in-Waiting' and the semicircle of photographs of the late King, her daughters and their children, and of her own family. While she is in residence at Clarence House, the Queen Mother's official day starts at about 10 am when she rings for her lady-in-waiting. Together they go through that part of the day's mail that is concerned with her patronage of various institutions and societies. When I asked for some details about this, I was shown a booklet which lists the hundreds of organizations of which the Queen Mother is president or patron. Each of these sends her at least an annual report which she conscientiously reads and to which, if needs be, she will send a reply. Another major portion of this part of her mail are the letters from people who want her to give them some item or other which can be auctioned at a bazaar or a fête. Then, I was told, there are many letters from people who feel that they have the right to ask for her personal assistance. Former members of one of her regiments write in to tell her that they have lost a job, been evicted from a house or had an accident which prevents them from continuing in employment – and they ask their former Colonel-in-Chief to help. Because of her intimate knowledge of the various charities and organizations that exist to help people who are in various states of need, she is able to put them into touch with SSAFA or some such charity.

She normally spends about an hour with her lady-in-waiting going through this section of her correspondence, and signing the letters which have been written in answer to mail received on previous days. Then, the lady-in-waiting having been sent off to prepare another lot of letters for signature, the Queen Mother rings for her private secretary, with whom she discusses the more official correspondence and the details of her immediate and future engagements.

The evening before my first visit she had spent almost four hours at a dinner and reception for the President of Rumania at Buckingham Palace. After lunch she was going to fly by helicopter to Hastings to play a part in the town's annual celebrations in honour of its fishermen and lifeboat service, where she was to make four separate appearances at receptions and two speeches before being flown back, late at night, to London. I understood what one of her staff meant when he said: "When I copy Queen Elizabeth's diary of public engagements, I just can't imagine how she fits it all in, and it makes me so angry with those people who don't appreciate how much the royal family does."

When discussing with her staff the nature of the Queen Mother's time-table, I could not avoid asking about her youthful inability to keep to time – even when the time-keeper was her father-in-law, King George V (p. 58). Always, and with everyone, this question raised a wry smile followed by a protesting, "But she's never late for anything. If she is supposed to be at the Albert Hall at 7.30 pm, then she'll be there. If the concert which she is to attend is due to start at 8 pm, then she will be in her place in time for it to start at that time. But," and here the speaker would shake a head, pucker up the lips and frown, "we often don't know how she does it." Her staff provide her with a detailed time-table for every public meeting. This will tell her that she has to get into the car at 7.12 pm, arrive at the cinema or hall at 7.37 pm, spend eight minutes chatting to people in the foyer before getting to her seat at 7.50 pm. "But she's been at this a long time, and she knows that it doesn't take eight minutes to shake hands with six people in the foyer, nor does it take five minutes to get up to her seat. So we hop about there like cats on hot bricks because she doesn't leave until 7.20 pm, and we are all worried in case, this time, it doesn't work and she really will be late. But so far she never has been" – the last words with an air of surprised incredulity by a man who has lived through many hours of anxiety.

Today Hastings, tomorrow perhaps a graduation ceremony, and the next day an official lunch with some City institution. The round of public engagements, as we saw in Chapter 25, is almost non-stop, and the centre of this activity is the working desk in the sitting-room at Clarence House. But Clarence House is also a State apartment. When her daughter was abroad and she acted as Counsellor of State and 'Deputy Queen', the Queen Mother received newly appointed ambassadors presenting their credentials for the first time, and here, nowadays, she receives the visits which such ambassadors conventionally make on the widow of the former King after they have first presented themselves to Queen Elizabeth II. Here too come British ambassadors when they return home on leave or retirement, bishops of the Anglican Church overseas, visiting statesmen and their wives, for some of whom the Queen Mother has to provide an official luncheon or dinner.

It costs a great deal of money to run this home and the Queen Mother receives an allowance from the Civil List. In 1979 she was granted £200,000. In 1969 Parliament appointed a Committee to examine the Civil List, which is the money which is awarded annually to the Queen and other working members of the royal family. In 1971 the Committee reported that the money was not, in any sense, an income for the people named in the List but was meant to cover 'operating expenses' incurred in the carrying out of public duties. The Queen Mother's allowance from the Civil List has to cover the salaries and wages of people working in Clarence House, such things as the postage on all the letters sent from the house each day as well as the gifts which she makes to the various societies of which she is president or patron. There is a minority who will complain about 'the cost of the monarchy'. The vast majority will continue to believe that it is money well spent and that "we get our money's worth from the Queen Mother and the rest of 'the royal firm'".

29

The grandmother

QUEEN ELIZABETH IS THE fourth great-grandmother queen of this century. Only the very old readers will remember Queen Victoria, of whom her grandchildren were so afraid that, as we have seen, the then Duke of York had to apologize for Prince Albert's choice of birthday.[1] By 1900 she had become a "mythical, legendary ancestral 'Gangan'" held in respectful fear by her grandchildren and, according to Wheeler-Bennett, regarded by her great-grandchildren "with a mixed reverence, awe and apprehension".[2] When they were children, Prince Edward (later the Duke of Windsor) and Prince Albert (the future George VI) were terrified of her. They often burst into tears in her presence and for no very obvious reason. This would drive the old Queen to ask angrily what she had done wrong now.

There is a healthier relationship between Queen Elizabeth and her grandchildren, and, if she lives to enjoy such visits, she will not cause her great-grandchildren to burst into tears.

Queen Alexandra was the second royal great-grandmother. (She died in 1925, a year before the birth of our present Queen, but she had two great-grandsons through her grand-daughter, the Princess Royal.) While her husband was still Prince of Wales, she was a lively and pleasant grandmother with whom the York children used to enjoy a relaxation from the stern *ménage* of their strict parents. Edward and Alexandra each in their own way made life at Sandringham and Marlborough House very pleasant for the young Princes Edward and Albert; the grandfather enjoyed riding, shooting, walking and boisterous games; with their grandmother the children enjoyed sing-songs, games of cards and other quiet indoor games.[3] But when she became Queen, Alexandra spent less time with her grandchildren, and after King Edward's death in 1910, she retreated into a seclusion from which she rarely emerged. She played little part in national life after 1910 and seems to have left few memories inside the royal family. Queen Elizabeth was only fifty-two when George VI died and, as we have seen, chose to play an active role. In the same way she has continued to be an active and involved grandmother.

The third of her predecessors as royal great-grandmother was Queen Mary. She and King George V had a very happy relationship with the two Princesses, Elizabeth and Margaret Rose. But even that relationship bore the stamp of 'Majesty' on which the then Queen was so insistent. The children had to curtsey to both their grandparents when entering and leaving their presence, even though, when with them, they were allowed a good deal of freedom – to play among Queen Mary's precious bric-à-brac in a way which she had never allowed her own children. "Lilibet" called the bearded King "Grandpa England", and he, as we have seen, enjoyed looking across the Park to 145 Piccadilly from where she waved a handkerchief each morning.

In 1937, when Queen Mary drove in the Coronation procession, in the coach with her was the ten-year-old Princess Elizabeth. Their 'togetherness' at this ceremony was no incidental accident. When 'the Yorks' had gone to Australia in 1927, the Princesses had spent part of the time with King George and Queen Mary, and the latter maintained this close contact with "Lilibet" throughout the rest of her life and played a large part in moulding her tastes and attitudes. She tried to give to her children and grandchildren her own concept of duty and of the respect which was due to 'Majesty'. She was, in 1936, the "strong, central point" without whom the family might have broken up during the Abdication Crisis. The new King and Queen were grateful for her support and advice, so that it is not surprising that, at least until the outbreak of war, she remained a major figure in national life and a major influence inside the royal family.

Queen Elizabeth has shown some of Queen Mary's characteristics – one of her friends called her "the great steadying force in the family" which calls to mind the view of Queen Mary expressed in 1936. Like Queen Mary she has a great sense of 'family', inherited in part from her own mother but strengthened no doubt by her close contact with Queen Mary after 1923. Like the last dowager queen, she too has that 'sense of duty' which the British people admired in Queen Mary and of which Woolton spoke when he met Queen Elizabeth during the War.[4]

But Queen Elizabeth is no mere reflection of her immediate predecessor. She has none of Queen Mary's frigid manner; "the smiling Duchess" has matured into the still-vivacious Queen Mother. Nor did she have that inner need to insist on her children's respect for 'Majesty'. Not for them the curtsey when they met their parents. She was more self-confident than Queen Mary, and she had no need for such outward signs of inner respect. However, she did insist that her children should pay that respect to their grandmother, Queen Mary, and, in her turn, the present Queen has insisted that the younger royals pay their grandmother the same respect. So it is that, for all her pleasant relationship with them, Prince Charles always bows when he enters her room while Princess Anne always curtsies.

She sees all her family together at Christmas, the major 'family' event. It was once spent at Sandringham, but the many royal marriages and births and the increase in the number of nephews and nieces has meant that Windsor is the only royal house that is large enough to hold them all. Here the Queen Mother sees the Queen, Prince Philip and their four children along with Captain Mark Phillips and her great-grandchild, the Gloucesters, the Kents and their younger relatives. Early in the New Year the family breaks up, and the Queen Mother goes with the Queen, Prince Philip and their sons to stay at Sandringham for the rest of January. Here, perhaps, she is reminded of the days when she and her husband had Prince Charles and, later, Princess Anne to stay with them when Princess Elizabeth and Prince Philip were away on some overseas visit. On her visit to Australia in 1954, Queen Elizabeth II was asked if she did not miss her children. She replied, "More than they miss us, I'm afraid. You see they have a doting grandmother."

At Sandringham the Queen Mother may remember the day of the King's death in 1952 when, on her instructions, Princess Anne and Prince Charles were kept in their nursery instead, as had been normal, of being taken to see their grandparents after breakfast. Puzzled by the crying of a maid, Prince Charles asked to see "Granny", who told him that his much-loved "Grandpa" had "gone away". The answer merely made the young Prince even more puzzled, so that he asked more questions. Why? Where? Why without saying goodbye? The Queen hugged him as she tried to hide her grief. She remembers that at that sad moment her grandson patted her hand and said, "Don't cry, Granny."[5]

It is not surprising that she has a special relationship with our present Queen's children – they were, after all, her first grandchildren, and since 1952 she has spent a good deal of her time with the Queen, with whom she shares a passion for horse racing and for whom she has a great sympathy in her monarchical role. But there is also something special about her relationship with the Snowdon children. Their mother, Princess Margaret, lived with her at Clarence House for the years before her marriage and has much of her mother's lively sense of humour. The Queen Mother had herself been a great party-goer when she "took London by storm" in the early 1920s. She approved of her younger daughter's zest for life and her long list of boy-friends. This gave her a particular relationship with this daughter and her children – the first of whom was born at Clarence House on 3rd November 1961, and with whom she had a very close contact in his early years. All her grandchildren have enjoyed staying with her when their parents have been away on official duty. Sometimes they have stayed at Clarence House; sometimes she has played grandmother-host at Balmoral or, more often, at

Birkhall, where the children have been able to escape from the more formal regime of Balmoral itself. Since her Castle of Mey has been renovated, they have enjoyed going to this northernmost royal house. Here, as at no other royal home, the children are free, for there are few neighbours, with all of whom, as we have seen, the Queen Mother has established a sense of friendship so that they do not intrude on the royal family's privacy. Here, as at no other home, there will be no journalist looking for the angry word or royal indiscretion. Nor will there be a lurking photographer waiting to 'snap' a sun-bathing prince or princess for the titillation of a particular type of reader.

I suggested to one of her staff that she had a particularly close relationship with Prince Charles. I was assured that this was so but was told that "she had a similar relationship with Princess Anne until her marriage".[6] Certainly, in all that one reads in newspapers, magazines and memoirs, and in all that one is told by those close to the family, it becomes clear that Prince Charles has a special place in her affections. When he was a little boy, she used to please him with simple conjuring tricks and by the sing-songs they enjoyed on car trips between Birkhall and Aberdeen Airport. In 1958, when the Queen Mother made her second visit to Australia, Prince Charles was in his first year at Cheam School. The Queen Mother was asked what she thought of her grandson, and she replied, "Oh he is a very gentle boy. He has a very kind heart, which, I think, is the essence of everything."[7] When she was visiting a hospital for babies, a doctor asked her if her grandchildren were as nice as they looked in their latest photograph. "I think so," said the Queen Mother. "Prince Charles is *particularly* nice."[8] When he was a new boy at Gordonstoun School, it was the Queen Mother who flew up to Birkhall and sent a car to pick him up when he was allowed to visit relatives for the first time. He spent most of his mid-term breaks with her, and she welcomed him and his friends to her home. Indeed, the boys became so familiar with her that, whenever she telephoned him at the school, he would be summoned with the call, "Charles! Granny's on the line!"[9] When he was at school in Timbertop in 1966, the Queen Mother made her third visit to Australia and spent some time with her favourite grandson. They met at Canberra in April 1966, the Queen Mother exclaiming, "It's good to see you again, Charles – why, I do believe you've grown a bit!"[10] Together they went to the Snowy Mountains, where their driver had to take avoiding action when an oncoming car almost drove into them. It was explained later that the other driver was "so busy looking at the Queen Mother that [he] crossed to the wrong side of the road".[11]

She sees much of herself in Prince Charles – a love for fishing, an appreciation of music, a sense of religion and of duty. It is not unimportant that on the morning of his twenty-first birthday Prince Charles got up early to go with Princess Anne and his grandmother to the Chapel Royal of St John in the Tower of London to make "an act of thanksgiving and dedication for his future life". But the Queen Mother also sees much of her late husband in this shy grandson, who has none of Princess Anne's boisterous nature nor the public confidence of his extrovert father. The Queen Mother who watched her introvert husband succeed in his role of monarch hopes that her grandson will repeat his success.

Prince Charles had been born in Buckingham Palace when his parents were waiting for their new home, Clarence House, to be modernized. Princess Anne was born in Clarence House on 15th August 1950. Indeed, there was, for a time, the hope that the new baby would arrive in time for the grandmother's fiftieth birthday, which would have linked the two very closely. But the fact that this child was born in the house which has since become her own London home gives the Queen Mother a special affinity with her first grand-daughter. She and Prince Charles form what has been described as the 'first' of our Queen's two families, with the much younger and more extrovert Princes Andrew (born on 19th February 1960) and Edward (born on 10th March 1964) being a 'second' family. In that sense, Princess Anne shared with Prince Charles a special relationship with their grandmother. As she has grown, Princess Anne has become an accomplished horsewoman and so retained a special link with her grandmother and one which Charles does not share to the same extent.

In April 1973 the Queen Mother took her part in the wedding ceremony of Princess Anne to Mark Phillips. In one sense this marriage took the Princess out of her grandmother's orbit; she has her own life to lead and has shown that she intends to become very much her own person. However, the birth of the first of the Queen Mother's great-grandchildren in 1977 created another link between the proud great-grandmother and her equally proud grand-daughter. Like Queen Victoria, Queen Alexandra and Queen Mary, our Queen Mother can feature in photographs of four generations!

30

The octogenarian

IN 1977 THE BRITISH PEOPLE took the opportunity to show how much they appreciated the institution of the monarchy. When it was first suggested that the Queen should be allowed to celebrate her Silver Jubilee, there were those who wondered whether the country could, or should, afford to spend money in this way while still deep in an economic crisis. There were others who questioned the holding of a Jubilee to honour what they saw as a meaningless institution which, they claimed, contributed little to national life.

It was interesting to chart the changes in such critics' opinions as the Jubilee of 1977 became such an evident success. Some claimed that the British people were not celebrating with the Queen but were congratulating themselves – for what was never specified, nor was it explained why they had had to wait until 1977 to do so. Other former critics became ardent celebrators and asked that street parties and other forms of communal rejoicing should become an annual ritual. These too failed to see that the success of the multifarious activities of Jubilee Year was precisely because it was just that – a special year in the history of the Crown and the people.

In 1976 there had been a large number of publications recalling the events of 1936 when King Edward VIII had abdicated. For older readers these were reminders of things past; for younger readers there was a chance to learn how much hope had been placed in a Prince of Wales who had not lived up to expectations and who had chosen to give up his throne for "the woman he loved". And from someone close to the Queen Mother came the wry comment that few, if any, of these publications paid much attention to the fact that if 1976 was the fortieth anniversary of the Abdication, it was also the fortieth anniversary of the accession of King George VI and Queen Elizabeth.

So, in 1976 and 1977, the people enjoyed their nostalgia as they re-lived the Abdication of 1936 and the accession of Queen Elizabeth II. But the Queen Mother's memory went back further than 1936. And even when she was reminded of the events of that momentous year her memories were not as bland as those of some who wrote about the departure of the Duke of Windsor. Her memory would certainly have gone back to 1923 when, reluctantly, she became a member of 'the royal firm'. She and her husband had been accorded a public celebration in 1948 in honour of their Silver Wedding, and, while celebrating the Jubilee of 1977, she may have recalled her own triumphal rides through the packed streets of the war-scarred City of London in 1948.

And when she played her part in helping to make her daughter's Jubilee the triumph that it was, she must have thought that she and King George VI would have had such a triumphant Silver Jubilee in 1961 if he had only lived to be sixty-seven. The Duke of Windsor had lived to be seventy-eight, the Duke of Gloucester died when he was seventy-four – so that she was entitled to think about what might have been for her and George VI if only he had lived a more normal span of life.

When I told some members of the Queen Mother's household that I intended to write this biography in honour of her eightieth birthday, they offered me their sympathy because, as they said, "nearly all the people who knew her have gone or are too old to be interviewed". She herself is fully aware of the effects of passing time – older friends and companions such as Lady Airlie, as well as contemporaries and younger people such as her brother David, have died. This has made all the more valuable the friendships of the few long-standing companions such as Lady Vyner with her home in Caithness.

During the massive popular celebrations of 1977 there was a special cheer of welcome for the Queen Mother whenever she appeared, whether as one of the many royals on their way to the Abbey or alone on a visit to some society or institution. The British people knew, instinctively, that this woman had played a major part in the life of the monarchy for the past sixty years or so. Their applause was their way of showing their gratitude for what she had done – and for the way in which she had done it – and their sympathy for her who had been deprived of the love and companionship of her husband when she was still only fifty-two. It is too easy to forget that she became the Queen Mother at exactly the age our present Queen had reached when in 1977 she celebrated the Silver Jubilee of her accession.

In 1972 Queen Elizabeth and Prince Philip celebrated their Silver Wedding. During her speech on that occasion the Queen had talked about the importance of the web of family relationships, between parents, children, grandparents and grandchildren, cousins, aunts and uncles. She said, "We all know the difficulties of achieving that 'happy family'." No one will deny the part played by the Queen Mother in the life of the royal family and in the life of the people of this country and the Commonwealth.

In 1976 there was a tendency to look back at the Abdication and to forget the accession. In 1977 there was, justifiably, a look-back at the accession of 1952 so that we ignored the death of George VI and the widowhood of the Queen Mother. Perhaps in 1980 there will be an opportunity to pay particular attention to the person, work and worth of the Queen Mother.

Bibliography

In addition to the files of newspapers and magazines, I have consulted the following books:

OFFICIAL ROYAL BIOGRAPHIES
NICOLSON, HAROLD, *King George V*, Constable, 1952
POPE-HENNESSY, SIR JAMES, *Queen Mary*, Allen & Unwin, 1959
WHEELER-BENNETT, SIR JOHN, *King George VI*, Macmillan, 1958

OTHER ROYAL BIOGRAPHIES
ASQUITH, LADY CYNTHIA, *Queen Elizabeth*, Hutchinson, 1937
BOLITHO, HECTOR, *King Edward VIII*, Eyre & Spottiswoode, 1937
BOOTHROYD, J. BASIL, *Philip, an informal biography*, Longmans, 1971
CATHCART, HELEN, *The Queen Mother*, W. H. Allen, 1965
DONALDSON, FRANCES, *Edward VIII*, Weidenfeld and Nicolson, 1974
DUFF, DAVID, *Elizabeth of Glamis*, Muller, 1973
GORE, JOHN, *King George V, A Personal Memoir*, Murray, 1941
JORDAN, RUTH, *Princess Margaret and her Family*, Robert Hale, 1974
LACEY, ROBERT, *Majesty*, Hutchinson, 1977
LAIRD, DOROTHY, *Queen Elizabeth, the Queen Mother*, Hodder & Stoughton, 1966
MORRAH, DERMOT, *The Royal Family in Africa*, Hutchinson, 1947
— *Princess Elizabeth, Duchess of Edinburgh*, Odhams, 1950
— *The Work of the Queen*, William Kimber, 1958
TOWNSEND, PETER, *The Last Emperor; The Decline & Fall of the British Empire*, Weidenfeld and Nicolson, 1976

ROYAL MEMOIRS
WINDSOR, THE DUCHESS OF, *The Heart has its Reasons*, Michael Joseph, 1956
WINDSOR, THE DUKE OF, *A King's Story*, Cassell, 1951

AUTOBIOGRAPHIES, MEMOIRS, DIARIES AND LETTERS
AIRLIE, MABELL, COUNTESS OF, *Thatched with Gold*, Hutchinson, 1962
ARGYLL, MARGARET, DUCHESS OF, *Forget Not*, W. H. Allen, 1975
ASQUITH, LADY CYNTHIA, *Diaries, 1915–18*, Hutchinson, 1968

ASQUITH, LADY CYNTHIA, *Haply I may Remember*, Barrie, 1950
— *Remember and be Glad*, Barrie, 1952
ATHOLL, DUCHESS OF, *Working Partnership*, Barker, 1958
ATTLEE, CLEMENT, *As It Happened*, Heinemann, 1954
BERKELEY, MOLLY, *Beaded Bubbles*, Hamish Hamilton, 1967
BLACK, SISTER CATHERINE, *King's Nurse, Beggar's Nurse*, Hurst & Blackett, 1939
CHANDOS, LORD, *The Memoirs of Lord Chandos*, Bodley Head, 1962
CHANNON, SIR HENRY, *The Diaries of Sir Henry Channon*. (ed. R. R. James) Weidenfeld and Nicolson, 1967
CHURCHILL, SIR WINSTON, *My Early Life*, Fontana, 1978
COLVILLE, LADY CYNTHIA, *Footsteps in Time*, Collins, 1976
— *A Crowded Life*, Evans, 1963
COOPER, LADY DIANA, *The Light of Common Day*, Rupert Hart-Davies, 1959
CRAWFORD, MARION, *The Little Princesses*, Cassell, 1950
CROSSMAN, RICHARD, *The Diaries of a Cabinet Minister; Vol. I. 1964–6*, Hamish Hamilton and Jonathan Cape, 1975
EDEN, ANTHONY (LORD AVON), *The Memoirs of the Right Hon. Sir Anthony Eden*, Cassell, 1960
FRANCIS, DICK, *The Sport of Queens*, Michael Joseph, 1974
GORELL, LORD, *One Man, Many Parts*, Odhams, 1956
GREY, VISCOUNT, *Twenty-Five Years, 1892–1916*, Hodder & Stoughton, 1926
HARDINGE, LADY HELEN, *Loyal to Three Kings*, William Kimber, 1967
HOME, LORD, *The Way the Wind Blows*, Collins, 1976
JONES, L. E., *An Edwardian Youth*, Macmillan, 1956
JONES, THOMAS, *A Diary with Letters, 1931–50*, Oxford University Press, 1969
KENNEDY, MRS ROSE FITZGERALD, *Times to Remember*, Collins, 1975
LEE OF FAREHAM, VISCOUNT, *A Good Innings*, John Murray, 1974
MACDONALD, MALCOLM, *People and Places*, Collins, 1969
MCGOVERN, JOHN, *Neither Fear nor Favour*, Blandford Press, 1960
MACMILLAN, HAROLD, *Tides of Fortune, 1945–55*, Macmillan, 1969
MOSLEY, SIR OSWALD, *My Life*, Nelson, 1968
NICOLSON, HAROLD, *Diary and Letters, 1931–9*, Collins, 1966
— *Diary and Letters, 1945–62*, Collins, 1968
PONSONBY, SIR FREDERICK, *Recollections of Three Reigns*, Eyre & Spottiswoode, 1951
REYNAUD, PAUL, *In the Thick of the Fight*, Cassell, 1953
RHONDDA, LADY, *Notes on the Way*, Macmillan, 1937
ROOSEVELT, MRS ELEANOR, *This I Remember*, New York, 1949
SPEER, ALBERT, *Inside the Third Reich*, Weidenfeld and Nicolson, 1971
STEVENSON, FRANCES, *Lloyd George; A Diary*, Hutchinson, 1971
THOMAS, SIR MILES, *Out on a Wing*, Michael Joseph, 1964
TOWNSEND, PETER, *Time and Chance*, Collins, 1978
VANDERBILT, GLORIA, AND FURNESS, LADY THELMA, *Double Exposure*, Muller, 1959
WOOLTON, LORD, *Memoirs*, Cassell, 1954

BIOGRAPHIES

BIRKENHEAD, LORD, *Walter Monckton*, Weidenfeld and Nicolson, 1969
BOYLE, ANDREW, *Only the Wind Blows; Reith of the BBC*, Hutchinson, 1972
FEILING, SIR KEITH, *Neville Chamberlain*, Macmillan, 1946
HYDE, H. MONTGOMERY, *The Unexpected Prime Minister*, Hart-Davies, McGibbon, 1973
JAMES, ROBERT RHODES, *Rosebery*, Weidenfeld and Nicolson, 1963
KUEBLER, KATHIE, *Meine Schulerin*
LANGHORNE, ELIZABETH, *Nancy Astor and her Friends*, Arthur Barker, 1974
LASH, JOSEPH, P., *Eleanor and Franklin*, André Deutsch, 1972
LOCKHART, J. G., *Cosmo Gordon Lang*, Hodder & Stoughton, 1949
MCCORMICK, D., *The Mask of Merlin*, Macdonald, 1963
MARTIN, R. G., *The Woman he Loved*, W. H. Allen, 1974
MORGAN, K. O. (ed.), *Lloyd George: Family Letters, 1885-1936*, Oxford University Press, 1973
PICKERSGILL, J. W. (ed.), *The Mackenzie King Record*, Oxford University Press, 1961
PRYCE-JONES, D., *Unity Mitford*, Weidenfeld and Nicolson, 1976
PURCELL, W., *Fisher of Lambeth*, Hodder & Stoughton, 1969
WATSON, F., *Dawson of Penn*, Chatto & Windus, 1951

GENERAL HISTORIES

MONTGOMERY, J., *The Twenties*, Allen & Unwin, 1970
MOWAT, C. L., *Britain between the Wars, 1918-40*, Methuen, 1966
MUGGERIDGE, M., *The Thirties*, Collins, 1967 ed.
READ, DONALD, *Edwardian England*, Harrap, 1972
TAYLOR, A. J. P., *English History 1914-45*, Oxford University Press, 1965

SPECIAL STUDIES

ANSON, W. E., *The Law and Custom of the Constitution*, 1886
BAGEHOT, WALTER, *The English Constitution*, Fontana, 1963
BEAVERBROOK, LORD, *The Abdication of King Edward VIII*, Hamish Hamilton, 1966
CALDER, ANGUS, *The People's War, 1939-45*, Jonathan Cape, 1969
CHURCHILL, SIR WINSTON S., *The Story of World War Two* (6 Vols.), Cassell, 1950-6
FRERE, J. A., *The British Monarchy at Home*, Gibbs & Phillips, 1963
INGLIS, BRIAN, *Abdication*, Macmillan, 1966
IRVING, DAVID, *Hitler's War*, Hodder & Stoughton, 1977
LONGMATE, NORMAN, *How We Lived Then*, Hutchinson, 1971
MARWICK, ARTHUR, *The Home Front*, Thames & Hudson, 1976
— *Women at War*, Fontana, 1977
MORRAH, DERMOT, *The Royal Family in Africa*, Hutchinson, 1947
MURRAY-BROWN, JEREMY, *The Monarchy and its Future*, Allen & Unwin, 1969
PETRIE, SIR CHARLES, *Monarchy in the Twentieth Century*, Eyre & Spottiswoode, 1952

ROWSE, A. L., *All Souls and Appeasement*, Macmillan, 1961
WILSHER, PETER, *The Pound in your Pocket, 1870–1970*, Cassell, 1970

OTHER BOOKS

BAILY, LESLIE, *BBC Scrapbook, 1918–39*, Allen & Unwin, 1968
BEAULIEU, LORD MONTAGU OF, *More Equal than Others*, Michael Joseph, 1970
GARDINER, A. G., *Certain People of Importance*, Jonathan Cape, 1926
JENKINS, SIMON, *Landlords to London*, Constable, 1975

Notes on Sources

INTRODUCTION *(pp. 13–14)*
1 *New Statesman*, 29th September 1951.
2 Wheeler-Bennett, p. 283.
3 Wheeler-Bennett, p. 297.

PART I
CHAPTER 1 (pp. 17–25)
1 Wheeler-Bennett, p. 152.
2 Asquith (1952), p. 4.
3 Beaulieu, p. 82.

CHAPTER 2 (pp. 26–33)
1 *The Times* Coronation Supplement, 1937.
2 Asquith (1937), p. 30.
3 Cathcart, p. 34.
4 Cathcart, p. 32.
5 Airlie, pp. 31–2.
6 Asquith (1937), p. 52.
7 Asquith (1937), p. 70.
8 Lacey, pp. 33–4.
9 Asquith (1937), p. 59.
10 Gorell, p. 170.
11 Laird, p. 33.
12 Laird, p. 33.
13 Asquith (1937), p. 59.
14 Asquith (1937), pp. 14–15.
15 Asquith (1937), p. 13.
16 Nicolson (1952), p. 365.
17 Atholl, quoted in Cathcart, p. 22.
18 Cathcart, p. 10.
19 Asquith (1937), pp. 42–3.
20 Mlle Lang, quoted in Cathcart, p. 38.

CHAPTER 3 (pp. 34–9)
1 Quoted in M. Harrison and O. M. Royston, *The Twentieth Century* (Allen & Unwin, 1967), p. 79.

2 Argyll, p. 28.
3 Kuebler, quoted in Cathcart, pp. 48–9.
4 Wheeler-Bennett, p. 69.
5 Kuebler, quoted in Cathcart, pp. 48–9.
6 Nicolson (1952), p. 247.
7 Quoted in N. Mansergh, *The Coming of the First World War* (Longmans, 1949), p. 235.
8 Asquith (1937), p. 87.
9 Asquith (1937), p. 103.
10 Asquith (1937), p. 117.

PART II
CHAPTER 4 (pp. 43–50)
1 Wheeler-Bennett, p. 6.
2 Wheeler-Bennett, p. 7.
3 Wheeler-Bennett, p. 13.
4 Wheeler-Bennett, p. 16.
5 Wheeler-Bennett, p. 16.
6 Wheeler-Bennett, p. 18.
7 Gathorne-Hardy, p. 237.
8 Wheeler-Bennett, p. 17.
9 Wheeler-Bennett, p. 18.
10 Wheeler-Bennett, p. 32.
11 Wheeler-Bennett, p. 32.
12 Wheeler-Bennett, p. 33.
13 Wheeler-Bennett, p. 39.
14 Wheeler-Bennett, p. 41.
15 Morgan (ed.) p. 153.
16 Wheeler-Bennett, p. 57.
17 Wheeler-Bennett, p. 69.
18 Wheeler-Bennett, p. 77.
19 Wheeler-Bennett, p. 93.
20 Wheeler-Bennett, p. 96.
21 Wheeler-Bennett, p. 131.

22 Wheeler-Bennett, p. 140.
23 Wheeler-Bennett, p. 167.

CHAPTER 5 (pp. 51–60)
1 Asquith (1968), p. 421.
2 Quoted in Lacey, p. 46.
3 Wheeler-Bennett, pp. 149–50.
4 Airlie, p. 166.
5 Airlie, p. 166.
6 Colville, p. 128.
7 Airlie, pp. 166–7.
8 Airlie, p. 167.
9 Wheeler-Bennett, p. 150.
10 Airlie, p. 167.
11 Airlie, pp. 166–7.
12 Wheeler-Bennett, p. 148.
13 Berkeley, p. 51.
14 Wheeler-Bennett, p. 150.
15 Airlie, p. 167.
16 Cathcart, p. 84.
17 Wheeler-Bennett, p. 150.
18 Wheeler-Bennett, pp. 150–1.
19 Airlie, p. 168.
20 Court Circular, 16th January 1923.
21 Duff, p. 62.
22 Quoted in Laird, p. 59.
23 The Star, quoted in Duff, p. 63.
24 Nicolson (1952), p. 51.
25 Wheeler-Bennett, p. 151.
26 Wheeler-Bennett, p. 151.
27 Watson, p. 285.
28 Royal Marriages Act, 1772.
29 The Times, 13th February 1923.
30 Quoted in Laird, p. 45.
31 The Times, quoted in Laird, p. 46.
32 Wheeler-Bennett, p. 152.
33 Wheeler-Bennett, p. 153.
34 Wheeler-Bennett, pp. 153–4.
35 Quoted in Laird, p. 56.

CHAPTER 6 (pp. 61–9)
1 Wheeler-Bennett, p. 154.
2 Wheeler-Bennett, p. 154.
3 Wheeler-Bennett, p. 154.
4 Duff, p. 79.
5 Wheeler-Bennett, p. 189.
6 The Times Coronation Supplement, 1937.
7 Laird, p. 68.
8 Windsor (1951), p. 182.
9 Cooper, p. 73.
10 Lee, pp. 272–3.
11 Wheeler-Bennett, p. 155.
12 Wheeler-Bennett, p. 214.

CHAPTER 7 (pp. 70–5)
1 Wheeler-Bennett, p. 191.
2 Wheeler-Bennett, p. 194.
3 Quoted in Laird, p. 80.
4 Wheeler-Bennett, p. 198.
5 Wheeler-Bennett, p. 198.
6 Wheeler-Bennett, p. 208.
7 Duff, p. 99.
8 Yorkshire Herald, 25th June 1925.
9 Wheeler-Bennett, p. 209.
10 Quoted in Montgomery, p. 234.
11 Wheeler-Bennett, p. 209.
12 Wheeler-Bennett, p. 209.
13 Airlie, p. 179.
14 The Times, 22nd April 1926.
15 Wheeler-Bennett, p. 209.
16 Wheeler-Bennett, p. 210.

CHAPTER 8 (pp. 76–82)
1 Rudyard Kipling, The English Flag.
2 Quoted in Nicolson (1952), p. 471.
3 Wheeler-Bennett, p. 212
4 Watson, p. 285.
5 Wheeler-Bennett, p. 214.
6 Wheeler-Bennett, p. 216.
7 New Zealand newspapers quoted in Laird, p. 99.
8 Wheeler-Bennett, p. 218.
9 Wheeler-Bennett, p. 218.
10 Wheeler-Bennett, p. 219.
11 Wheeler-Bennett, pp. 218–19; see also p. 224.
12 Wheeler-Bennett, p. 220.
13 Quoted in Laird, pp. 101–2.
14 Wheeler-Bennett, p. 223.
15 Wheeler-Bennett, pp. 227–8.
16 Wheeler-Bennett, p. 230.
17 Quoted in Laird, p. 107.
18 Laird, p. 99.
19 Wheeler-Bennett, p. 215.
20 Gardiner, pp. 61–2.
21 Quoted in Laird, p. 108.

CHAPTER 9 (pp. 83–90)
1 Lee, pp. 278–9.
2 Colville, p. 132: see also Chapter 25, Quote 2.
3 Quoted in Laird, p. 118.
4 Quoted in Laird, p. 121.
5 The Scotsman, 21st May 1929.
6 Airlie, p. 188.
7 Donaldson, p. 59.
8 Donaldson, p. 59 and Lacey p. 69.
9 Airlie, p. 184.
10 Airlie, p. 183.

11 Airlie, pp. 184–6.
12 Wheeler-Bennett, p. 253.
13 Wheeler-Bennett, p. 253.

CHAPTER 10 *(pp. 91–6)*
1 Wheeler-Bennett, p. 254.
2 Laird, p. 129.
3 Quoted in Laird, p. 131.
4 Vanderbilt and Furness quoted in
  Cathcart, p. 122.
5 Crawford quoted in Cathcart, p. 123.
6 Crawford, p. 19.
7 Quoted in Duff, p. 150; see also
  Lacey, p. 64.
8 Asquith, 1937, quoted in Lacey,
  p. 60.
9 Nicolson, 1966, p. 239.
10 Wheeler-Bennett, p. 239.
11 Crawford quoted in Cathcart, p. 123.
12 Airlie, p. 197.

PART III
CHAPTER 11 *(pp. 99–104)*
1 Nicolson (1952), p. 524.
2 Black, p. 170, quoted in Nicolson
  (1953), p. 525.
3 Jones, p. 148.
4 Nicolson (1952), p. 526.
5 Nicolson (1952), p. 530.
6 Jones, p. 164.
7 Wheeler-Bennett, p. 264.
8 Crawford, p. 32.
9 Wheeler-Bennett, p. 265.
10 *Daily Express*, 21st January 1936.
11 Pope-Hennessy, p. 612.
12 Jones, p. 166.
13 Pope-Hennessy, p. 612.
14 Jones, p. 167.
15 Mowat, p. 563.
16 Jones, p. 167.

CHAPTER 12 *(pp. 105–10)*
1 Gardiner, pp. 61–2.
2 *Hansard*, 23rd January 1936.
3 Jones, p. 164.
4 Lee, pp. 138–9.
5 Hardinge, p. 61.
6 Lacey, p. 81.
7 Jones, p. 162.
8 Jones, p. 162.
9 Jones, pp. 163–4.
10 Bolitho, pp. 210 and 225.
11 Jones, p. 166.
12 Lee, p. 331.

13 Quoted in Lacey, p. 104.
14 Lacey, p. 76.
15 Donaldson, pp. 207–8.
16 Airlie, p. 197.
17 Airlie, p. 197.
18 Nicolson (1966), p. 231.
19 Jones, p. 164.
20 Windsor (1951), p. 267.
21 Lee, p. 331.
22 Donaldson, p. 181.

CHAPTER 13 *(pp. 111–19)*
1 Donaldson, p. 177; Lacey, p. 82.
2 Quoted in Mowat, p. 582.
3 Nicolson (1966), pp. 239–40.
4 Nicolson (1966), p. 249.
5 Jones, p. 162.
6 Donaldson, p. 194.
7 Pryce-Jones, p. 117.
8 Speer, p. 72; Pryce-Jones, p. 150.
9 Donaldson, pp. 192–206.
10 Ribbentrop, quoted in Donaldson,
   p. 204.
11 Lacey, pp. 88–9.
12 Watson, quoted in Cathcart, p. 129.
13 Donaldson, p. 189.
14 *Evening News*, 18th July 1969, quoted
   in Lacey, p. 84.
15 Airlie, p. 198.
16 Nicolson, 1966, p. 262.
17 Hardinge, pp. 102–3.
18 Windsor, 1956, pp. 224–5.
19 Crawford, p. 36.
20 Channon, p. 79.
21 Lockhart, quoted in Cathcart,
   pp. 134–5.
22 Donaldson, p. 215.
23 Channon, p. 79.
24 Airlie, pp. 198–9.
25 Wheeler-Bennett, p. 277.

CHAPTER 14 *(pp. 120–6)*
1 Nicolson (1966), p. 276.
2 Hardinge, p. 149.
3 Nicolson (1966), p. 270.
4 Wheeler-Bennett, p. 280.
5 Windsor (1951), p. 334.
6 Walter Monckton, quoted in
  Donaldson, p. 216.
7 Donaldson, p. 250.
8 Pope-Hennessy, p. 575.
9 Wheeler-Bennett, p. 285.
10 Windsor (1951), p. 335.
11 Cathcart, p. 140.

12 *News Chronicle*, quoted in Baily, p. 166.
13 Nicolson (1966), p. 273.
14 Jones, p. 287.
15 Hyde, p. 568.
16 Nicolson (1966), p. 274.
17 Jones, p. 296.
18 Gardiner, pp. 61–2.
19 Jones, p. 288.
20 Wheeler-Bennett, pp. 283–4.
21 *The Times*, 30th November 1936.
22 Quoted in Wheeler-Bennett, p. 284.
23 Quoted in Lacey, p. 99.
24 Nicolson (1966), p. 275.
25 Nicolson (1966), p. 276.
26 Lacey, pp. 101–3.
27 *The Sunday Times*, 24th April 1966.
28 Nicolson (1966), p. 277.
29 Wheeler-Bennett, p. 286.
30 Lockhart, p. 407.

CHAPTER 15 (pp. 127–33)
 1 Windsor (1956), p. 225.
 2 Lacey, pp. 101–2; and Wheeler-Bennett, pp. 308–9.
 3 Morrah (1950), p. 52; Morrah (1958), p. 10; Lacey, p. 102.
 4 Jones, p. 302.
 5 *The Times*, 14th December 1936.
 6 Wheeler-Bennett, p. 310.
 7 Windsor (1956), p. 288.
 8 Windsor (1956), p. 356.
 9 Taylor, p. 402.
10 Wheeler-Bennett, p. 295.
11 Quoted in Donaldson, pp. 310–11.
12 Donaldson, p. 317.
13 Donaldson, p. 317.
14 Stevenson (1971), p. 327.
15 *London Gazette*, 28th May 1937.
16 Windsor (1956), p. 298.
17 Quoted in Donaldson, p. 341.
18 Nicholson (1966), p. 345.

PART IV
CHAPTER 16 (pp. 137–43)
 1 Wheeler-Bennett, p. 288.
 2 Wheeler-Bennett, p. 288.
 3 Wheeler-Bennett, pp. 293–4.
 4 Attlee (1954), pp. 210–11.
 5 *Forward*, 13th November 1937.
 6 *Daily Herald*, 6th December 1936.
 7 Airlie, p. 202.
 8 Churchill, p. 12.
 9 Wheeler-Bennett, p. 299.

10 Wheeler-Bennett, p. 283.
11 Wheeler-Bennett, p. 297.
12 Pope-Hennessy, p. 582.
13 Quoted in Taylor, p. 402.
14 Windsor (1951), p. 279.
15 Quoted in Lacey, p. 109; see also Walter Monckton, quoted in Donaldson, p. 216.
16 *Hansard*, 10th December 1936.
17 Lockhart, p. 417, Wheeler-Bennett, p. 311.
18 Rhondda, pp. 173–4.
19 Nicolson (1966), p. 294.
20 Wheeler-Bennett, p. 316.

CHAPTER 17 (pp. 144–51)
 1 Anson, p. 362.
 2 Asquith (1937), quoted in Lacey, p. 105.
 3 Airlie, p. 203.
 4 Crawford, p. 39.
 5 Quoted in Laird, p. 188.
 6 Airlie, p. 205.
 7 Pope-Hennessy, p. 583.
 8 Wheeler-Bennett, p. 298.
 9 Wheeler-Bennett, p. 297.
10 Attlee (1954), p. 210.
11 Quoted in Laird, p. 160.
12 Quoted in Laird, pp. 157–8.
13 *Northern Whig and Belfast Post*
14 Wheeler-Bennett, p. 296.
15 Windsor (1951), p. 287.
16 Wheeler-Bennett, p. 311.
17 Wheeler-Bennett, p. 312.
18 Purcell, p. 250.

CHAPTER 18 (pp. 152–8)
 1 Kennedy, p. 241.
 2 Kennedy, pp. 243–5.
 3 Cooper, pp. 190–3.
 4 Ponsonby, pp. 170–3.
 5 Cooper, p. 221.
 6 Reynaud, p. 590.
 7 Jones, p. 409.
 8 *The Times*, 27th September 1938.
 9 Nicolson (1966), pp. 363–4.
10 339. H.C. Deb. 5s., pp. 359–73.

CHAPTER 19 (pp. 159–64)
 1 Wheeler-Bennett, p. 357.
 2 Wheeler-Bennett, p. 364.
 3 Wheeler-Bennett, p. 364.
 4 H.C. Deb., 31st March 1939, col. 2415.

5 Wheeler-Bennett, p. 372.
6 *The Times*, 28th April 1938.
7 Kennedy, p. 264.
8 Wheeler-Bennett, p. 380.
9 Wheeler-Bennett, p. 380.
10 Wheeler-Bennett, p. 383.
11 Wheeler-Bennett, p. 384.
12 Wheeler-Bennett, p. 384.
13 Wheeler-Bennett, p. 387.
14 Wheeler-Bennett, pp. 388–9.
15 Wheeler-Bennett, p. 392.
16 Nicolson (1966), p. 398.
17 Wheeler-Bennett, pp. 395–6.
18 Wheeler-Bennett, pp. 397–9.

PART V

CHAPTER 20 (pp. 167–75)
1 Wheeler-Bennett, p. 401.
2 Quoted in Cathcart, pp. 161–2.
3 Wheeler-Bennett, pp. 406–7.
4 Quoted in Laird, p. 207.
5 Quoted in Cathcart, p. 163.
6 Quoted in Cathcart, p. 163.
7 Quoted in Laird, p. 209.
8 Quoted in Laird, p. 210.
9 Woolton, p. 223.
10 Quoted in Laird, p. 210.
11 Quoted in Cathcart, p. 165.
12 Quoted in Duff, p. 238.
13 Duff, pp. 237–78; Cathcart, p. 166.
14 Wheeler-Bennett, p. 467.
15 Wheeler-Bennett, p. 470.
16 Wheeler-Bennett, p. 470.
17 Wheeler-Bennett, p. 470.
18 Wheeler-Bennett, pp. 429–30.
19 Duff, p. 236.
20 Wheeler-Bennett, p. 568.
21 *Glasgow Herald*, quoted in Laird, p. 224.
22 Wheeler-Bennett, p. 610.
23 Quoted in Laird, p. 228.
24 Wheeler-Bennett, p. 419.
25 Laird, pp. 230–1; Cathcart, p. 173.
26 Wheeler-Bennett, p. 626.
27 Donaldson, p. 377.

CHAPTER 21 (pp. 176–80)
1 Wheeler-Bennett, pp. 406–7.
2 Lash, p. 658.
3 Lash, p. 658.
4 Wheeler-Bennett, p. 550.
5 Roosevelt (1949), quoted in Wheeler-Bennett, p. 551.

6 Lash, p. 669.
7 Roosevelt (1949), quoted in Wheeler-Bennett, p. 551.
8 Wheeler-Bennett, p. 551.
9 Wheeler-Bennett, p. 551.
10 Roosevelt (1949), quoted in Wheeler-Bennett, p. 552.

CHAPTER 22 (pp. 181–7)
1 Churchill (1956), quoted in Wheeler-Bennett, p. 629.
2 Pickersgill, quoted in Cathcart, p. 176.
3 Wheeler-Bennett, p. 470.
4 Quoted in Laird, p. 231.
5 Quoted in Duff, p. 241.
6 Pickersgill, quoted in Cathcart, p. 177.
7 Pickersgill, quoted in Cathcart, p. 176.
8 Wheeler-Bennett, p. 654.
9 Airlie, p. 224.
10 Nicolson (1968), p. 115.
11 *The Times*, 4th June 1946.
12 Airlie, pp. 223–4.
13 Airlie, pp. 219–20.
14 Airlie, p. 225.
15 Wheeler-Bennett, p. 626.
16 Airlie, p. 225.
17 Morrah (1947), quoted in Duff, pp. 269–70.
18 Quoted in Cathcart, pp. 184–5.
19 Lacey, p. 160.

CHAPTER 23 (pp. 188–94)
1 *London Gazette*, 10th July 1947.
2 Crawford, p. 59.
3 Boothroyd, p. 136.
4 Nicolson (1952), pp. 249–52.
5 Nicolson (1952), pp. 309–10.
6 Lacey, p. 129.
7 Lacey, p. 130.
8 Airlie, p. 227.
9 Quoted in Wheeler-Bennett, p. 748.
10 Quoted in Wheeler-Bennett, p. 749.
11 Crawford, p. 92.
12 Channon, pp. 286–7.
13 Wheeler-Bennett, p. 749.
14 Airlie, pp. 227–8.
15 Wheeler-Bennett, p. 751.
16 Airlie, p. 226.
17 *Country Life*, 20th November 1947.
18 Wheeler-Bennett, pp. 754–5.
19 Quoted in Lacey, p. 162.
20 Quoted in Duff, p. 286.
21 Wheeler-Bennett, p. 762.

CHAPTER 24 (pp. 195–200)
1 Quoted in Laird, p. 256.
2 Quoted in Laird, pp. 256–7.
3 Wheeler-Bennett, p. 766.
4 Nicolson (1968), p. 167.
5 Attlee, p. 211.
6 The Times, 4th August 1950.
7 Wheeler-Bennett, p. 788.
8 Nicolson (1968), p. 209.
9 Quoted in Laird, p. 265.
10 Chandos, p. 425.
11 Thomas, pp. 306–7.
12 Airlie, p. 235.
13 Quoted in Lacey, p. 182.
14 Quoted in Laird, p. 268.

PART VI
CHAPTER 25 (pp. 203–10)
1 Dylan Thomas, Selected Works (Dent, 1976).
2 Colville, p. 132; and see Chapter 9, quote 2.
3 Duff, p. 310.
4 Personal interview.
5 Lacey, p. 204.
6 Laird, p. 171.
7 Thomas, pp. 312–13.
8 Quoted in Laird, p. 178.
9 Quoted in Cathcart, p. 223.
10 Quoted in Duff, p. 326.
11 McGovern, quoted in Cathcart, p. 224.
12 Quoted in Cathcart, p. 227.
13 Woolton, p. 320.
14 Crossman, p. 330.
15 Lacey, p. 330.
16 Nicolson (1968), p. 354.

CHAPTER 26 (pp. 211–16)
1 Most of the information in this chapter was given in private interviews.
2 Most of the information in this chapter was given in private interviews.
3 Quoted in Duff, p. 341.

4 Quoted in Duff, p. 344.
5 Personal interview; see also Cathcart, p. 206.
6 Duff, p. 344.
7 Gorell.
8 Francis, pp. 224ff.
9 Nicolson (1968), p. 198.
10 Francis, p. 198.
11 Quoted in Laird, p. 284.

CHAPTER 27 (pp. 217–24)
1 Personal interview.
2 Quoted in Cathcart, p. 219.
3 Quoted in Duff, p. 319.
4 Personal interview.
5 Airlie, p. 225.
6 Channon, p. 439.
7 Royal Marriages Act, 1772.
8 The People, 11th June 1953.
9 Lacey, p. 231.
10 The Times, 22nd October 1955.
11 Nicolson (1968), p. 290.
12 Townsend (1978).
13 Frere, p. 154.

CHAPTER 28 (pp. 225–30)
This chapter is based on a series of interviews at and visits to Clarence House.

CHAPTER 29 (pp. 231–5)
This chapter is based on research which I did for my book Prince Charles (Weidenfeld and Nicolson, 1978).
1 Wheeler-Bennett, p. 7.
2 Wheeler-Bennett, p. 19.
3 Wheeler-Bennett, p. 21.
4 Woolton, p. 223.
5 Wakeford, pp. 36–7.
6 Personal interview.
7 Quoted in Wakeford, p. 86.
8 Quoted in Wakeford, p. 86.
9 Quoted in Wakeford, p. 157.
10 Quoted in Wakeford, p. 182.
11 Duff, p. 376.

Index